William Elder

Aphasia and the Cerebral Speech Mechanism

William Elder

Aphasia and the Cerebral Speech Mechanism

ISBN/EAN: 9783744759793

Printed in Europe, USA, Canada, Australia, Japan

Cover: Foto ©ninafisch / pixelio.de

More available books at **www.hansebooks.com**

APHASIA

AND

THE CEREBRAL SPEECH MECHANISM

APHASIA

AND

THE CEREBRAL SPEECH MECHANISM

BY

WILLIAM ELDER, M.D., F.R.C.P. Ed.
PHYSICIAN TO LEITH HOSPITAL

WITH ILLUSTRATIONS

LONDON
H. K. LEWIS, 136 GOWER STREET, W.C.
1897

London: H. K. Lewis, 136, Gower Street, W.C.

TO

THE MEMORY

OF

MY FATHER

FROM WHOSE LIPS I EARLY RECEIVED MY

FIRST INSTRUCTION

IN

SCIENTIFIC TRUTH.

PREFACE.

THE greater part of this work consists of my Edinburgh University M.D. Thesis. I put it before the Medical Profession as an attempt to elucidate a very difficult but very interesting subject—a subject which, if we thoroughly understood it, would, I believe, give us the key to a knowledge of a great part of the mechanism of cerebral functions.

The work does not aim at a description of all the disorders of speech; its scope has been confined to the central mechanism concerned in speech written and spoken, the disturbances of that mechanism, and the localisation of the lesions which produce those disturbances.

Special attention has been devoted to the differential diagnosis of the clinical varieties of aphasia, and wherever possible the varieties have been illustrated by cases of my own observation.

For much valuable assistance in reporting the cases I am indebted to Doctors A. W. Cameron, Hill Buchan,

Angus Macdonald, and Eason, House Physicians, Leith Hospital; to Dr. George Elder, Edinburgh, for help in many ways; and to Dr. James Pearse, Trowbridge, Wilts, for the laborious duty of preparing an Index.

4, JOHN'S PLACE, LEITH,
February, 1897.

CONTENTS.

	PAGE
HISTORICAL INTRODUCTION	1

CHAPTER I.
THE RECEPTION, RETENTION, AND PRODUCTION OF SPEECH . . . 8

CHAPTER II.
RECEPTION, RETENTION, AND PRODUCTION SPEECH ROUTES 15

CHAPTER III.
MECHANISM OF SPEECH, AS SHOWN BY ITS DISORGANISATION 58

CHAPTER IV.
CLINICAL VARIETIES OF APHASIA . 94

CHAPTER V.
I. AUDITORY APHASIA 96

CHAPTER VI.
II. CONDUCTION APHASIA . . . 141

CHAPTER VII.

III. VISUAL APHASIA, WORD-BLINDNESS, OR CÉCITÉ VERBALE . . . 151

CHAPTER VIII.

IV. APHEMIA, MOTOR APHASIA, BROCA'S APHASIA . 178

CHAPTER IX.

V. AGRAPHIA (GRAPHIC APHASIA) AND THE QUESTION OF THE EXISTENCE OF A SPECIAL GRAPHIC CENTRE 200

CHAPTER X.

DISTURBANCES OF THE MUSIC FACULTY, AMUSIA, ETC. . . 238

CHAPTER XI.

APHASIA FROM A SURGICAL POINT OF VIEW . 244

BIBLIOGRAPHY . . 254

INDEX 257

LIST OF ILLUSTRATIONS

FIG.		PAGE
1.	Diagrammatic Representation of Reception and Production of Language	13
2.	Lateral Surface Left Cerebral Hemisphere, showing Position of Auditory Centre	16
3.	Showing the Semidecussation of the Optic Nerves	21
4.	Showing the Position of the Visual Perceptive Centres	25
5.	Lateral Surface Left Hemisphere, showing the Relative Position of the two Primary Perceptive Centres	26
6.	Lateral Surface Left Hemisphere	29
7.	Lateral Surface Left Hemisphere in Case I.	33
8.	Photograph of Brain in Case I.	35
9.	Diagrammatic Representation of the Course of the Fibres in the Motor Speech Tract	39
10.	Horizontal Section of Brain (after Flechsig) through the Internal Capsule and Basal Ganglia	41
11.	Vertical Section of Left Hemisphere in Anterior Parietal Region, showing Position of Lesion in Case II.	46
12.	Lateral Surface Left Hemisphere. Diagrammatic Representation of the Centres concerned in the Reception and Production of Speech	55
13.	Diagrammatic Representation of Speech Mechanism	61
14.	Lichtheim's two Diagrams of the Speech Mechanism	64
15.	Diagram after Lichtheim	65
16.	Photograph of Left Cerebral Hemisphere of Case V.	110
17.	Diagrammatic Representation of the Sensory Connections of the Naming Mechanism	124

LIST OF ILLUSTRATIONS.

FIG.		PAGE
18.	Diagrammatic Representation of Connections of Naming Mechanism on the Receptive Side	125
19.	Localisation of the Lesion in Mills' Case.	131
20.	Lateral Surface Left Hemisphere, showing the Position of the Area of the Cortex affected in Case VI.	135
21.	Volitional Writing of Case VII.	144
21A.	Writing of Case VII. to Dictation and to Copy	145
22.	Diagrammatic Representation of the Course of the Optic Fibres, modified from Déjerine	156
23.	Copy of Specimens of Attempts at Writing by Case IX.	168
23A.	Copy of Specimens of Attempts at Writing by Case IX.	169
24.	Writing of Case XII., showing Complete Recovery from Agraphia	183
24A.	Mirror Writing of Case XVA..	facing p. 220
25.	Copy of Writing of Case XVI. on 15th Oct., 1896	
26.	,, ,, 16th ,,	
27.	,, ,, 17th ,,	facing p. 228
28.	,, ,, 20th ,,	
29.	,, ,, 9th Nov., 1896	
30.	Lateral Surface Left Hemisphere, showing an Area in which a Lesion of any Size is very apt to produce some Form of Speech Disturbance	245

APHASIA AND THE CEREBRAL SPEECH MECHANISM.

HISTORICAL INTRODUCTION.

THE power that man possesses of communicating his thoughts to his fellow-men by means of language is one of the most characteristic of the many points that distinguish him from the lower animals. That some of the lower animals do possess the power of communicating with each other there can be little doubt, but it can hardly be said of them that they possess the faculty of speech.

Although necessarily experiments on animals can only, therefore, throw light indirectly on our knowledge of the mechanism of speech in man, still such experiments have given a considerable impetus to our knowledge of speech disturbances. That knowledge, however, has been acquired to a much greater extent by accurate clinical and pathological observation in the human subject. The discussion of speech disturbances has been very intimately associated with the discussion of the question as to whether the different faculties are localised or not localised in the cerebral hemispheres.

Flourens[1] more than fifty years ago stated "that the

---

[1] Ferrier, *Med. Chir. Trans.*, Vol. LXVII., 1884, p. 35.

organ of mind, like the mind itself, was one and indivisible, there being no differentiation of function, but each and every part possessed of the potentialities, and capable of exercising every function, pertaining to the whole." This view was accepted for many years, and although many facts in cerebral pathology were inexplicable under the non-localisation theory, still observers did not possess sufficient information to upset it altogether. It was not till 1861, when Broca[1] recorded his cases of aphasia localising the lesion to one part of the left hemisphere, that the opinions of the opponents of the non-localising observers began to gain ground.

Previous to Broca's time many theories had been propounded as to the cause of disturbances in speech. Lordat[2] in 1820, who himself became aphasic later, ascribed this affection, not to paralysis of the tongue, but to incoordination of the muscles used in speaking. Bouillaud,[3] following a theory of Gall, a few years later located, as a result of his clinical observation, the faculty of language in the frontal lobes of the brain.

Dax in 1836,[4] from the observation of cases, stated that patients suffering from aphasia along with paralysis were always paralysed on the right side, and that therefore the faculty of language was situated in the left side of the brain. G. Dax (son of the elder Dax) made another step forwards when he located the lesion that causes aphasia in the anterior and outer part of the middle lobe of the left cerebral hemisphere. This was in 1863, two years

[1] *Bulletins de la Société Anatomique*, August 1861.
[2] *Rev. pér. de la Société de Paris*, December 1820, p. 317.
[3] *Treatise on Encephalitis.*
[4] *Gazette Hebdomadaire*, Paris, Avril 1865, No. 17 (republished).

after Broca had published his two famous cases: the first [1] where the lesion was in the left frontal lobe, and the second [2] where it was more limited, viz. to the posterior part of the second and third left frontal convolutions.[3]

Clinical observers from this time began to pay particular attention to this region, and many cases were published which confirmed more or less the accuracy of Broca's views; but as time went on the number of cases which did not conform to the views of Broca also began to accumulate, and it became necessary to modify the view that all disturbances of speech were due to lesions of Broca's convolution. Charcot, who had produced ten or twelve successive cases confirmatory of Broca's views, gave an account of a case where Broca's convolution was intact, but where there was a lesion in the posterior part of the island of Reil and the lower marginal convolution. Broca himself had assisted at the post-mortem examination of this case, and acknowledged the accuracy of Charcot's observation (Trousseau). Cases also began to be recorded where lesions in the right cerebral hemisphere in the region corresponding to Broca's convolution occurred without disturbances of speech, showing that the speech centres were located on the left side only. To show how difficult it was for clinical observers to accept Broca's views, the following quotation is from the famous lectures of Trousseau on aphasia [4]: "You see, gentlemen, that I have kept back none of M. Broca's arguments, and that I have allowed them to be stretched almost to the limits of

[1] *Bulletins de la Société Anatomique*, August 1861.
[2] *Ibid.*, November 1861.
[3] Trousseau, *Clinical Med.*, Vol. I. (New Sydenham Soc., 1867), p. 252.
[4] *Ibid.*, p. 252.

absurdity, for is it possible in physiology to admit that in an organ so exquisitely symmetrical as the brain there may be in one of the hemispheres a portion discharging a function which does not appertain to the other hemisphere? Analogy and common sense would protest against such a conclusion, and although in almost all the cases of aphasia which have come under my observation the paralysis (when present) always affected the right side, and I was therefore obliged to admit a lesion of the left hemisphere, I could not accede to M. Broca's strange doctrine."

Trousseau summarises the position of the subject at that time thus[1]: "Aphasia is produced in nearly all cases by an injury to the frontal lobes, as Professor Bouillaud has shown; the lesion, as Dr. Marc Dax has established, is almost exclusively confined to the left hemisphere; whilst its most frequent seat is the posterior part of the third left convolution, as M. Broca was the first to point out." Many cases in the next few years were accurately observed, and the results of many post-mortems recorded in this country, in France, and in Germany, by such observers as Broadbent,[2] Sanders,[3] Hughlings Jackson,[4] Gairdner,[5] Ogle,[6] and Bastian,[7] and from these it was seen that it was necessary to differentiate several varieties of aphasia.

[1] *Clinical Med.*, Vol. I. (New Sydenham Soc., 1867), p. 253.
[2] "Cerebral Mechanism of Speech and Thought," *Med. Chir. Trans.*, 1872.
[3] *Edin. Med. Journal*, 1866.
[4] *Lond. Hosp. Clin. Lectures and Reports*, 1864.
[5] *Proceedings of the Glasgow Philosophical Society*, 1865-68, p. 87.
[6] "Aphasia and Agraphia," *St. George's Hospital Reports*, Vol. II., p. 83.
[7] *Med. Chir. Rev.*, Vol. XLIII., p. 299.

Wernicke[1] in 1874 published his classical paper pointing out clearly that aphasia could be divided into two distinct forms, namely motor and sensory; that whilst the first is produced by a lesion in Broca's convolution, the sensory form is produced by a lesion in the first temporal convolution. He also very clearly pointed out several subvarieties of these two principal forms. Thus the upholders of the localisation theory of cerebral functions gradually got stronger evidence from a study of aphasia in support of their position, but in the next few years the question was raised from a position of doubt to one of certainty, because about this time began those experiments on the brains of the lower animals which are associated with the names of Fritsch and Hitzig, Ferrier, Horsley, Beevor, Semon, Krausse, and François Franck.

Cerebral non-localisation may be said to have been finally vanquished at the International Medical Congress in London in 1881, when Goltz of Strasburg,[2] the chief of the few remaining champions of the Flourentian system, produced a dog which he had operated on, and "which he exhibited before the physiological world as a practical refutation of the theory of localisation."[3] It was found, however, at the post-mortem of this dog that the cortical areas had not been destroyed so completely as Goltz had believed. At the same Congress Ferrier produced two monkeys, in one of which he had destroyed the motor areas, and there had resulted not only hemiplegia, but also late rigidity. In the other the superior temporo-sphenoidal

---

[1] *Der Aphasische Symptomen Complex*, 1874
[2] *Trans. Internat. Medic. Congress*, 1881, Vol. I.
[3] Ferrier, *Med. Chir. Trans.*, Vol. LXVII., 1884.

convolutions had been destroyed, with the result that the animal had been rendered deaf.[1]

Meanwhile perhaps the ablest monograph up to this time on aphasia was published by Kussmaul[2] in 1877, in which he added another to the chief varieties of aphasia, viz. word-blindness. Both Broadbent[3] and Wernicke[4] had described cases of this kind, but they had not clearly differentiated it from the other varieties.

In 1877 Barlow[5] published his case, which proved that, although the motor speech centre is situated in Broca's convolution on the left side, it was quite possible when Broca's convolution was destroyed for the corresponding part of the right hemisphere to take up its function. In 1881 Madame Skwortzoff, in her able Thesis to the Faculty of Medicine in Paris,[6] contributed most valuable observations of cases of word-blindness and word-deafness. In 1885 Grainger Stewart[7] gave an excellent *résumé* of the subject, and in the same year appeared Lichtheim's well-known paper,[8] in which he differentiated seven different varieties of aphasia; and in 1886 Wernicke[9] contributed further observations on the subject. In recent years probably the ablest contributions on aphasia have been published in France, chiefly on word-blindness and

---

[1] Ferrier, *Med. Chir. Trans.*, Vol. LXVII., 1884.

[2] Ziemssen, *Cycl. of Pract. Med.*, Amer. edition, Vol. XIV.

[3] "Cerebral Mechanism of Speech and Thought," *Med. Chir. Trans.*, 1872.

[4] *Der Aphasische Symptomen Complex*, 1874.

[5] *Brit. Med. Journ.*, Vol. I., 1877.

[6] *De la Cécité et de la Surdité des Mots dans l'Aphasie.*

[7] *An Introduction to a Study of Diseases of the Nervous System.*

[8] *Brain*, January 1885.

[9] *Fortsch. der Med.*, II., 1886, p. 463.

agraphia, by Déjerine,[1] Sérieux,[2] and Pitres,[3] in which the former prove the existence of two distinct forms of word-blindness produced by lesions in two situations, and at the same time attempt to disprove the existence of agraphia pure and simple as an independent form of aphasia. Pitres, on the other hand, argues strongly for the existence of a special graphic centre. Henschen in 1890,[4] in his excellent work on Cerebral Pathology, contributed many valuable observations on the pathological localisation of aphasic lesions. Wyllie in 1894,[5] in his able work on Disorders of Speech, produced the most accurate and comprehensive account of the whole subject that has yet been published. In that work the contributions of the French School to the subject of word-blindness were brought clearly before the profession in this country, and an article by Hinshelwood[6] on word-blindness and visual memory contributed in December 1895 to the *Lancet*, besides again bringing the work of Déjerine, Sérieux, and Henschen on word-blindness before the English profession, added several other important observations to those already published.

[1] *Compt. Rendus de la Soc. de Biolog.*, 1891 and 1892.
[2] *Ibid.*
[3] *Revue de Médecine*, 1884, p. 864.
[4] *Pathologie des Gehirns.* Upsala, 1890.
[5] *Disorders of Speech.* Edinburgh, 1894.
[6] *Lancet*, December 21, 1895.

CHAPTER I.

THE RECEPTION, RETENTION, AND PRODUCTION OF SPEECH.

IN considering the mechanism of speech it is perhaps best to study it, not as found in its more perfect form in the adult, but rather to study it in the child who is acquiring it. The child hears words and understands the meaning of those words for a considerable time before it is able to intelligently produce words, although it may accidentally produce sounds which are words. The process, therefore, of reception goes before that of production of language. And here I wish at once to make it clear that language in this sense means all the methods by which man is enabled to communicate his thoughts to his fellow-man. Speech written and spoken is of course the most commonly used of all these methods, and is therefore taken as the type; but the other methods, such as by signs and by muscular movements as used by the deaf, and by tactile sensations as used by the blind, have an analogous mechanism called into action. The acquiring and production of music is an analogous process to that of the acquiring and production of language, and it also will be briefly considered later.

Speech is acquired by means of the sensory organs. The child first gets its knowledge of language by the ears. The mother speaks and the child hears the sound and gradually gets to understand the meaning of that particular sound after it has been repeated on several occasions along with its associations. It is enabled to do so by means of memory. This is brought about by the next process in learning a language, viz. what I have called retention of speech, or storing up of the impressions of the sound images of the word spoken. Now it is generally supposed that on receipt of a sensory impression, whether from an ordinary sensory nerve, from a nerve of the muscular sense or of a special sense, a lasting effect is brought about in a particular cell or cells of the cerebrum, so that the impression can either be revived from within the brain or from without on a future occasion. This recalling or reviving is therefore the memory for the past sensation. One of the best ways to recall this past impression is to repeat a similar impression, when at once the previous one is recalled to memory. The repetition of the same sound to the child therefore recalls to its memory the previous sound, and at the same time the associations of the previous sound, and it is so enabled to learn the meaning of the sound. After it knows once the meaning, such meaning is associated with the sound and its other associations, so that in the next repetition of the sound the child recalls the meaning much more readily. It is easily, therefore, understood how repetition of sounds and repetition of the circumstances which recall their meaning, and repetition of the meanings themselves, make the individual gradually more expert in the recognition of sounds, and in the recognition of their meaning.

And what applies to hearing and hearing sounds applies to all the other sensations and sensory impressions which it is possible for the brain to receive—as, for instance, when we once see anything we probably remember it and recognise it on seeing it a second time, but after seeing it on many occasions we recognise it much more readily. Later on I shall refer to memory for muscular movements. A similar process is concerned in their revival and reproduction, the cerebral cells receiving the impressions of the muscular movements through the nerves of the muscular sense, as Bastian holds.

Let me here state that memory in this sense need not necessarily be conscious memory. The individual may not be conscious of ever having received the previous sensory impression. Such memory may only be called up by means of cells which are in a lower level in the cerebral functions than those which are concerned in consciousness.

Again going back to the case of the child. The mother speaks to it, and it gradually stores up in its cerebral cells the sensory impressions of the word sounds which it hears, and gradually recognises the sound of one word after another, and the meaning associated with such sounds. The next process is the production of language. I shall not enter here into an account of the interesting process that most children go through in the production of a language for themselves. They gradually give up that baby language, and by imitating those who speak, they are enabled to reproduce the same sounds which they have heard others produce, and the associations of such sounds are recalled just as if another had produced them. Now a child is enabled to learn to speak from seeing the movements of the mouth, lips, etc., of those who speak to it. It probably does not notice each individual movement and try to imitate each movement, but it sees that sounds are produced by movements. It attempts to produce sounds, and probably also makes attempts at producing a particular sound; and it is enabled to correct itself by means of its hearing, and by gradual imitation it pronounces the words correctly. Often I have no doubt the correct sound is stumbled on accidentally, is recognised by the child and reproduced. Deaf mutes are dumb because they are primarily deaf. They have never heard sounds, and therefore they never try to reproduce them, but that they have the power to produce words is shown by the fact that they can by perseverance be taught to speak. From what I have already said it will be seen that sight plays also a part, although perhaps not so important a one in the acquiring of spoken speech. But sight plays a much more important part in the acquiring of the other forms of speech later on in the life of the child. Written and printed speech is acquired primarily by means of sight. The child sees a particular form or sign, viz. a letter. He associates it with a particular sound by hearing it pronounced. He gradually puts one or two letters together, and joins the one sound to the other to form a word with its associated meaning; and these sight impressions are stored in the cerebral cells, are linked to the sound impressions also stored in the cerebral cells, and can be recalled to memory either from within or from without, from hearing or from seeing. As the sensory impressions of sounds are received, stored up, and the sounds reproduced by the child, so the sensory impressions of these signs or letters written or printed are received, stored up, and the letters reproduced by the child.

The production is done by imitation, analogously to learning to speak, but here it is a case of copying the form of the letters, in other words learning to write. The child imitates the design of the letters, tracing them bit by bit, but through time by means of memory of the impressions received from the muscular movements concerned in past attempts it becomes more expert, until it is able to write proficiently.

A blind agraphic patient is thus analogous to a deaf mute. Is there any case where a child was a blind mute? I have not seen any notice taken of such a condition, but I think that if a case which Dr. Broadbent[1] published as a case of congenital aphasia be studied, it will be seen that the boy was a blind mute. He was not able to speak, although he could hear and understand words, but he could not read letters. The case was published before word-blindness had been described, and perhaps it is too much to draw my conclusion from description only.

It will thus be seen—1st. That speech is received by the brain by two routes, viz. by the ears and auditory nerves and by the eyes and optic nerves. 2nd. That these sensory impressions are stored up in the memory, and are associated so that the memory or another sensory impression of the one can recall the memory or sensory impression of the other. For instance, when the letter O is seen, the sound of O is at once recalled in the auditory memory. Or again, when one thinks of the sound of O, that is, recalls it to memory, the sign O at once is revived in the visual memory, and *vice versa*. 3rd. That speech is produced by the brain by two routes, viz. by speaking and by writing.

It is also to be understood of course that language that

[1] "Cerebral Mechanism of Speech and Thought," *Med. Chir. Trans.*, 1872.

reaches the brain cells by sight can be produced by either production route, and language received by hearing can be produced by either production route. This can easily be indicated by means of a simple diagram (see Fig. 1).

These are the usual routes used, but other not so common routes can be and are cultivated; for instance,

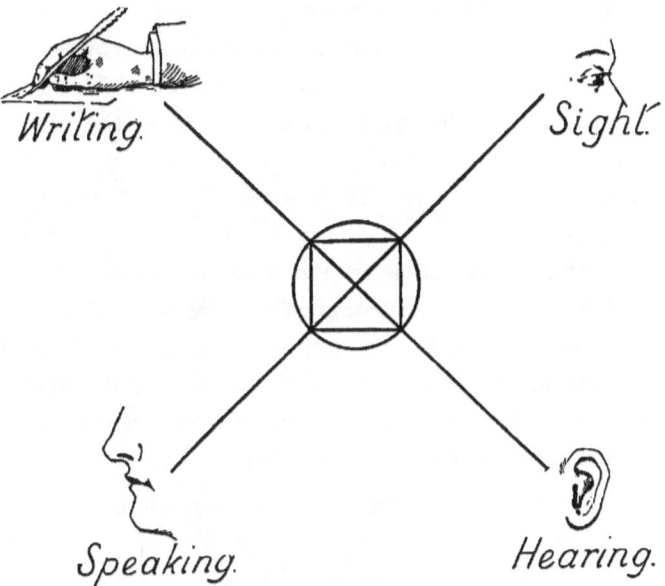

FIG. I.—DIAGRAMMATIC REPRESENTATION OF RECEPTION AND PRODUCTION OF LANGUAGE.

by means of other signs than those of printed or written symbols, as by gestures where the reception route is the same, viz. that of sight, but the production may be done by the whole body or any part of it. Deaf mutes are taught to speak by "reading" the lips, and hearing is not required for this process. A much more marked example, however, of change of route is the teaching of the blind to read by means of the tactile and muscular sensations of the fingers. The sensory nerves of the fingers (tactile and those of the muscular sense) are here used instead of the optic nerves, but the production route is the usual one, viz. the route used in ordinary oral articulation.

Such is a short outline of the method by which speech is acquired, the motor and sensory impressions of speech retained, and revived in the memory at a later period so that they can be reproduced either by speaking or by writing. It is generally believed that the same cells which receive the impressions must be called into action in the reviving of such impressions, and that the process of reviving in each cell probably consists in a repetition of the original process in that cell. This view was well put by Bastian[1] in his able contribution on the muscular sense where he stated that "when past impressions are revived as ideas or recollections, precisely the same parts of the hemispheres, the same nerve fibres, and the same nerve cells must be called into activity as were previously concerned in the perception of the original impression."

[1] *Brit. Med. Journ.*, Vol. I., 1869, p. 394.

CHAPTER II.

RECEPTION, RETENTION, AND PRODUCTION SPEECH ROUTES.

HAVING given an outline of the means by which speech is received, retained in the memory, and reproduced, I shall now proceed to give an outline of the different routes in the brain concerned in speech reception and production. I shall look at this part of the subject from an anatomical, physiological, and pathological, as well as clinical, point of view.

I. AUDITORY ROUTE.

And first then let us trace the auditory route from the ear to the auditory centres in the cerebral hemispheres. The tract of this, as well as of the other cranial nerves, has been studied very carefully in recent years, experimentally and microscopically, as well as clinically, by such well-known observers as Flechsig, Meynert, Bruce, and Hans Held, and its course has now been pretty well made out. Without entering into minute and complicated details, it may be stated briefly that it has been found that the auditory nerve really consists of two parts. One part which originates in the vestibule and the semicircular canals is the nerve of equilibration. It becomes the anterior root of the auditory nerve and goes to the cerebellum, and need not further be considered here.

The posterior root or auditory nerve proper originates in the organ of Corti in the cochlea, passes into the bulb to the lateral tubercle and accessory nucleus of the same side, then passes to the opposite side and by way of the fillet, posterior quadrageminal body, internal geniculate body, and cerebral radiations to the posterior half or two-thirds of the first and second temporo-sphenoidal convolutions.

It has been shown experimentally by Ferrier [1] that the

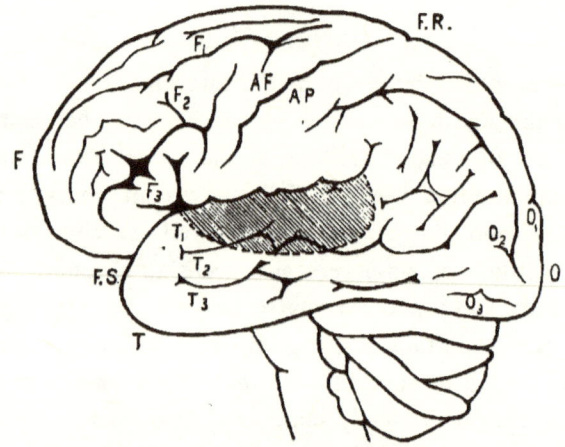

FIG. 2.—LATERAL SURFACE LEFT CEREBRAL HEMISPHERE. THE SHADED PORTION SHOWS THE POSITION OF AUDITORY CENTRE.

position of the centre for hearing is in the first temporo-sphenoidal convolution, as is indicated in the accompanying diagram (see Fig. 2). Ferrier by stimulating that particular region proved that the animal behaved just as if it had heard a sound in the opposite ear, and by extirpation of the same region in monkeys he rendered the animals either deaf or less sensitive to sounds in the opposite ear. He also showed that extirpation of that

[1] *Functions of the Brain.*

region on both sides produced total deafness. Schäfer and Sanger Brown[1] from their experiments on six monkeys disputed Ferrier's results, but Ferrier[2] maintained that bilateral extirpation of the superior temporo-sphenoidal convolution rendered the animal at first completely deaf, and later, although not insensible to sonorous vibrations, it was quite indifferent to sounds that formerly used to recall some meaning to it. Munk[3] placed the position of the auditory centre much in the same region, but extending slightly lower than Ferrier.

Clinical evidence on this subject has also shown that the centre is in this region. Mills[4] records the case of a man deaf for thirty years, whose brain showed atrophy of the superior temporo-sphenoidal convolution on both sides, and particularly the left. Wernicke and Friedlander[5] have published a case of a woman who as a result of an apoplexy had right hemiplegia, word-deafness, aphasia, and paraphasia, and a few months later had a second attack affecting the other side, with the result that she was rendered completely deaf. At the post-mortem both superior temporo-sphenoidal convolutions were affected. Mills[6] records another case in which a patient fifteen years before her death had an apoplectic attack which left her word-deaf, but not deaf to sounds or

[1] *Brain*, January and April 1888, and *Proceed. of Phys. Society*, No. 2, 1887.
[2] *Brain*, April 1888, and *Croonian Lectures*, p. 80.
[3] *Verhandlungen der Berliner physiol. Gesellschaft*, 1878; and *Ueber die Functionen des Grosshirns, Gesammelte Mittheilungen*, Berlin, 1881.
[4] *Univ. Med. Mag.*, November 1889, Vol. II., p. 69.
[5] *Fortschritte der Medicin*, Bd. I., No. 6, March 15th, 1883; quoted in *Brain*, April 1888, p. 19.
[6] *Univ. Med. Mag.*, 1891, Vol. IV., p. 105.

music. Six years afterwards she had another attack, which, however, was on the other side, as she had left-sided hemiplegia chiefly affecting the arm, and became now almost totally deaf. The post-mortem revealed the presence of a destructive lesion of the first and second temporo-sphenoidal convolutions on both sides, thus accounting for the symptoms during life and confirming the localisation of the auditory centres to this region, a region slightly greater in extent than that marked out by Ferrier[1] from his experiments on monkeys.

From what has been already said it will be seen, that there is a cortical auditory centre in both hemispheres, and experiments have shown that the ears are bilaterally represented. How this is brought about it is not exactly known, but probably there is an arrangement of the auditory fibres much like what will be seen later on in connection with the optic fibres, viz. a semidecussation. Ferrier, who is an upholder of this view, says that "unilateral extirpation never gives rise to permanent deafness of the one ear; but though I have on many occasions, after extirpation of the auditory area in one hemisphere, observed loss or impairment of hearing in the opposite ear, I have never been able to detect the slightest impairment of hearing in the ear of the same side." Clinical evidence from a study of word-deafness and cortical lesions, such as give rise to hemiplegia, would lead us to the same conclusion, because it is necessary for a lesion to destroy the centres in both hemispheres in order to render either ear totally deaf, although, as we shall see later, the centre for word-hearing is situated in the left hemisphere only. This is just what would have been expected from a study

[1] *Functions of the Brain.*

of the principle involved in the hypothesis of Broadbent,[1] which has been called Broadbent's law, and is generally recognised to hold good with regard to the motor centres and their innervation, but which is equally applicable to the sensory centres. It was propounded in 1866 by Broadbent before the experiments on animals had shifted the motor centres from the basal ganglia to the cortex, and Broadbent's words have to be considered in that light, but they are sufficiently clear. "Where the muscles of the corresponding parts on opposite sides of the body constantly act in concert, and act independently either not at all or with difficulty, the nerve nuclei of these muscles are so connected with commissural fibres, as to be *pro tanto* a single nucleus. This combined nucleus will have a set of fibres from each corpus striatum, and will usually be called into action by both, but it will be capable of being excited by either singly, more or less completely according as the commissural connection between the two halves is more or less perfect." Again, in 1872,[2] he states his hypothesis very distinctly with regard to the special senses. "But there is a peculiarity in the nerve nuclei or sense centres of the special senses: they are bilaterally associated. This at least is especially the case with the two intellectual senses of sight and hearing, and offers an explanation of the absence of unilateral blindness or deafness in hemiplegia, with marked loss of common sensation in the limbs and trunk. The fused nerve nuclei will constitute a common sense centre which will send up fibres to each half of the cerebrum,

---

[1] *Brit. and For. Med. Chir. Rev.*, April 1866; "Cerebral Mechanism of Speech and Thought," *Med. Chir. Trans.*, 1872.
[2] *Ibid.*, p. 189.

and thus impressions will travel equally to the two hemispheres," etc. In considering the motor side of speech disturbances I shall probably have to refer to this law again.

The conclusions we can draw, therefore, from the facts stated in connection with the localisation of the auditory centre in man are :—

1. That the auditory centre is situated in the first and second temporo-sphenoidal convolutions (see Fig. 2).
2. That there is a centre in both hemispheres.
3. That each ear is bilaterally represented.

We shall at this point leave the auditory route in the meantime, and shall next take up the second route by which sensory impressions of language reach the brain, viz. the visual route.

II. VISUAL ROUTE.

If the course of the auditory route has given rise to much discussion, that of the visual has given rise to even more. The optic nerve fibres begin in the retina and pass to the optic commissure or chiasma, where there is a semidecussation of the fibres. The decussated fibres along with the fibres that have not decussated are then continued in one bundle as the optic tract. This tract winds round the cerebral peduncles, and divides at the postero-inferior part of the optic thalamus into two bundles of fibres. A small internal bundle goes to the internal geniculate body and the posterior quadrageminal body. The larger more external passes into the external geniculate body, the anterior quadrageminal body, and the posterior part of the optic thalamus. From these three masses of grey matter springs the large bundle of fibres which goes by the name of the optic radiations or the radiations of Gratiolet. These fibres pass into the posterior part of the internal capsule, pass backwards external to the posterior horn of the lateral ventricle, and end in the cortical region of the occipital lobe, chiefly in the cuneus and the most posterior part of the lobe.[1] The arrange-

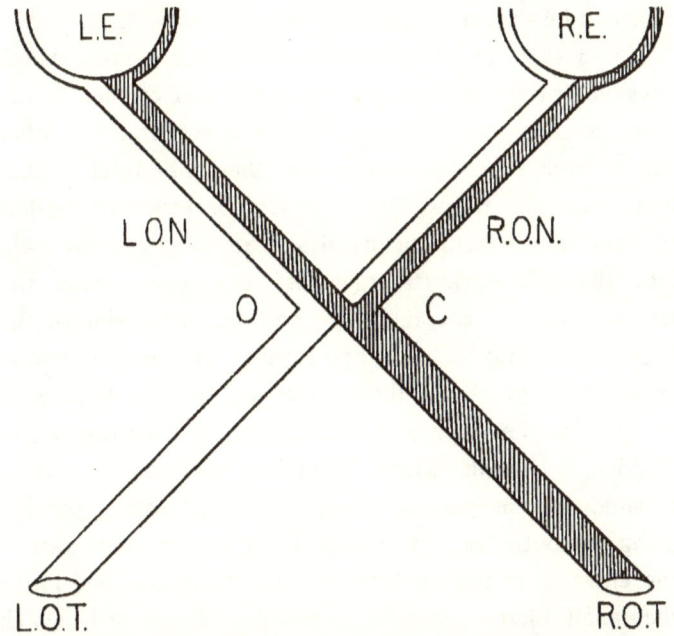

FIG. 3.—SHOWING THE SEMIDECUSSATION OF THE OPTIC NERVES.

L E. Left eye; R E. Right eye; L O N. Left optic nerve; R O N. Right optic nerve; L O T. Left optic tract; R O T. Right optic tract; O C. Optic chiasma.

ment of the fibres in the optic commissure has been pretty well made out. It was held by Brown Sequard and others that there was complete decussation at the chiasma, but it has been distinctly proved in recent years

[1] Déjerine, *Compt. Rendus de la Soc. de Biolog.*, 1891 and 1892.

that there is only a semidecussation. It has been found that the optic fibres of one half of the retina of each eye cross to the opposite side, whereas the optic fibres from the other half of the retina do not cross over. The fibres from the internal or nasal half of the retina cross over, whilst the fibres from the temporal or external half of the retina do not cross over but remain on the same side. This can be shown by a simple diagram (see Fig. 3).

The result of this is that the optic fibres which physiologically act together from the half of each retina pass into one optic tract, whilst the fibres from the other half of each retina pass into the other optic tract. That is to say, the fibres from the temporal side of the left eye and those from the nasal side of the right eye pass into the left optic tract, whilst the fibres from the temporal side of the right eye and the nasal side of the left eye pass into the right optic tract. In the commissure in addition to these fibres there is another bundle of fibres, viz. the inferior commissure or commissure of Gudden, a bundle which is purely commissural. It is situated in the posterior angle of the chiasma; passing along one optic tract, it crosses along the posterior part of the chiasma to the optic tract of the other side, and forms the small internal bundle, previously mentioned, which goes to the internal geniculate body and the posterior quadrageminal body. These fibres are simply commissural for these two bodies on each side, and have been traced from them to the temporal lobes,[1] and need not further be considered here.

It has been shown experimentally that, whilst division of one optic nerve produces complete blindness in one eye,

[1] Monakow, *Opticus u. Sehcentren*. *Arch. f. Psych.*, XVI.

division of one optic tract produces blindness in one half of each retina, viz. what is called homonymous lateral hemianopia. If the left optic tract be divided left lateral homonymous hemianopia is produced—that is to say, the temporal side of the left retina and the nasal side of the right retina are rendered blind. As rays of light from the right side of the patient fall on that half of the retina in each eye, the patient is thus blind to objects in his right field of vision. He is said to have right lateral homonymous hemianopsia, hemianopsia being the term applied to blindness in half of the field of vision, whilst hemianopia is applied to blindness in half of the retina.

The same symptoms are produced by division of the fibres in any part of their course from the optic commissure to their termination in the cortex of the occipital lobe. It has been found also that extirpation of the eyeball is followed by ascending degeneration in the optic nerve of the same side and of half of the optic tract, as far as the external geniculate body, the anterior quadrageminal body, and the optic thalamus, but it does not extend to the optic radiations. Excision of both eyes is followed by ascending degeneration of both tracts as far as the same ganglia,[1] so that these ganglia are the first centres on the visual route. On the other hand, descending degeneration of the fibres follows lesions of the cortical terminations of the radiations of Gratiolet. The fibres in the optical radiations and also the posterior part of the optic thalamus degenerate, and in young animals, and sometimes in man, such degeneration extends to the external geniculate and quadrageminal bodies, the optic tracts and optic nerve of the same side as

[1] Monakow, *Opticus u. Sehcentren.* *Arch. f. Psych.*, XVI.

well as the optic nerve of the opposite side.[1] Much discussion has taken place in recent years as to the precise position of the centre for sight. Ferrier,[2] as result of his experiments, located it in animals in the angular gyrus. Munk,[3] on the other hand, stated that the visual centre was in the outer convex part of the occipital lobe. Horsley and Schäfer[4] found that extensive lesions both of the occipital and of the temporal lobe were invariably followed by visual disturbances taking the form when the operation was confined to one side of the brain of bilateral homonymous hemianopsia, but in nearly every case the hemianopsia was merely temporary. The most marked results were obtained when the occipital lobes were the seat of operation, extensive unilateral lesions producing amblyopia, but only temporary. Schäfer and Sanger Brown[5] in their experiments destroyed both angular gyri without any change in vision. It has been found that both Ferrier and Munk were right in their localisation, because the primary perceptive visual centres have been proved to be in the occipital lobes, and the specialised visual centre, viz. that for words, signs, etc., in the angular gyrus.

In recent years, from a careful study of clinical, pathological, and experimental evidence, the primary visual

---

[1] Monakow, quoted by Déjerine, *Compt. Rendus de la Soc. de Biolog.*, 1891 and 1892.

[2] *Philos. Trans.*, Part II., 1884, and Part II., 1895; and *Brain*, 1888.

[3] *Verhandlungen der Berliner physiol. Gesellschaft*, 1878; and *Ueber die Functionen des Grosshirns, Gesammelte Mittheilungen*, Berlin, 1881.

[4] Quoted by Mills, *Nervous Diseases*, by American Authors. Edited by Dercum, 1895.

[5] *Brain*, January and April 1888, and *Proceed. of Phys. Soc.*, No. 2, 1887.

perceptive centres have been localised in man chiefly to the internal surface of the occipital lobes. Henschen,[1] from a careful study of a large number of cases, arrives at the conclusion that only part of the radiations of Gratiolet are visual, and part have to do with the reflexes of the eye. The visual part is ventrally situated in the radiations, and goes to the neighbourhood of the calcarine fissure. He holds that a lesion in this neighbourhood produces complete hemianopsia, and quotes one of his cases where

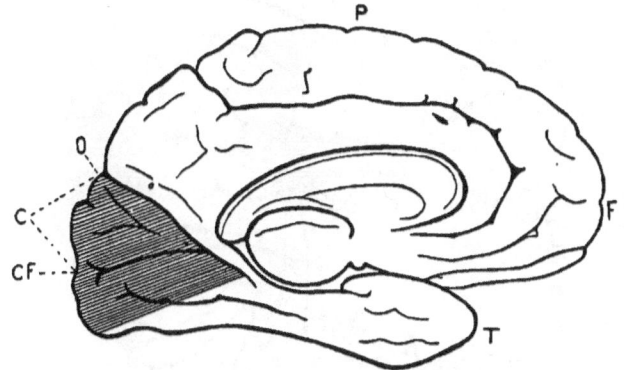

FIG. 4.—THE POSITION OF THE VISUAL PERCEPTIVE CENTRES IS SHADED IN THE DIAGRAM.

F. Frontal, P. Parietal, O. Occipital, T. Temporo-sphenoidal lobes; C. Cuneus; CF. Calcarine fissure.

the cortex and only the cortex in this region was involved with complete hemianopsia. He also believes that the retinal field can be divided into different quadrants, each having its special representation in the optical radiations and in this cortical region, and, contrary to the opinion of Ferrier, who locates it in the angular gyrus, he holds that the macula is represented here also. Vialet[2] also agrees

[1] *Brain*, LXI. and LXII., 1893; Vol. XVI., p. 170.
[2] *Les Centres Cérébraux de la Vision, et l'Appareil*, p. 355.

with Henschen that the calcarine fissure is about the middle of the cortical visual centre of man.[1] The position of the centre is seen in the accompanying diagram (Fig. 4).

The conclusions to be drawn, therefore, from a consideration of all the evidence on visual centres are these:—

1. That the perceptive or primary visual centre in man is in the cortex of the occipital lobe, and most probably

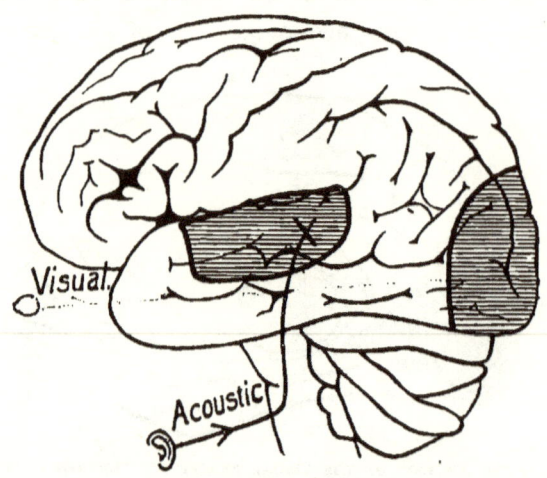

FIG. 5.—LATERAL SURFACE LEFT HEMISPHERE.

The cross is placed in the centres for visual and auditory sensations, the areas being faintly shaded. The blue line represents the optic nerves; the red line represents the auditory nerves.

on the internal surface of that lobe in the immediate neighbourhood of the calcarine fissure.

2. That there is a centre in both hemispheres.

3. That one half of both retinæ is represented in each hemisphere.

4. That as both eyes act together there are probably commissural fibres connecting the centre in one hemi-

[1] *Nervous Diseases*, by American Authors. Edited by Dercum, 1895.

sphere with the centre in the other hemisphere, through the corpus callosum; but these have not yet definitely been made out.

The accompanying diagram (Fig. 5) shows the relative position of the two primary perceptive centres, and it will now be convenient to take up the consideration of the two routes by which speech is produced by the brain, before discussing the means by which these centres are linked together, and in what way speech is able to be received and transmitted, from the sensory or receptive centres to the motor or productive centres.

III. MOTOR SPEECH ROUTE.

And first then let us take up the route concerned in the production of spoken speech. In the act of speaking there are three distinct mechanisms called into action, viz. the respiratory, the vocal, and the oral articulative. A blast of air is forced by the expiratory muscles through the trachea and larynx, and the vocal mechanism acts so as to produce voice or sound by means of movements of the vocal cords. The voice-laden air passes into the pharynx and mouth, and is there acted on by the oral articulative mechanism so as to produce words.

It is therefore necessary, in order to a proper understanding of the speech production route, to trace the innervation of these three mechanisms. I have elsewhere [1] entered into a discussion as to the cerebral localisation of the respiratory centre, and shall only say here, that although it is believed that the respiratory mechanism has a cortical centre, the precise position of it has not yet been made out. Following Broadbent's law, however,

---

[1] Elder, *Edinburgh Hospital Reports*, Vol. III., 1895.

it must be bilaterally represented, and therefore must be very rarely completely disorganised. As respiration requires to go on continually in order that the individual may live, there is a primary centre in the bulb which carries on the usual respiratory movements necessary for life. In the paper quoted I have given some reasons for supposing that the cortical centre for the respiratory movements for speech is situated in the motor areas, but evidence on this point is still very much wanted.

In this connection I may mention a symptom which will be found detailed in Case III.,[1] viz. an occasional deep expiration when the patient was doing anything, either voluntarily or by request. I have noticed this symptom in hemiplegias, aphasias, and other cerebral cases, but I am not aware of its significance, nor am I aware that it has been previously noted. The only explanation I can suggest is that it is due to some impairment of the functions of the respiratory centres, or fibres passing from them to the bulb.

On the other hand, experimental physiology has done much in recent years to locate exactly the position of the centres for the vocal mechanism, as well as the oral articulative mechanism. Before the days when Fritsch and Hitzig began their experiments on the brains of living animals, the motor centres were generally believed to be in the basal ganglia; but since that time the researches of Ferrier,[2] Horsley and Beevor,[3] Horsley and Semon,[4] Krausse,[5] François Franck,[6] and Risien Russell[7] have

---

[1] Page 50.   [2] *Functions of the Brain.*
[3] *Phil. Trans. of Royal Society*, London, 1890.   [4] *Ibid.*
[5] *Arch. f. Anat. u. Physiol.*, 1884.
[6] *Leçons sur les Fonctions Motrices du Cerveau*, Paris, 1887.
[7] *Brit. Med. Journ.*, August 1895.

completely established the fact that the motor centres are situated in the neighbourhood of the fissure of Rolando.

Amongst the muscles whose centres have been so localised are those concerned in the production of speech both spoken and written.

Ferrier[1] locates the centres "*for the lips and tongue as in articulation*" in the foot of the third frontal convolution,

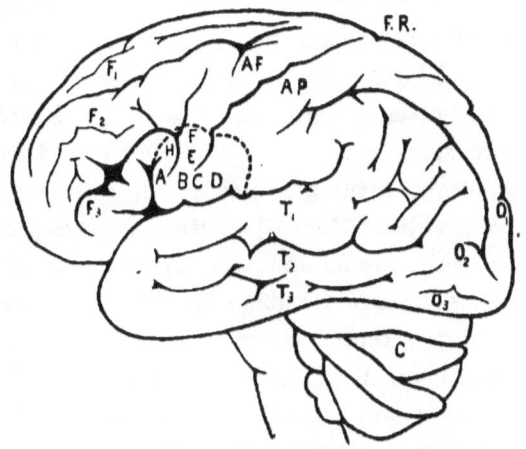

FIG. 6.—LATERAL SURFACE LEFT HEMISPHERE (AFTER WYLLIE).

A. Psycho-motor speech centre ; B. Adductor centre of vocal cords ; C D. Centres for tongue, mouth, etc.; E. Lower face and angle of mouth ; F. Upper face ; H. Abductor centre of vocal cords.

the foot of the ascending frontal and the foot of the ascending parietal (A B C D, Fig. 6), whilst Horsley and Beevor[2] and Horsley and Semon[3] locate the centre for these movements in the same region, but they do not include the posterior part or foot of the third frontal (A) in this centre. Horsley and Semon[4] showed very clearly

[1] *Functions of the Brain.*
[2] *Phil. Trans. of Royal Society*, London, 1890.
[3] *Ibid.*
[4] *Ibid.*

that the anterior part of the foot of the ascending frontal convolution (B, Fig. 6) was the centre for adduction of the vocal cords, and that they were completely bilaterally represented in the hemispheres, so that stimulation of this region on one side produced adduction of both, and that destruction of this region on one side did not produce paralysis of the adduction movements of either side. Several cases have been published against this view in which lesion of this area on one side is said to have produced paralysis of one vocal cord. Such cases have been published by Déjerine,[1] by Garel,[2] and by Garel and Dor.[3]

Semon,[4] however, pointed out that these observations cannot be reliable, because lesion of the whole of this region, as in hemiplegia, never produces paralysis of one vocal cord. Recently Risien Russell[5] by very careful experiments has located the centre for abduction of the vocal cords, not far from this same area, viz. about H (Fig. 6); but he found that the adductor centre was much more active than the abductor, and hence the difficulty in differentiating the two centres. Horsley and Beevor[6] found that the remainder of the lower part of the ascending frontal convolution as well as the lower part of the ascending parietal was the centre for movements of the tongue and throat and for opening and closing the mouth (C D), and that immediately above these areas was an area for the lower face and angle of the mouth, and higher up still a centre (F) for the upper part of the face (see Fig. 6). These were the

[1] *Compt. Rendus Soc. de Biolog.*, Paris, March 1891.
[2] *Ann. d. Mal de l'Oreille du Larynx, etc.*, May 1886.
[3] *Ibid.*, April 1890.
[4] *Virchow's Festschrift*, Bd. III., s. 432.
[5] *Brit. Med. Journ.*, August 1895.
[6] *Phil. Trans. of Royal Society*, London, 1890.

positions of the centres in the anthropoid apes and higher animals, and it was generally supposed that the foot of the third frontal and the cortex immediately behind were the parts of the human brain which corresponded to these centres; the oral articulative mechanism was therefore supposed to have its centre in Broca's convolution, and hence lesion of this region on the left side was supposed to produce always motor aphasia. Wyllie[1] pointed out that whilst Ferrier, probably from clinical as well as experimental evidence, included the foot of the third frontal in the oral articulative centre, other observers did not, and he therefore threw out the hypothesis that the foot of the third frontal is the centre for the psycho-motor images of speech, lesion of which produces motor aphasia, whilst the oral articulative mechanism has its centre in the lower part of the ascending frontal and the lower part of the ascending parietal (B C D E). In the *Edinburgh Hospital Reports* for 1895 I published a case which went a long way to confirm the hypothesis of Wyllie, and as the subject is of considerable importance I give a note of the case here.

CASE I. (*Personal Observation*).—Thomas T., æt. 60, admitted into Leith Hospital May 16th, 1895, complaining of difficulty in speaking. The day before his admission his speech suddenly became indistinct and blurred, and it was observed that the saliva trickled from his mouth. These appear to have been the only symptoms. He went to work, but returned home at midday, not feeling able for it. Next day he was no better, and he asked assistance in putting on his coat. He walked to the hospital, about three hundred yards, and was admitted. On

[1] *Disorders of Speech*, p. 301. Edinburgh, 1894.

admission patient looked feeble, rather stupid and dazed, but conscious, and understood all that was being said. The saliva was trickling from the mouth. There was paresis of the right side of the face and angle of the mouth, not involving the orbicularis palpebrarum, the patient being able to close his eyes quite well. He spoke in a very thick blurred manner, so that it was difficult for him to pronounce the words distinctly. This, however, was seen to be due simply to a difficulty he had in moving the tongue, lips, and other muscles of articulation as readily as he wished to. *There was no true aphasia.* He knew what was being said; he knew what he was going to say, tried to say it, and always succeeded in saying it, but the words were blurred and indistinct. He had difficulty in swallowing even liquids. His voice was unimpaired; there was no hoarseness or other indication that the movements of the vocal cords were in any way affected. He could protrude his tongue, although it came out rather slowly. It did not point distinctly to either side. There was no paralysis of the arm or leg. Sensation remained unimpaired. On the 19th the general appearance of patient was a little better, speech thicker, trouble in swallowing considerable, facial paresis present. The patient gradually got weaker, without showing any new symptoms except dilatation of the right pupil, general livid flushing on the right side of the face, and hypostatic congestion of the lungs. On the 22nd he became comatose and died.

The diagnosis was made of a lesion in the white substance of the left hemisphere, cutting off the fibres passing from the cortex in the lower part of the fissure of Rolando to the internal capsule.

The result of the post-mortem showed that not only were these fibres involved, but the *cortical substance itself* at the lower part of the ascending frontal and ascending parietal convolutions *was destroyed without producing aphasia*. The following is the post-mortem report: On removing the skull-cap the dura was not adherent; the veins on surface of the brain were seen to be full. In the lower part of the ascending frontal convolution, about

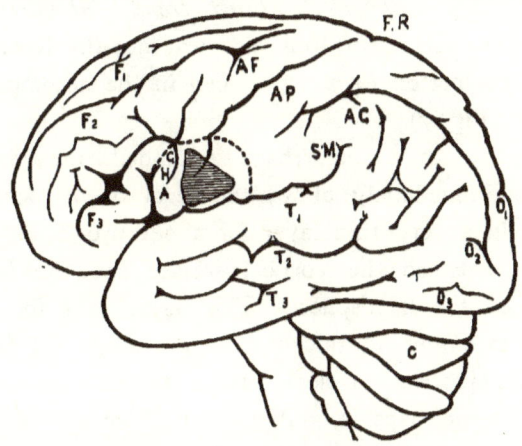

FIG. 7.—LATERAL SURFACE LEFT HEMISPHERE IN CASE I.

The shaded portion shows where the hæmorrhage had destroyed or completely undermined the cortex.

half an inch from the Sylvian fissure, a blood clot was seen which had just pushed its way through the cortex at that particular spot, and it could be seen before cutting into the hemisphere that the cortical substance all around was quite thin, most of it having been destroyed. On slicing the brain horizontally a blood clot, of about a dessert-spoonful in quantity, was found at the level of the lower part of the ascending frontal and ascending parietal convolutions. It had destroyed almost entirely the cortical substance of the lower end of these convolutions, from the Sylvian fissure to as high up as the level of the fissure that divides the second from the third frontal convolution. It extended a little higher up in front than it did behind. It did not quite involve the whole of the lower end of the ascending frontal, as it did not quite reach the precentral sulcus, *there remaining intact a strip of cortex adjoining the foot of the third frontal. The foot of the third frontal also remained intact.* The island of Reil also was not involved. The area of the cortex involved is seen in the accompanying diagram (Fig. 7).

Internally the hæmorrhage extended inwards and forwards immediately above the level of the lenticular nucleus in a very thin layer for about two-thirds of the distance between the cortical surface and the internal surface of the hemisphere. This layer was for about half of its extent no thicker than a penny. Its farthest internal point was in close relation to the anterior limb of the internal capsule, and quite in front of the motor tract.

Fig. 8 is a photograph of the brain in section showing the position of the hæmorrhage.

There was no lesion in the pons or any other part of the central nervous system.

Since publishing the above I have come across a case much similar. In the recently published *Text-Book on Nervous Diseases*, by American Authors, edited by Dercum (1895), Mills quotes a case (page 409) observed by himself as confirmatory of Wyllie's hypothesis. He says: " In a case of typical orolingual paralysis recorded by me, the patient had distinct facial paralysis in the muscles supplied by the lower distribution of the seventh nerve, and also lingual paresis; probably also slight want of control over the right orbicularis palpebrarum. He had some power over the nasal dilator, and good control of masseter, pterygoid, and temporal movements. Articulation was distinctly involved because of orolingual mono-paresis. He could talk, but pronounced certain words indistinctly. He had

FIG. 8.—PHOTOGRAPH OF BRAIN IN CASE I. HORIZONTAL SECTION THROUGH LEFT HEMISPHERE.
The position of the blood clot is darker in the photograph.

no difficulty in propositionising. (That is, there was no true motor aphasia.) A focus of strictly cortical yellowish softening was found involving the lower extremities of both central convolutions (the ascending frontal and ascending parietal) both on their external and Sylvian surfaces, and a soft one, half an inch in diameter, about the middle of the internal portion of the insula. The softening reached into the central fissure, thus taking in a posterior inferior strip of the second frontal convolution. Its greatest height was one and a half inches upward from the Sylvian fissure, its width along this fissure one and a quarter inches. The anterior limit of the lesion was a fourth of an inch caudad of the pre-sylvian fissure." This case is so very like my case in the position of the lesion and in the symptoms that I find that Mills draws almost the same conclusion from his case that I did from mine, viz. that the psycho-motor speech area, or, as he calls it, following Broadbent, the propositionising centre, is in the foot of the third frontal, whilst the vocal and oral articulative centres, or, as he calls them, the utterance centre, are situated in the lower part of the ascending frontal and lower part of the ascending parietal convolutions. "Utterance centre," although a convenient term, is not, I think, a physiologically accurate one, because I believe there are several centres in this area and not only one utterance centre. There is the centre for adduction and the centre for abduction of the vocal cords, the centres for movements of the tongue, throat, lips, and cheeks, and these centres are quite capable of acting independently, but in speech production they are acted on by the psycho-motor (Wyllie) or propositionising (Broadbent) centre in the foot of the third frontal, which centre does all the cell grouping or regulating, or coordinating of these centres so that the correct word or words are produced.

Wyllie's terms, therefore, of "psycho-motor" for the propositionising centre and "executory-motor" or "vocal and oral articulative mechanism" for the utterance centres are more physiologically correct.

Granted that these two centres exist, then they must be joined together by connecting fibres, which in all probability lie either immediately beneath the cortex or in the cortex itself. As it is generally supposed that corresponding parts of the cortex of each hemisphere are also linked together, the foot of the third frontal on the left side is probably joined to the corresponding part on the right side by commissural fibres through the corpus callosum. The lower parts of the ascending frontal and ascending parietal convolutions for the same reason are probably connected with the corresponding parts on the opposite side by commissural fibres, also through the corpus callosum. It probably is by means of these fibres that there is a more or less bilateral representation, but it is possible that the bilateral representation may be partly if not wholly brought about by commissural fibres in the bulb. The importance of these commissural fibres will appear when lesions in this region are considered. Tracing now the course of the motor speech route from the propositionising or psycho-motor centre in the foot of the left third frontal, the nervous energy passes posteriorly to the vocal and oral articulative centres on the same side where the proper cell grouping takes place for the production of the correct words. The vocal and oral articulative mechanism centres on the opposite side must also be acted on by the same psycho-motor centre in the same way and at the same time, but in what way the nerve influence reaches the right side has not hitherto been known. Besides proving the precise position of the vocal and oral articulative centre, the case I have published, as also Mills', proves that the energy to reach the right side passes from the foot of the third left frontal to the foot of the third right frontal, and thence to the vocal and oral articulative mechanism on the right side; or, what is not so likely, it passes from the third left frontal directly to the vocal and oral articulative centres on the right side; or, what is least probable of all, it passes from the psycho-motor centre on the left side to the vocal centre on the same side, and then to the vocal and oral articulative centres on the opposite side. I draw this conclusion because the lesion in my case of destruction of the left oral articulative centre (the vocal centre escaped destruction) produced only mono-paresis of the oral articulative mechanism, and not complete paralysis, as would have been the case if the whole of the fibres from the foot of the third frontal on the left side had to pass through this destroyed centre first before reaching the other side. The case would have shown all the symptoms of a subcortical motor aphasia, instead of simply being one of dysarthria, if this conclusion is not correct.

That the commissural fibres high up in the cerebrum are of great importance is also seen from the fact that lesion in the fibres from the oral articulative centre on the right side produces the same symptoms as the same lesion on the left side, viz. dysarthria, showing that the commissural fibres in the pons are not quite sufficient for the innervation of both sides. If these latter commissural fibres were sufficient, then lesion of the fibres on any side above the pons would not produce any paresis of the oral articulative mechanism, because the nervous energy could reach the pons by the side which remained intact. It has been found, however, that more nervous energy passes down the fibres on the left side than on the right, as lesion on the left side produces more marked dysarthria than the same lesion on the right side, and also that a right-sided lesion is sooner recovered from than a left-

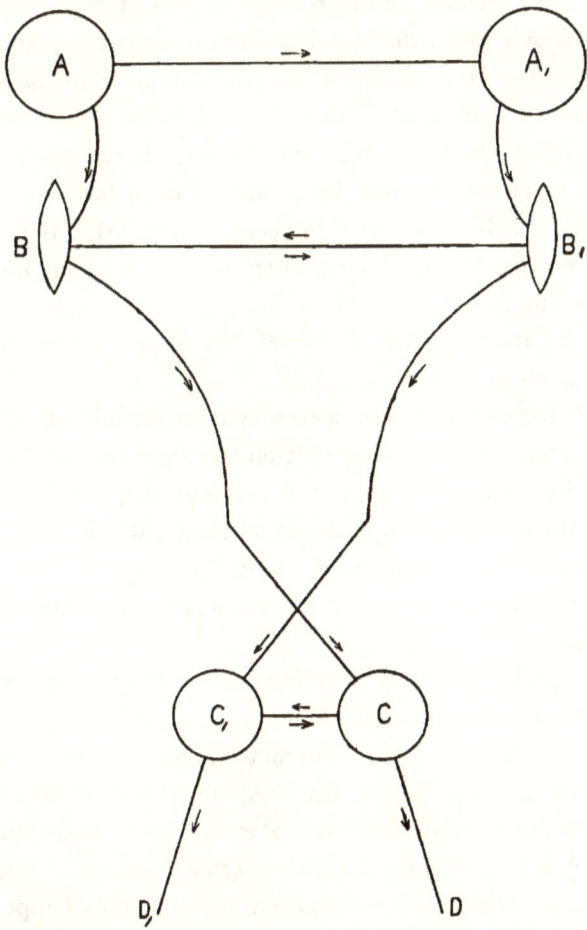

FIG. 9.—DIAGRAMMATIC REPRESENTATION OF THE COURSE OF THE FIBRES IN THE MOTOR SPEECH TRACT. FOR DESCRIPTION SEE TEXT.

sided one. Lichtheim,[1] who of course treats Broca's convolution as one centre and not as containing several

[1] *Brain*, January 1885, p. 480.

centres, shows that there must be decussating fibres crossing high up in the cerebrum. He says: Now if the fibres from Broca's centre reached the basal organs down the left side only, the usual persistent aphasic symptoms would arise from lesion of the left peduncle or internal capsule as uniformly as they do from those of the centre itself. But we know that this is only exceptionally the case; hence there must be a partial decussation of the speech tract from left to right hemisphere within the brain itself, so that the left internal capsule does not contain the whole bundle of these fibres. Fig. 9 is a diagrammatic representation of the course of the fibres of the motor spoken-speech tract.

A is the psycho-motor speech area on the left side.

A_1 is the corresponding part on the right side.

B, the vocal and oral articulative centres on the left side.

B_1, the corresponding centres on the right side.

C_1 and C, the centres in the bulb.

D_1 and D, the nerves to the vocal and oral articulative muscles.

In speaking the production route I suppose to be A B C D and A A_1 B_1 C_1 D_1.

If A is destroyed complete motor aphasia is produced.

If lesion cuts off A from A_1 and from B complete infra-pictorial or subcortical motor aphasia is produced.

If A is cut off from B alone or from A_1 alone, B and A_1 remaining intact, probably no symptoms or only temporary ones would be produced, owing to the commissural fibres between B and B_1; but no case of this has been recorded, the area is so limited.

If B is destroyed or B C, or if B_1 is destroyed or $B_1 C_1$, dysarthria results.

If B C and B_1C_1 are both destroyed anarthria and pseudo-bulbar paralysis result.

From the vocal and oral articulative centres the outgoing fibres pass in the centrum ovale over the lenticular nucleus to the internal capsule, and Horsley and Beevor [1]

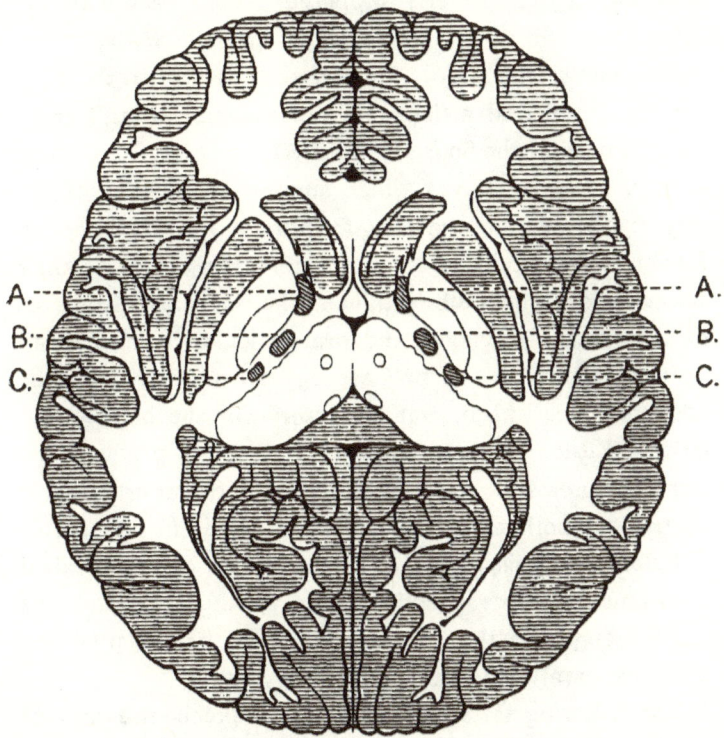

FIG. 10.—HORIZONTAL SECTION OF BRAIN (AFTER FLECHSIG) THROUGH THE INTERNAL CAPSULE AND BASAL GANGLIA.

A shows position in internal capsule of the fibres for tongue and mouth; B shows position for wrist, fingers, thumb, etc.; C shows position for adductors of the vocal cords.

have shown that the fibres for the oral articulative mechanism are situated at the knee of the internal capsule,

[1] *Phil. Trans. of Royal Society*, London, 1890.

whilst Horsley and Semon[1] have shown that the fibres for adduction of the vocal cords are situated in almost exactly the middle of the posterior limb of the capsule (see Fig. 10).

The fibres do not form any connections with the corpus striatum, as was formerly supposed. They pass with the other motor fibres into the crus cerebri, where the motor tract occupies the middle third of the crusta. In the pons the vocal and oral articulative fibres decussate and enter motor nuclei in the floor of the fourth ventricle, from which arise the cranial nerves which supply the muscles of the larynx, the throat, the tongue, mouth, lips, and cheeks. Lesion of these fibres on one side in any part of their course above the bulb produces the same symptoms as destruction of the vocal and oral articulative mechanism centres themselves, as in Case I., viz. no change in the adductor mechanism, but dysarthria in the oral articulative. Lesion of these fibres on both sides produces the same symptoms as lesion of the vocal and oral articulative centres on both sides, viz. anarthria, and the symptoms of bulbar paralysis, a form of disease which has been called by French authors pseudo-bulbar paralysis. Below the motor ganglia in the bulb, lesion of the nerves produces of course paralysis in the muscles they supply.

The following are short notes of two excellent examples of dysarthria in patients where the lesions were in all probability in two different parts of the motor speech tract. In the first the lesion was diagnosed and proved at the post-mortem examination to be in the fibres passing from the executory-motor centres in the lower part of the ascending frontal and ascending parietal convolutions to

[1] *Phil. Trans. of Royal Society*, London, 1890.

the internal capsule; I concluded that it was much in the same position as in Case I. (Fig. 8), and the post-mortem showed that it was slightly nearer the internal capsule. Besides dysarthria there was paresis of the right hand and face, and there was also slight disturbance of the psycho-motor centre (A, Fig. 9), because the patient occasionally had difficulty in recalling the pronunciation of the word, as well as "slurring" it once it was recalled. She could read and understand what she read, as well as understand spoken speech. The case might have had a lesion of the cortex as well as of the substance, as in Case I.; but the fact that the arm was so much involved, as well as the face and muscles of oral articulation, together with the fact that the patient was never very ill until the onset of the congestive symptoms which preceded death, showed that the cause of the symptoms was probably a small lesion, and therefore was more likely in the white substance where the fibres from the different areas converge. It must, however, as I have said, have been sufficiently near the cortex to have disturbed the functions of Broca's convolution. The patient could not use the right hand sufficiently to write with that, but she wrote with the left hand as readily as any one can with it, although it is very interesting to notice that she wrote from right to left instead of from left to right. This is very interesting to contrast with the next patient, who wrote with her left hand from left to right. Such writing can be read on holding it up before the mirror, and she was therefore a case of mirror writing. She wrote in that way because it was more convenient for her, and probably would have done so with her left hand before the onset of her illness. I have tested many patients and others in this way, and find that a certain proportion, especially of well educated people, are mirror writers with the left hand. This patient had been a very well educated woman and had had much practice in writing. I shall, however, have more to say on this point when considering mirror writing.

CASE II. *(Personal Observation).—Dysarthria, paresis of right arm and right side of face. Post-mortem.*

B. N. L., æt. 31, admitted to Leith Hospital October 23rd, 1896, with paresis of the right arm and right side of face and difficulty in speaking. The history was that shortly before admission she had suddenly lost the power of the right arm, so that she could not raise the hand to the mouth. She was not unconscious. The power came back for a short time again, so that she could grasp a hand and raise her hand to her mouth; but it very soon disappeared, and she remained in the condition in which she was admitted, viz. she had not complete paralysis of the right hand, but the movements of the hand were slow and not nearly so extensive as they ought to be. She could raise her hand slowly to her mouth. She grasped one's hand slowly and feebly, whilst the movements of her left hand were normal. There was also evident paresis of the right side of her face, most marked about the angle of the mouth. There was no paralysis of either leg.

Her speech was slow, hesitating, and slurring in character. She had evident difficulty with the finer movements necessary to produce distinct pronunciation, so that test sentences such as " British Constitution " were imperfectly pronounced. In addition to this, however, there was a very slight difficulty in recalling the pronunciation of some words, so that there was evidently a disturbance of the functions of the psycho-motor speech centre, believed at the time to be due to a lesion near to Broca's convolution.

The paresis of arm, hand, and face gradually improved from the date of admission to November 2nd, when she suddenly became worse and rapidly passed into coma. In this comatose condition the left side seemed to be more limp and flaccid than the right, so that it was doubtful whether these acute symptoms were not due to a lesion in the right internal capsule. As the patient, however, was quite comatose it was difficult to be certain as to the left-sided paralysis. Soon after the onset of the comatose condition bedsores began to form on the right side of the back and buttock. There was a rapid rise of temperature to 104° on the 4th, and she died with a high temperature on November 6th.

The diagnosis that was made was a lesion in the white substance of the left hemisphere, in the fibres passing from the convolutions at the lower half of the fissure of Rolando to the internal capsule, accounting for the symptoms during the first ten days in hospital, whilst the sudden aggravation of her illness might either be due to a fresh lesion in the internal capsule of the other side or to an attack of congestive meningitis.

At the post-mortem there was found a slightly thickened dura-mater, with increase of arachnoid fluid and congestion of the superficial veins. Over the vertex of the hemispheres, on each side of the longitudinal fissure, the membranes were found adherent to the brain substance, so that on tearing them off small shreds of cortical substance were torn off along with them. There was a considerable amount of milky opalescent fluid in the fissures between the convolutions, and this was especially marked at the beginning of the Sylvian and Rolandic fissures on the left side. The milkiness was seen to be due to shreddy lymph.

On making a transverse section of the left hemisphere a small patch of acute softening about the size of a small marble was seen in the white substance of the hemisphere immediately external to and above the corpus striatum. The ventricle was normal, as was also the internal capsule. There was no lesion found in the right hemisphere, and none in the pons or other part of the brain. The seat of the lesion is seen in Fig. 11.

Evidently this lesion accounted for the primary symptoms, and the later severe symptoms were due to the meningitis which was so evident over both hemispheres.

The next case, also one of dysarthria, presented some points of great interest. The lesion in her I presume to have been considerably lower down in the motor tract. There was marked dysarthria in her also, but there was no impairment at all of the psycho-motor speech area. She had no true motor aphasia, and, like the previous case, she could have written if she had had the use of her right hand. With her left hand she wrote slowly in the usual way. Like the previous

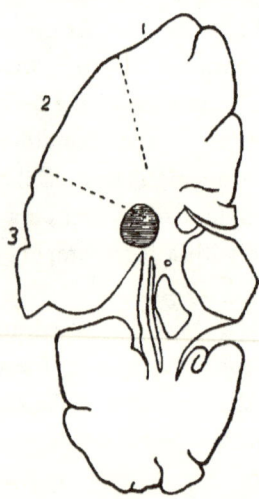

FIG. 11.—VERTICAL SECTION OF LEFT HEMISPHERE IN ANTERIOR PARIETAL REGION.

The shaded portion shows the patch of acute softening, Case II. 1. Cortical motor area for the leg; 2. Cortical motor area for the arm; 3. Cortical motor area for the face.

case, she could read and understand what she read and what was said to her quite well.

What, however, makes it certain that the lesion was farther down than in the previous case was the extensive nature of the tracts involved. She had complete hemiplegia and hemianæsthesia. She not only had complete motor paralysis of all the muscles of the arm and leg on the right side, but she had also paresis of the muscles of the right side of the face and mouth, just as results from central paralysis of one facial. She had, in addition, hemianæsthesia on the right side. She had insensibility to common sensation, to heat and cold, and to pain, and also loss of muscular sense on the right side.

In spite of the extensive involvement of sensory and motor nerves, her general cerebral symptoms were not marked, showing that the lesion was not a very large one.

Taking all these facts together, therefore, the seat of the lesion must have been in a position where the sensory and motor fibres were near each other. They get near together about the lower part of the internal capsule, the crus cerebri, and the pons. As the position must have been above the crossing of the seventh nerve, and as there were no eye symptoms, the probabilities are that it was above the level of the pons, and probably therefore in the crus or lower part of the internal capsule.

CASE III. (*Personal Observation*).—*Dysarthria, hemiplegia, hemianæsthesia.*

N. E., æt. 64, cook, admitted to Leith Hospital October 18th, 1896, with the following history :—

Three days before admission, whilst patient was sweeping the lobby in the early morning, she took a pain in the left side of the head and felt very giddy. She was quite conscious, and has remained so. Her niece saw her on the afternoon of the onset of her illness, and says that the patient was unable to move the right arm and leg, and also that her mouth was drawn to the left side. She was cold on the right side, but next day the coldness began to disappear. She slept well during the night, and was drowsy through the day. She was able to drink milk through a feeding cup.

On admission to the hospital the following was her condition :—

There was complete motor and sensory paralysis of the right side of body, arms, and legs; a high degree of facial paralysis, especially in the lower part of the face. Pupils were equal, and reacting to light and accommodation. Knee-jerks were almost absent on the affected side. There were commencing bedsores on the right side of the back and buttocks. There was no incontinence of urine or fæces. Speech was slurring and difficult to make out because of paresis of the lips, tongue, etc., and also from the fact that she was without her false teeth.

On the 25th the following was her condition :—

There was almost complete anæsthesia of the right side, including face, arms, body, and legs; the anæsthesia extending close up to the middle line both in front and behind; complete hemiplegia of right arm, leg, and face; right side of face flattened, and angle of mouth drawn to left side. Frontalis muscles of both sides moved at will, and muscles of right side of face moved better the higher up they were in position. Had slurring speech (dysarthria). Occasionally whilst being examined gave a deep sigh. Was insensible to heat and cold and pain, as well as to ordinary sensation on the right side. Muscular sense on right side had also gone.

1. She could read aloud and silently, understanding what she read.

2. She could hear and understand words perfectly.

3. Had difficulty in pronouncing words, slurring the syllables (dysarthria), but had no difficulty in recalling how they should be pronounced. When reading and speaking she often made a deep expiration like a sigh.

4. Could not move her right hand, and therefore was not able to write with it, but with the left hand she wrote slowly from left to right (in the usual way), although the writing was very shaky.

Oct. 26.—The knee reflexes on the right side were slightly exaggerated. No ankle clonus. Had no sensation of pain on the right side even when a pin was stuck through the skin into the muscle.

Could move the right leg at knee slightly.

Oct. 27.—Still was able to move the right leg a little, and some return of sensation about and below the knee and in the sole of the foot.

Oct. 28.—Slight return of sensation on the right side of face towards the middle line and in sole of foot. Could move the hip, knee, and toes. Ankle clonus was elicited.

Nov. 4.—Sensation in leg slightly improved, as also in the arm. Moved the whole leg slightly. There was distinct ankle clonus, and increased reflexes on the right side. There was a distinct movement of the leg on tickling the sole, although she herself felt it little (a reflex movement). Her speech was not so slurring, and her general intelligence not so dulled.

Had still a tendency to give a deep sigh when undergoing examination.

Pupils reacted to light and accommodation. There was no aphasia.

Nov. 7.—Sensation and motor power in right side was improving. Felt tickling of soles of feet distinctly. Was speaking better, and had a brighter expression.

Nov. 10.—Moved the thumb and index fingers slightly, and there was a gradual increase of her motor power, and return of sensory functions in affected side. The bedsores were rapidly healing.

She gradually improved, and on December 21st she was able to move her arm and leg, although slowly and with difficulty. She could stretch out her hand and grasp a hand of another, and could slightly press the hand. The sensory functions had almost completely returned. The right side of the body perspired a little more freely than the left. Her speech was nearly normal, the dysarthria having almost entirely disappeared. Common sensation, sense of heat and cold, the muscular sense, and sense of pain seemed to return about the same time and gradually.

This case was a very unusual one, as it is very rarely one finds complete hemiplegia along with complete hemianæsthesia. Into that subject it is not my intention to enter, however, here. In the absence of a post-mortem examination one cannot be absolutely definite as to the site of the lesion, but the probabilities are that it was in the crus cerebri or lower part of the internal capsule, for the reason stated previously.

One symptom I may mention here which was very marked in this case, and that was the tendency the patient had to give a deep sigh or a forcible expiration now and again when she was doing anything, as, for instance, when speaking or when being examined. This symptom I have referred to and have suggested an explanation of when I was considering the respiratory centres; whatever its significance may be, it was certainly very evident in this case.

The conclusions we are now in a position to draw from a consideration of the spoken-speech production route are the following :—

1. That the psycho-motor speech centre is in the foot of the third left frontal convolution.

2. That the vocal and oral articulative centres are immediately behind it in the lower part of the ascending frontal and the lower part of the ascending parietal convolutions on both sides

3. That whilst the vocal or phonation mechanism is completely bilaterally represented, the oral articulative mechanism is not so completely bilaterally represented in the hemispheres.

4. That the psycho-motor centre is connected directly with the vocal and oral articulative centres on the left side, and either directly, or more probably indirectly, through the less active psycho-motor speech area on the right side, by means of connecting or commissural fibres, with the vocal and oral articulative centres on the right side.

5. That lesion of the oral articulative centres on either side, or fibres from them down to the bulb, only produces difficulty in articulation (dysarthria), and not true aphasia, whereas a lesion of the psycho-motor centre, or of the fibres coming from it connecting it both to the vocal and oral articulative centres on the same and opposite

sides, produces complete motor aphasia. Later on it will be shown, however, that the symptoms of a lesion of the psycho-motor centre itself (cortical motor aphasia) differ from the symptoms of a lesion of the fibres connecting this centre with the vocal and oral articulative centres (subcortical or infra-pictorial motor aphasia).

IV. GRAPHIC PRODUCTION ROUTE.

Let me now shortly describe the other speech production route, viz. the route for writing. In writing the right hand is used by most people, and the centre is therefore usually situated in the left hemisphere. Ferrier localises the centre for the hand across the middle of the ascending frontal and ascending parietal convolutions, opposite the posterior extremity of the second frontal. In accordance with Broadbent's law, the hand is unilaterally represented in the hemispheres, stimulation of the centre in one hemisphere producing only movements in the opposite hand. Whilst the right hand only is used for writing, we can, to a certain extent, trace letters and form words with the left hand. This I believe in most cases is merely an act of tracing or copying, because the person who is using the left hand, even although there is no copy before him, raises the visual picture memory of the letters in his cerebrum. It is, I believe, the same process that is gone through where we try to substitute the left hand for the right in an action for which the right hand has become specialised: the action is not done neatly and promptly, and as it were automatically, but rather by imitating each individual movement of the right hand. This is done either from imitating directly the movements of the right hand, or by raising up in memory the picture of its former movements. As I pointed out when discussing Case II., some people on attempting to write with the left hand naturally write from right to left, so that the writing can be read easily when reflected in a mirror. Later I shall have more to say on this subject, however, as well as on the whole subject of writing and agraphia. I shall give reasons for supposing that, analogous to the psycho-motor speech centre in the third left frontal, there is in all probability a psycho-motor writing centre which does all the cell grouping for regulating the movements of the hand and fingers, so that the proper letter is written. This subject, however, will be best considered along with word-blindness and agraphia, and I shall only say here that some, although far from conclusive, evidence has been produced in favour of this centre being situated in the posterior part of the second left frontal convolution in right-handed persons. From the motor centres for the hand the fibres pass to the internal capsule, where they occupy an area in the posterior limb a little behind the knee, whence they pass down with the other motor fibres in the motor tract to the spinal cord, crossing to the opposite side at the decussation of the pyramids, and need not further be considered here.

CONCLUSIONS AS TO THE RECEPTION AND PRODUCTION SPEECH ROUTES.

We have now considered the two routes for the reception of speech and the two routes for the production of speech, and we have been able to localise the terminations and origins of these routes in the cerebral cortex.

We have found that the hearing centres are in both hemispheres in the posterior half of the first and second temporal convolutions, and that the visual centres are in both hemispheres in the occipital lobes in the neighbourhood of the calcarine fissure; that analogous to these primary receptive centres—or that part of the cortex where the incoming nerve fibres reach the nerve cells first—we have on the motor side two areas where the nerve fibres leave the nerve cells in the cortex: viz. the lower part of the ascending frontal and ascending parietal convolutions in both hemispheres, the beginning of the spoken speech tract; and the middle of the ascending frontal and ascending parietal convolutions in the left hemisphere (owing to the right hand only being usually used for writing), the beginning of the writing speech tract. These areas have been indicated in Fig. 12 by a X. We have seen also that on the production side there is a higher or specialised centre, the psycho-motor speech centre, situated in the left hemisphere only, in the foot of the third frontal, and that there also probably is a higher or specialised psycho-motor writing centre in the posterior part of the second frontal. Analogous to these, many cases have proved that on the receptive side also there are two higher or specialised centres: one, the word-hearing centre, situated in the same region as, but more limited in area than, the hearing centre, and on one (the left) side only; and the other, the word-seeing centre, situated in the angular gyrus and posterior part of the supra-marginal convolution, on one (the left) side only. We shall find evidence of these latter facts later, when we consider the various forms of aphasia.

CEREBRAL SPEECH MECHANISM. 55

I have indicated these four specialised centres by a circle in the diagram (Fig. 12), and connected them with their lower centres, and indicated the course of the speech routes on the receptive side up to these areas and on the production side from these areas.

To complete our consideration of the different routes and to show how these centres are connected it will be

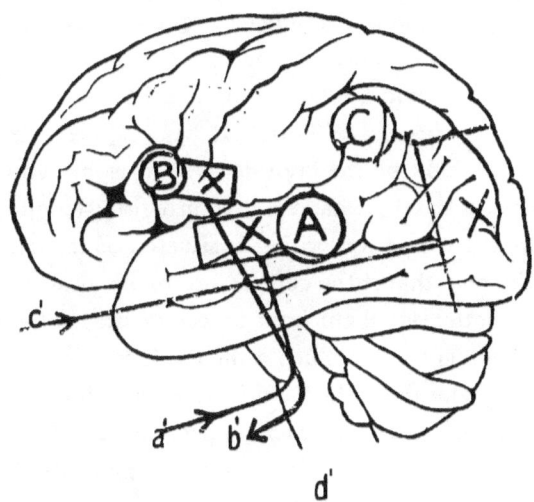

FIG. 12.—LATERAL SURFACE LEFT HEMISPHERE. DIAGRAMMATIC REPRESENTATION OF THE CENTRES CONCERNED IN THE RECEPTION AND PRODUCTION OF SPEECH.

The circles show the higher speech centres; the crosses are placed in the receptive areas for auditory and visual sensations, and on the production side in the motor areas for the movements concerned in speech production.

A. Auditory centre; C. Visual word centre; B. Psycho-motor speech centre; D. Supposed psycho-motor graphic centre. a'. Auditory, c'. Optic nerves; b'. Nerve fibres to oral articulatory muscles; d'. Fibres to the hand.

best to enter into a consideration of lesions of these different areas and the connecting fibres between them, lesions which give rise to the various forms of aphasia.

Dextral Pre-eminence.

Before entering on the subject of aphasia, however, it will be well to say a few words as to why the specialised speech centres are situated in the left hemisphere. Various explanations of this have been suggested. Wyllie[1] agrees with the theory first suggested by Dr. Moxon,[2] that the explanation is to be found in a study of the Faculty of Attention, and that if it is sufficient for the purpose of speech that the speech memories be only stored on one side of the brain, then it would be more economical for nature to train one side only instead of both. It has also been suggested that the left side of the brain is used in right-handed persons because the right hand is used in writing language, and therefore the centre for writing is situated on the left side of the brain, and that if the centres are to be localised to one side it is better for them from an economical point of view to be on the left side. Such a theory, however, besides not explaining why the right hand is used for writing and other actions in preference to the left, is defective also from a physiological point of view, because the writing centre is one of the very last to acquire its special function in the production of speech. The child learns to speak before it learns to write, and such speech is stored on the left side. The explanation of why the left side of the brain is used in writing as in speaking must be sought for in a consideration of the whole subject of dextral pre-eminence. Many explanations have been offered as to why the right hand takes the foremost place, and why either hand is not used indiscriminately. It has been found that not only are the majority of men right-handed, but they also show a preference for the right leg.

[1] *Disorders of Speech*, p. 248. Edinburgh, 1894.
[2] *Brit. and Foreign Med. Chir. Rev.*, 1866.

Ogle[1] found that not only do the right limbs take a pre-eminent place in man, but that the same dextral pre-eminence is found in some of the lower animals, notably in monkeys and parrots. After carefully considering most of the theories as to dextral pre-eminence, he arrives at the conclusion that the cause of it is to be found in structural anatomy. The left hemisphere is found to be larger and more convoluted than the right; the left carotid and left vertebral arteries are larger than the right; and he thought he found the explanation of this in the fact that the left carotid came off from the arch of the aorta directly, and more in a line with the current of blood in the aorta, whereas the right carotid is a branch of the innominate, which latter vessel at its origin from the aorta is not so directly in a line with, and would offer more resistance to, the blood current.

This explanation is certainly very ingenious, but it has yet to be proved whether it is the correct one. All that we know at present is that the left side of the brain takes the lead in the large majority of the human race, and that it very decidedly does so in the reception and production of speech. It has been found, however, that most left-handed persons have their speech centres situated in the right hemisphere, and this in spite of the fact that many of them use the right hand for writing, showing that writing has not such a decided determining influence as some suppose. This has been found in many cases of left hemiplegia with aphasia where post-mortems have taken place. The very few exceptional cases which have been published would probably be found, if every circumstance were known, to be not really exceptions at all.

[1] *Med. Chir. Trans.*, LIV., 1871.

CHAPTER III.

MECHANISM OF SPEECH, AS SHOWN BY ITS DISORGANISATION.

HAVING localised the speech reception and the speech production centres to special areas in the cerebral cortex, I shall now endeavour by a study of cases of aphasia to show the mechanism by which speech and thought are received, stored up, and produced by the brain.

Since the time of Broca's cases our knowledge of the localisation of the cerebral speech mechanism has gradually been added to. Broca described one form of aphasia, a form which has since borne the name of Broca's type or motor aphasia. James Russell[1] in 1864 was the first to show that, besides the form of motor aphasia described by Broca, there was another form where there was loss of the memory of words. Ogle[2] for the latter form gave the name of amnemonic and for the former ataxic aphasia. "Amnesic" was soon, however, substituted for "amnemonic," and "amnesia," or loss of the memory of words, is still much used in connection with aphasia.

Wernicke[3] divided the different forms of aphasia into three varieties : 1st, motor aphasia ; 2nd, sensory aphasia ; and 3rd, a form where the conduction fibres between the

[1] *Brit. Med. Journ.*, 1864.
[2] "Aphasia and Agraphia," *St. George's Hospital Reports*, Vol. II., pp. 83-121.
[3] *Der Aphasische Symptomen Complex*, 1874.

sensory area and the motor area or Broca's convolution were involved in a lesion. This form he called "Leitungs-aphasie." Wernicke also localised his sensory form to the temporal lobe, and the conduction form probably to the island of Reil.

Word-blindness was first described by Kussmaul[1] in 1877, but it was not till later that the lesion was localised. Agraphia was noticed in many aphasic patients, and was believed to be a symptom which might be exhibited by all forms of aphasia. In recent years the tendency of clinical observers has been towards recognising it as a special variety of aphasia, but perhaps the greatest authority on it and word-blindness, Déjerine,[2] has shown that, although it is a prominent symptom in the other forms of aphasia, the cases are very few if there are any where it is the only symptom.

Clinical observation has therefore shown that there are five chief forms of aphasia, and four of these forms are produced by a lesion or disorganisation of the four centres which we have already from a study of speech in the child theoretically found to exist, and from physiological, experimental, and pathological evidence have localised in special parts of the left cerebral cortex.

These primary varieties of aphasia are the following :—

1. Auditory aphasia, or word-deafness.

2. Visual aphasia, or word-blindness.

3. Motor aphasia, or aphemia, or the blotting out of the motor images of words.

4. Agraphia, or the blotting out of the motor graphic images of words.

[1] Ziemssen, *Cycl. of Pract. Med.*, Amer. edition, Vol. XIV.
[2] *Compt. Rendus de la Soc. de Biolog.*, 1891 and 1892.

5. Conduction aphasia, or lesion of the fibres connecting the auditory and visual to the motor and graphic centres.

The two first will be seen to be sensory, and consist in a lesion of the cortical regions where the receptive speech routes terminate, and the next two to be motor, and due to a lesion of the cortical regions at the commencement of the two production speech routes. Auditory aphasia, or word-deafness, is thus due to a lesion in the upper part of the temporo-sphenoidal convolution, whilst word-blindness is due to a lesion in the supra-marginal convolution and angular gyrus; aphemia to a lesion in the psycho-motor centre or foot of the left third frontal, and typical agraphia to a lesion in the posterior part of the second left frontal; whilst conduction aphasia cases are usually due to lesions in the neighbourhood of the island of Reil and floor of the Sylvian fissure.

Lesions limited, however, to each of these areas are very rare, so that in most cases we have more than one of these areas involved—and, besides, the fibres connecting these areas are also often involved—so that there are great varieties in the symptoms produced, even in cases where the chief lesions are in the same region. From a careful study of the mechanism of speech, however, it is theoretically necessary to add another and higher mechanism than these four centres, viz. the mechanism by which the intelligence is called into action or by which the concepts are elaborated, which has gone by various names by various authors, but for which perhaps the best name is the "ideational" mechanism.

Probably there is not one ideational centre alone, but rather many higher centres, concerned in the elaboration of ideas. We, however, know very little as to the

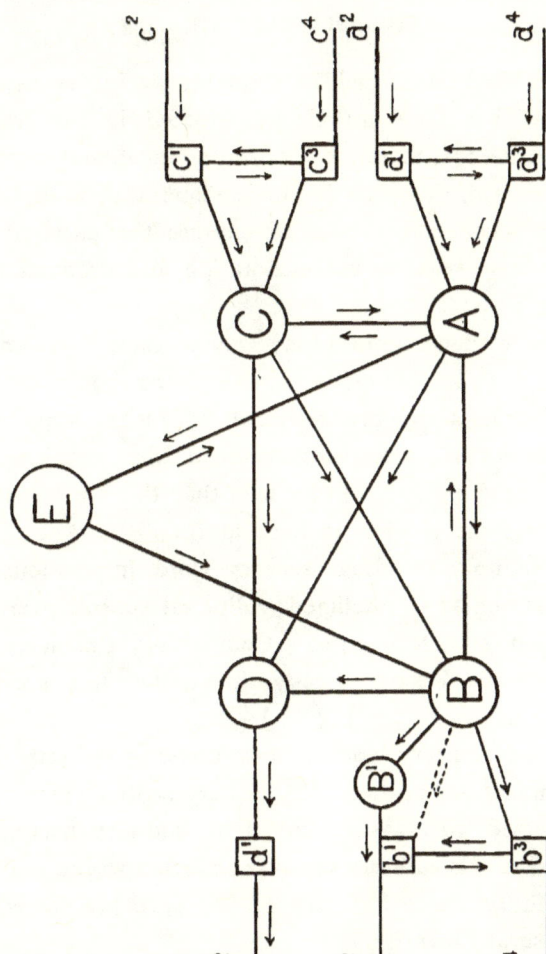

FIG. 13.—DIAGRAMMATIC REPRESENTATION OF SPEECH MECHANISM. FOR DESCRIPTION SEE TEXT.

higher centres concerned in thought, but it is usually supposed that they are chiefly situated in the frontal lobes. Although, therefore, the words "ideational mechanism" are used, it is to be understood that such terms are simply convenient ones to express the parts of the cerebrum concerned in the elaboration and production of thoughts and ideas.

Clinical evidence goes a long way to show that there is such a mechanism, because some symptoms shown by some aphasic patients are only explicable on such a hypothesis. Going back to our consideration of the acquiring of speech by the child, it will be seen that this mechanism is necessary if the child is to have an intelligent knowledge of the auditory or visual sensory word impressions received, as well as an intelligent volitional control over the production speech centres. Completing, therefore, the schema which I have already drawn out in a previous part of this work (see Fig. 13),—

A is the auditory word centre, receiving auditory word impressions from a^1, the right auditory centre, which again is connected with a^2—a^1, the right auditory nerve, and from a^3, the left auditory centre, connected with a^4—a^3, the left auditory nerve. a^1 and a^3 are probably joined by commissural fibres.

C is the visual word centre, receiving visual word impressions from c^1, the right visual centre, and c^2—c^1, the right optic tract, and from c^3, the left visual centre, and c^4—c^3, the left optic tract. c^1 and c^3 are probably joined by commissural fibres.

B is the psycho-motor speech centre connected with the executory motor centres, b^3, and motor fibres, b^3—b^4, passing to internal capsule from vocal and oral articulative centres on left side, and connected with b^1, the executory motor centres on the right side, through B^1, the psycho-motor centre, and b^1—b^2, the motor fibres passing to internal capsule from the executory motor centres on the right side. b^1 and b^3, the executory motor centres, are probably also joined by commissural fibres.

D is the psycho-motor graphic centre connected with d^1, the centre for the movements of the hand, and d^1—d^2, the fibres passing from it to internal capsule.

E represents the ideational concept or elaborating mechanism, and I have connected it with A, the auditory word centre, and B, the psycho-motor speech centre, and indirectly through these two with C, the visual word centre, and D, the graphic motor centre; it may be directly connected with these centres, but these direct connections are not the ones usually used—as, for instance, in ordinary intelligent reading in silence, probably in most cases an internal silent articulation of the words, as probably also an internal recalling of the sound of the word, takes place, showing that if the process does not take place through these centres, then by constant association the motor and auditory images are revived by a process of radiation to and from those centres.

The actual arrangement, however, may be even more complicated than this schema shows, and it is necessary to have these centres connected in these various ways in order to produce a schema that will be in accord with all the clinical facts. Many of these diagrams have been produced much similar in their principal parts, but differing in some of the connections according to the opinion of the authors as to the internal mechanism of speech.

Lichtheim's diagram is perhaps better known than any

other, and is generally accepted as being, if not entirely, nearly correct. He really produced two diagrams, differing in one small detail, viz. in the route of volitional writing, as will be seen from the two drawings in Fig. 14.

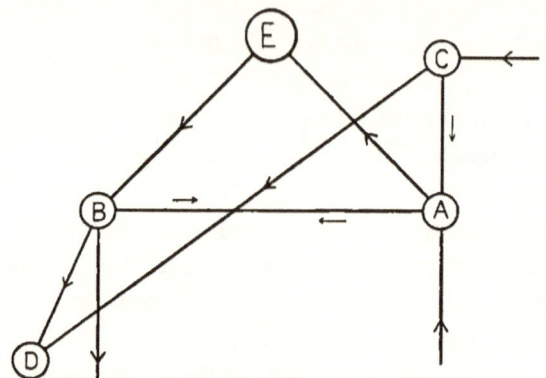

FIG. 14.—LICHTHEIM'S FIRST DIAGRAM.

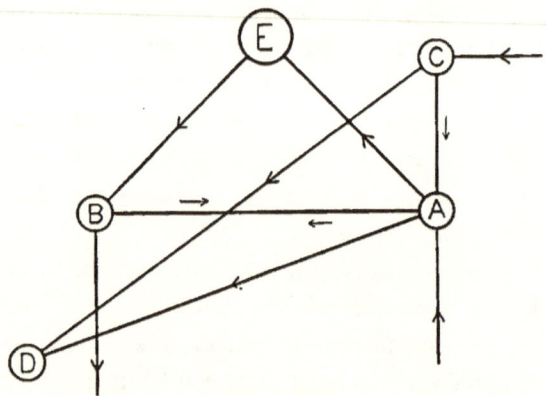

FIG. 14.—LICHTHEIM'S SECOND DIAGRAM.

In the one the route for volitional writing passed from the intellectual centres to Broca's centre, and thence to the graphic centre; in the other the route passed through Broca's centre, thence to the auditory centre, and on to the graphic. In the schema which I have sketched, and which agrees in this detail with that of Mills,[1] both of these views are adopted.

It will be seen that if a variety of aphasia could be produced by a lesion either of any or any number of these centres or connecting fibres, the varieties of aphasia would be very numerous indeed. Clinically it has been found that there are cases exhibiting symptoms which one

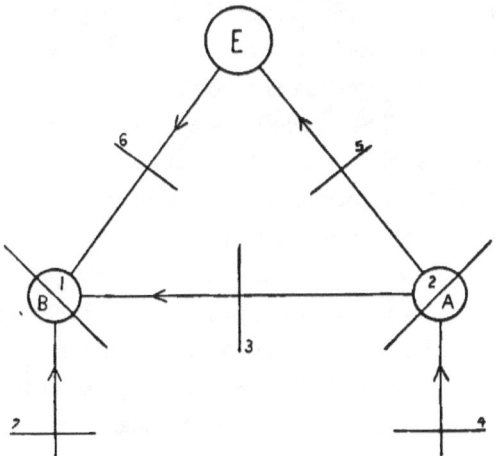

FIG. 15.—DIAGRAM AFTER LICHTHEIM.
The cross lines show the position of lesions.

would expect in many of these possible varieties, showing that probably it is possible anatomically to produce them by a pathological process.

Lichtheim, taking only the auditory and the motor centres along with the ideational mechanism, and putting aside the visual and graphic centres, concluded that seven different forms of aphasia can be produced by lesions, and that these seven varieties actually occur.

[1] *Nervous Diseases*, by American Authors. Edited by Dercum, 1895.

The accompanying drawing (Fig. 15) taken from Lichtheim's paper shows the varieties, the cross lines being in the position where the lesions are supposed to take place. Wyllie[1] admits that 1, 2, and 3 have been distinctly established as varieties that do occur, and that Lichtheim's cases go a long way to show that 4, 5, 6, and 7 also may occur. Wernicke, who had adopted Lichtheim's view, gave these different varieties of aphasia distinctive names, but Wyllie suggested that the word "pictorial" should be substituted for "cortical" in Wernicke's classification. The suggestion is a good one, and is not nearly so confusing. These varieties are (the first nomenclature being Wyllie's, the second Wernicke's):—

1. Pictorial auditory, or Cortical sensory.
2. Pictorial motor, or Cortical motor.
3. Inter-pictorial, or Conduction or Leitungsaphasie.
4. Infra-pictorial auditory, or Subcortical sensory.
5. Supra-pictorial auditory, or Transcortical sensory.
6. Supra-pictorial motor, or Transcortical motor.
7. Infra-pictorial motor, or Subcortical motor.

Probably a better term for 3, instead of simply inter-pictorial, would be inter-pictorial auditory-motor.

It will be seen that if written speech is treated in the same way it is quite possible, putting aside spoken speech in the meantime altogether, to theoretically produce seven forms of lesion here also, and Wernicke[2] has also pointed out those possible varieties. I have applied the principle of Wyllie's nomenclature to these different forms. They are:—

1. Pictorial visual aphasia, or Cortical alexia.
2. Pictorial graphic, or Cortical agraphia.

---

[1] *Disorders of Speech.* Edinburgh, 1894.
[2] *Fortsch. der Med.*, II., 1886, p. 463 (quoted by Wyllie).

3. Inter-pictorial visual-graphic, or Conduction agraphia.
4. Infra-pictorial visual, or Subcortical alexia.
5. Supra-pictorial visual, or Transcortical alexia.
6. Supra-pictorial graphic, or Transcortical agraphia.
7. Infra-pictorial graphic, or Subcortical agraphia.

It will be seen later that whilst Déjerine and others have proved that 1 and 4 do exist, and that there is some evidence to show that 2 also does occur, the others have hitherto been considered to be highly problematical as separate lesions. I shall, however, later describe a case (Case X.) which probably ought to be classified in group 5, viz. a supra-pictorial visual aphasia; and I shall point out whilst discussing agraphia that cases of 6. supra-pictorial graphic do occur, and have been described, although the seat of the lesion has not been pointed out. I shall record one such case which has come under my notice (Case XVI.), and shall endeavour to show that cases of motor aphasia with agraphia where the aphasic symptoms are recovered from but the agraphia persists can be fairly considered to belong to this variety.

The Significance of each Symptom exhibited by Cases of Aphasia.

Leaving this in the meantime, however, let us now consider what are the symptoms that may be produced theoretically by a disturbance of any part of the central speech mechanism. Looking at our schema, and considering that any of the centres or connections may be destroyed in a case of aphasia, the answers to the following questions will make clear what form of aphasia the patient is suffering from and where the lesion probably is.

They embrace practically all the main questions that

have to be answered in the investigation of an aphasic case, although there are several subsidiary ones which are dependent on the answers to some of these principal ones. These questions are :—

1. Can the patient hear sounds of any kind?
2. Can the patient hear words spoken?
3. Can the patient understand words spoken?
4. Can the patient see objects of any kind?
5. Can the patient see words written or printed? (Can he read words silently?)
6. Can the patient understand words written or printed? (Can he read intelligently?)
7. Can the patient speak voluntarily?
8. Can the patient repeat words?
9. Can the patient speak words read? that is, can he read aloud?
10. Can the patient write voluntarily?
11. Can the patient write to dictation?
12. Can the patient copy?

One other question, although dependent on the answers to 7, 8, and 9, is of so much importance that it will be as well to mention it here, viz. If he can't speak voluntarily, repeat what he hears, or read aloud, does he know how the word is to be articulated, as, for instance, how many syllables it contains? That may be answered by his breathing or pressing the hand once for every syllable the word contains (*L'expérience Proust—Lichtheim*).

These questions, as will be seen, are arranged in the order in which they would be put by an investigator who was studying the mechanism of speech in the way in which we have approached it, viz. by studying first the reception routes and then the production routes.

I shall take up each of these questions separately, and shall show the significance of the answers to each of them. In doing so I shall refer to the diagram which I have previously drawn (see Fig. 13).

1. Can the patient hear sounds of any kind?

It is necessary to get an answer to this in order to find out whether sounds reach his cerebral hemispheres at all. If he hears sounds, then one or both ears and one or both auditory nerves and hearing centres must be intact, a^2—a^1 and a^4—a^3. As previously ascertained, the auditory nerves are bilaterally represented in the hemispheres, so that if the patient is deaf to sounds the lesion must be double, and either both ears, a^2 and a^4, both auditory nerves and tracts, a^2—a^1 and a^4—a^3, or both acoustic centres, a^1 and a^2, in the first and second temporo-sphenoidal convolutions must be affected. A deaf mute is such a case, and I have made reference to several other such cases of double central lesion when I was considering the localisation of the auditory centres. Such central double lesions must be rare, but disorganisation of the organ of hearing in both ears is not quite so rare. Lesion of both auditory nerves and tracts is probably the rarest of all these lesions.

It will be convenient to take the next two questions together.

2. Can the patient hear words spoken?

3. Can the patient understand words spoken?

Having ascertained that he can hear sounds, it is next necessary to ascertain whether he can hear words. In most cases of course this is quite easily ascertained by simply putting questions to the patient. The best way is to ask the patient to do something or other, such as to touch the nose, ear, etc.; but there are theoretically some cases who could not do this, and still the auditory word centre would be intact, because such a question implies that the person *understands the word heard*. By looking at the schema it will be seen that it implies that A E is intact. It is possible, however, for A E to be interrupted (supra-pictorial auditory aphasia) and A remain intact. If the lesion was limited to A E, then the patient would be able to repeat words without understanding them or to write words to dictation without understanding them; such a case has been described by Lichtheim,[1] but probably it is the only one on record. In a case of this sort it would be found that the patient would only be able to repeat or write to dictation word by word or very short sentences. The repetition of a long sentence implies that the word has reached his intelligence E, and so if the link A E was broken, only short sentences or words could be repeated, as it were reflexly. Practically, therefore, it is easy making out whether the patient hears words or not. If he can hear sounds and not words, then the lesion is in one of two places.

1st. *An infra-pictorial auditory or subcortical aphasia* cutting off both a^1 and a^3 from A. Such a case must be very rare, because, as we have already found, both the word-hearing and the general acoustic centres are in the same region, although cases have shown that the word-hearing centre is more limited in area, and probably only in the posterior third of the first temporo-sphenoidal convolution. A case of this lesion has been described by Lichtheim.[2]

2nd. *A cortical or pictorial auditory aphasia* destroying

---

[1] *Brain*, January 1885, p. 454
[2] *Ibid.*, Case IV., p. 461.

the word-hearing centre A. Such cases are not uncommon, although they are usually not entirely limited to this region. Later I shall give an account of several such cases which I have personally observed. It may be noted here also that the patient may be able to hear words and not music, and to hear music and not words. This point will also be illustrated in one of my cases.

4. Can the patient see objects of any kind?

If he cannot, then there is in all probability a double lesion, or at all events a lesion bilateral in its results. A single lesion destroying entirely the optic chiasma, or both optic nerves or optic tracts, would of course produce the same results as double lesions affecting both eyes, both optic nerves or optic tracts, both quadrageminal bodies, both radiations of Gratiolet, or both visual centres in the occipital lobes c^2—c^1 and c^4—c^3. A lesion affecting one side only above the chiasma would produce homonymous hemianopia. I shall have more to say on this subject when I consider word-blindness.

5. Can the patient see words?

If the patient cannot see words he will not be able to read, and it will be found later on that he may not be able to write. Writing is the test for whether the cause of his word-blindness is subcortical, that is infra-pictorial (in c^1—C and c^3—C), or cortical, that is pictorial visual aphasia (in C). If the lesion is subcortical, cutting off C from the visual centres in both hemispheres (c^1 and c^3), the patient, whilst not seeing letters, figures, and words as letters, figures, or words written or printed, is able to write letters, figures, and words voluntarily in their written or printed form, and to write to dictation; whilst if the lesion is cortical or pictorial (in C) he cannot see letters, figures, or words, nor can he write voluntarily or to dictation. He can, however, copy letters, figures, and words as he would any design, because he sees letters, figures, and words only as objects and not as letters, figures, and words. I shall have more to say on this, however, when I consider word-blindness, and also on other peculiarities of some cases where there is blindness for words and not for letters, and in others blindness for words and letters and not for figures.

6. Can the patient understand words written or printed? that is, can he read intelligently?

The patient may be able to see words and yet not understand them. Such a condition might be ascertained by either writing or printing some request, or by both, such as "Put out your tongue," and although if the lesion was limited to the fibres between C and E he might be able to read aloud what you had written, he would not understand the meaning of your request. He might also be able to rewrite it and yet not understand it. A practical writing test, however, would be to ask him to write from printed copy. Such a patient would probably not be able to change the printed characters into written characters, because the letters and words would not have reached his intelligence. He would copy printed into printed characters, and written into written characters. Such a patient would have supra-pictorial visual aphasia; but this condition must be very rare as an organic lesion, although we all know such a functional condition, the result of inattention. I have not been able to find one case of this variety in medical literature, but later I shall describe a case (Case X.) that is explicable under the theory that it was a supra-pictorial visual aphasia (lesion of C—A). Another source of confusion would occur, however, because the patient, if he could read aloud, would hear what he had read, and would be able to ascertain the meaning by means of the auditory centre. This was very distinctly shown in Cases VIII. and X. In the schema the course of the fibres from the visual word centre has been drawn through the auditory word centre A, and through the psycho-motor centre B, because it is almost certain that in intelligent reading both the auditory and the articulatory images of the word are raised, whether that is done by radiation from the visual centre C or ideational mechanism E, or because the path of the fibres between C and E passes through either A or B or both. Most of us certainly know that we can read even whole pages without understanding what we have read, even although we may be reading aloud. The meaning of what we may be reading, however, is not so apt to escape us if we read aloud as it is if we read in silence, showing that words heard and seen at the same time reach the intelligence easier than when read in silence only.

7, 8, and 9 are best considered together.

7. Can the patient speak voluntarily?
8. Repeat words? And—
9. Read aloud?

It will of course be necessary to ascertain whether the patient *is able* to speak, and not simply whether he *does* speak or not. He may not be able to speak voluntarily nor to repeat on account of amnesia verbalis, or word-deafness, nor to read aloud on account of word-blindness. Again, suppose the patient is not able to speak voluntarily, then it is possible theoretically that he might be able to repeat words heard or to read aloud. Several such cases have been recorded, notably one by Lichtheim[1] and one by Hammond.[2] These cases are supra-pictorial motor aphasias, and result from a lesion of the fibres connecting E, the ideational mechanism, with B, the psycho-motor speech centre. Such a patient would not be able to write voluntarily, but would be able to write to dictation and to copy. It is to be noted here also, however, that although the patient might be able to repeat words and to write to dictation, such repetition and writing would have to be done at once, and only if the words were spoken word by word or in very short sentences. If he is not able to speak voluntarily, nor repeat words, nor read aloud, then the lesion is either in the psycho-motor articulatory centre B itself, or in the fibres from B to the executory motor centres b^3 on the left and b^1 on the right side. If in the psycho-motor centre B, the patient has no knowledge of how the words ought to be articulated (*motor cortical or pictorial motor or Broca's aphasia pure*); he would also have agraphia.

If the lesion is in the fibres from the psycho-motor to the executory motor articulatory centres (*infra-pictorial or subcortical motor aphasia*), he would know how the word should be articulated, that is, he would know how many syllables it contained, and he would be able to indicate that by breathing or pressing the hand once for each syllable ("*L'expérience Proust—Lichtheim*"). He would also be able to write voluntarily, write to dictation and to copy. Again, the patient may be able to speak voluntarily, to repeat, to read aloud, and to write voluntarily and to dictation, all of which, however, in a disturbed

---

[1] *Brain*, January 1885, Case II.
[2] *Diseases of the Nervous System*, 7th Edition, Chap. VII

and imperfect manner. This is due to a cutting off of the connection between the auditory centre A and the psycho-motor articulatory centre B; and as the fibres from C to B have probably nearly the same if not actually the same course, these fibres may also be involved. This form of aphasia is the conduction aphasia or interpictorial of Wyllie. A prominent symptom in this form is paraphasia and paragraphia. Although the patient is able to speak and to write, he uses many wrong words.

When a patient is not able to articulate words properly (slurring, etc.), but knows how to pronounce them, the lesion is either in the executory motor speech centres, or in the nerve tracts in the production route lower down—as in Cases I., II., and III., previously described and discussed.

10. Can the patient write voluntarily?
11. Can the patient write to dictation?
12. Can the patient copy?

These questions also are best considered together. The patient may not be able to write expertly because he cannot use the right hand. He may not be able to write except by simply tracing from copy. In that case the lesion may be in C, the visual word centre, or it may be in D, the psycho-motor graphic centre. It is very doubtful whether any true simple case of the latter has occurred; one case recorded by Henschen had also a lesion in the angular gyrus, which might have accounted for the agraphia. Several other cases will be alluded to later when considering the whole question of agraphia. Again, if the patient cannot write voluntarily nor write to dictation the lesion may be in the fibres connecting D, the graphic centre, with B, the psycho-motor speech centre. This would be the position of the lesion if there was no disturbance of voluntary speech, of repeating words, or of reading aloud. Such cases I shall show later do occur as remains of pictorial motor aphasia, and I shall record one such case. If there was also disturbance of voluntary speech, of repeating words, and reading aloud, the lesion would be as already considered under voluntary speech. If the lesion was in C, the word-seeing centre itself, the patient would be word-blind as well as not able to write voluntarily nor to dictation, although able to copy by tracing. If in the connecting fibres between C, the word-seeing centre, and D, the graphic centre, whether such fibres pass directly (C D) or indirectly (C B D) by B, the psycho-motor centre, or (C A B D) by A, the auditory centre, and B, the psycho-motor centre, the patient, although not word-blind, probably also might not be able to write voluntarily nor to dictation, but might be able to copy by tracing. Some form of paragraphia would probably also be shown by the patient. These symptoms result from the fact that the visual images of the letters and words are very essential for writing expertly, as I shall point out when I consider agraphia. If the patient was able to write voluntarily and to dictation, but not to copy except perhaps by tracing, the lesion would be subcortical to the word-seeing centre, c^1 C, c^3 C ; such a patient would be word-blind, but not agraphic.

It is very necessary that it be noted in every case whether the patient is able to copy perfectly, or only copy as he would a map, a design, or a drawing. If he retains the faculty of copying perfectly, he can copy printed characters into written characters, and *vice versa*. In this case he must have retained the power of understanding what he sees and writes, whereas it is not necessary that he understand what he copies when he simply traces the letters as he would a drawing. It is to be understood, therefore, that when I say that a patient can copy, I mean that he can copy print into manuscript writing and *vice versa*, whereas if he cannot I shall say that he copies by tracing as he would a drawing or design.

DIFFERENTIAL DIAGNOSIS OF THE VARIETIES OF APHASIA.

Having shown how the answers to each of these twelve questions affect the localisation of the lesion in aphasic patients, it will be well to summarise these results, and show what reply to each of these questions would be given by an investigator, firstly, of each of the seven varieties of aphasia described by Wernicke and Lichtheim, and re-named by Wyllie; and, secondly, of seven other possible varieties.

I wish to state here, however, that whilst some of these varieties have been proved by post-mortem examination to occur, our knowledge of many of them is very imperfect. Much pathological work has yet to be done in order to increase our knowledge on this subject.

Cases observed clinically have shown symptoms in accordance with the symptoms of most of those varieties, and I shall record later many such cases of my own observation. This method of subdivision is therefore a convenient one clinically. It is also in accordance with the theory of cerebral speech mechanism that I have endeavoured to describe, and as our knowledge increases I believe that it will be found to be more and more in accordance with the cerebral mechanism of speech as shown by pathology.

Many aphasia cases, on account probably of the situation or the size of the lesion, show symptoms which cannot be classed as belonging to one of those groups, but to more than one, so that there are many mixed cases. I believe that if clinical observers would carefully note in which of the groups a case ought to be classed, and, if the opportunity of a post-mortem examination occurred, noted exactly the localisation of the lesion in the cerebrum, our knowledge of the cerebral speech mechanism would rapidly become more precise. The lesions, however, which would probably be the most useful in helping us in our work of localisation are just those lesions which patients most frequently recover from, being small and limited in area.

Questions 1. Can the patient hear sounds of any kind? and 4. Can the patient see objects of any kind? may be put aside in this connection, because they are simply put in order to ascertain whether it is a case of aphasia we have to deal with at all. The answer is presumed in each case to have been in the affirmative.

The symptoms of seven varieties are given in Lichtheim's paper, but I shall here take the varieties of aphasia in the order in which we would find them approaching the subject from the receptive side, just as we have done in the investigation of each part of our subject.

I. *Infra-pictorial Auditory Aphasia.* (The Subcortical Sensory of Wernicke.) Lesion of a^1 A and a^3 A in schema (Fig. 13).

2. The patient cannot hear words.

3. The patient cannot understand words spoken.

5. The patient can see words (read silently).

6. The patient can understand words written.

7. The patient can speak voluntarily.

8. The patient cannot repeat words.

9. The patient can speak words read, *i.e.* he can read aloud.

10. The patient can write voluntarily.

11. The patient cannot write to dictation.

12. The patient can copy.

5, 6, 7, 9, 10, 12, are thus answered in the affirmative; 2, 3, 8, and 11, in the negative.

II. *Pictorial Auditory.* (Cortical Sensory Aphasia of Wernicke.) Lesion of A in the schema (Fig. 13).

2. The patient cannot hear words.

3. The patient cannot understand words spoken.

5. The patient can see words (read in silence).

6. The patient cannot understand words written (read intelligently).

7. The patient can speak voluntarily.

8. The patient cannot repeat words.

9. The patient cannot speak words read—that is, read aloud.

10. The patient can write voluntarily.

11. The patient cannot write to dictation.

12. The patient cannot copy printed into written words, but can copy written words by tracing.

5, 7, 10, are thus answered in the affirmative; 2, 3, 6, 8, 9, 11, and 12, in the negative.

Such a patient, although he can both speak and write voluntarily, usually shows great disturbances of spoken speech and writing. He usually shows amnesia verbalis, and uses a great many wrong words and wrong syllables, both in speaking and writing—that is, he has paraphasia and paragraphia.

These symptoms result from the fact that the auditory word images are very essential both for perfect spoken and written speech, being the primary speech images, as pointed out in an earlier part of this work.

It is stated that he would be able to see words—that is, read silently—but it is very difficult seeing how this could be ascertained, as he could not read intelligently and probably would not be able to read aloud. The facts, however, would probably be as stated, because the angular gyrus would be intact, and he would be able to write voluntarily, although, as I have stated, imperfectly.

From these symptoms it will be seen how difficult it is to distinguish between a case of this variety pure and simple, and a case where the visual word centre is also involved.

III. *Supra-pictorial Auditory.* (Transcortical Sensory of Wernicke.) Lesion in A E (Fig. 13).

2. The patient can hear words.
3. The patient cannot understand words spoken.
5. The patient can see words.
6. The patient cannot understand written words.
7. The patient can speak voluntarily.
8. The patient can repeat words spoken.
9. The patient can read aloud.
10. The patient can write voluntarily.
11. The patient can write to dictation.
12. The patient can copy only by tracing, as he cannot understand written words.

2, 5, 7, 8, 9, 10, 11, are answered in the affirmative; 3, 6, and 12, in the negative; but as volitional speaking and volitional writing are done directly from the ideational mechanism E, the latter being cut off from the auditory centre, there is paraphasia and paragraphia. Although the patient can repeat, read aloud, and write to dictation, these actions are done mechanically and not intelligently. They must, therefore, be done at once, because the words cannot reach the intelligence. A long phrase, therefore, cannot be repeated nor written to dictation.

IV. *Inter-pictorial Auditory-motor.* (Inter-pictorial of Wyllie; Conduction or Leitungsaphasie of Wernicke.) Lesion in A B.

2. The patient can hear words.
3. The patient can understand words spoken.
5. The patient can see words (read in silence).
6. The patient can understand written words (read intelligently).
7. The patient can speak voluntarily.
8. The patient can repeat words.
9. The patient can read aloud.
10. The patient can write voluntarily.
11. The patient can write to dictation.
12. The patient can copy words.

2, 3, 5, 6, 7, 8, 9, 10, 11, 12—all the questions in fact —are thus answered in the affirmative, but there are disturbances in the performance of several of the acts to which these questions refer. 2, 3, 5, 6, and 12 are preserved, whilst there is considerable paraphasia and paragraphia in 7 (voluntary language) and 10 (voluntary writing), for the reason stated previously, that whilst the direct path from E (the ideational mechanism) to B (the psycho-motor articulatory centre) is intact, that through the word-hearing centre (A) to B is interrupted. There is also paraphasia and paragraphia in 8 (repeating words), 9 (reading aloud), and 11 (writing to dictation), because, instead of these acts being performed directly through the path A B, the path used is through A to E (the ideational mechanism), and thence by the voluntary path E B. It will thus be seen how essential the auditory word centre is in the production of correct voluntary language. The ideational mechanism seems to make use of the auditory word centre in the reviving of the correct word.

V. *Supra-pictorial Motor Aphasia* (Wyllie). (The Transcortical Motor of Wernicke.) Lesion in E B.

2. The patient can hear words.
3. The patient can understand words spoken.
5. The patient can see words.
6. The patient can understand words written.
7. The patient cannot speak voluntarily.
8. The patient can repeat words.
9. The patient can read aloud.
10. The patient cannot write voluntarily.
11. The patient can write to dictation.
12. The patient can copy by tracing, but doubtful if he can copy perfectly.

2, 3, 5, 6, 8, 9, and 11 are thus answered in the affirmative, whilst 7, 10, and 12 are answered in the negative. It seems to me that whilst in the inter-pictorial form (Leitungsaphasie—E A B interrupted with the path E B intact) voluntary speech and writing show paraphasia and paragraphia, whilst in this form (E B interrupted and E A B intact) both voluntary speech and writing are lost, the main course of the voluntary speech path is direct from E to B. Nevertheless, as we have already seen, it seems to be necessary to have the path from E through the auditory centre A and on to B also intact in order to have speech and writing without paraphasia or paragraphia.

It is doubtful whether he can copy perfectly. He can understand what he reads, but he cannot write voluntarily, and therefore it is probable he cannot convert printed characters into written ones. He can, however, write to dictation.

VI. *Pictorial Motor Aphasia* (Wyllie). (Cortical Motor Aphasia of Wernicke ; Motor Aphasia ; Broca's type of Aphasia.) Lesion of B.

2. The patient can hear words.
3. The patient can understand words spoken.
5. The patient can see words.
6. The patient can understand words written.
7. The patient cannot speak voluntarily.
8. The patient cannot repeat words.
9. The patient cannot read aloud.
10. The patient cannot write voluntarily.
11. The patient cannot write to dictation.
12. The patient can copy, not perfectly, but only by tracing.

2, 3, 5, and 6 are answered in the affirmative ; 7, 8, 9, 10, 11, and 12, in the negative.

These answers show that in most cases the path for writing in all probability passes through the psycho-motor articulatory centre B. Another point which has not altogether been settled is whether such a patient is able to read silently and understand what he is reading. According to the schema he can, but it is very doubtful whether all cases are able to do so or not. In the not very well educated individual probably the faculty of reading in silence and intelligently would be lost, because such persons almost invariably use articulation more or less audibly, or if not at all audibly then they are conscious of the movements necessary for the articulation of the words. Even most if not all educated persons are more or less conscious of the same thing, as well as of a more or less distinct auditory image of the word. Probably as a person gets more and more proficient at reading in silence such images get less and less distinct, but it is very doubtful whether they entirely disappear. Sometimes when a language is acquired almost entirely by reading and not by hearing or speaking, as, for instance, in the acquiring of a foreign language, such articulative images may not be called up on reading foreign words. Some persons have acquired foreign languages in this way, and don't recall the articulative images because they have never used articulation in the acquiring of the language. This must apply more distinctly to a language where the sounds and pronunciation of the words are different from the person's native language. The same remarks apply to the faculty of writing silently. The oral articulative images of the letters or syllables are probably always raised in the memory; hence the faculty of writing is almost if not always affected when the psycho-motor speech centre B is destroyed.

VII. *Infra-pictorial Motor Aphasia* (Wyllie). (Subcortical Motor Aphasia of Wernicke.) Lesion in B—b^3 and B—b^1.

2. The patient can hear words.
3. The patient can understand words spoken.
5. The patient can see words.
6. The patient can understand words written.
7. The patient cannot speak voluntarily.
8. The patient cannot repeat words spoken.
9. The patient cannot read aloud.
10. The patient can write voluntarily.
11. The patient can write to dictation.
12. The patient can copy.

2, 3, 5, 6, 10, 11, and 12 are answered in the affirmative; 7, 8, and 9, in the negative.

This therefore differs from the cortical variety in that the faculty of writing remains intact. The patient is able to indicate how the words ought to be articulated; he knows the number of syllables the words contain. The faculty of writing is preserved because the psycho-motor speech centre is intact, but only cut off from the executory motor centres of its own and the opposite side. Two functional cases with these symptoms I shall describe later.

I shall now take the seven varieties of written speech lesions in the same order as I have considered the spoken speech lesions, viz. from the reception to the production side.

VIII. *Infra-pictorial Visual Aphasia* (Wyllie). (Sub-cortical Alexia of Wernicke; *Cécité Verbale Pure* of Déjerine and French authors.) Lesion in c^1—C and c^3—C.

This is one of the best known of the varieties of aphasia, having been very carefully observed by Déjerine,[1] Sérieux,[2] etc. It is usually accompanied by hemianopsia, owing to

[1] *Compt. Rendus de la Soc. de Biolog.*, 1891 and 1892.   [2] *Ibid.*

an involvement of the radiations of Gratiolet as well as the fibres subcortical to the angular gyrus.

2. The patient can hear words.
3. The patient can understand words spoken.
5. The patient cannot see words.
6. The patient cannot understand words written.
7. The patient can speak voluntarily.
8. The patient can repeat words.
9. The patient cannot read aloud.
10. The patient can write voluntarily.
11. The patient can write to dictation.
12. The patient can copy (only imperfectly as in tracing a design).

2, 3, 7, 8, 10, and 11 are answered in the affirmative; 5 6, 9, and 12, in the negative.

The difference between this form and the next is that the patient can write voluntarily and to dictation when the lesion is subcortical, whereas he cannot do so when it is a cortical lesion.

IX. *Pictorial Visual Aphasia.* (Cortical Alexia of Wernicke; *Cécité Verbale avec Agraphie* of Déjerine, etc.) Lesion of C.

2. The patient can hear words.
3. The patient can understand words spoken.
5. The patient cannot see words.
6. The patient cannot understand words written or printed.
7. The patient can speak voluntarily.
8. The patient can repeat words.
9. The patient cannot read aloud.
10. The patient cannot write voluntarily.

11. The patient cannot write to dictation.

12. The patient can copy only by tracing and very imperfectly.

2, 3, 7, and 8 are answered in the affirmative; 5, 6, 9, 10, 11, and 12, in the negative.

I shall have much more to say about these two forms when I consider word-blindness.

X. *Supra-pictorial Visual Aphasia.* (Transcortical Alexia of Wernicke.) Lesion in C—E, which probably passes through A, and therefore if the lesion was between A and E the symptoms would be the same as in III. Supra-pictorial auditory aphasia, and if A was involved the symptoms would be as in pictorial auditory, but if the lesion was between C, the visual, and A, the auditory centre, the symptoms would be

2. The patient can hear words.

3. The patient can understand words spoken.

5. The patient can see words written and printed.

6. The patient cannot understand words written or printed.

7. The patient can speak voluntarily.

8. The patient can repeat words spoken.

9. The patient can probably read aloud.

10. The patient probably cannot write voluntarily.

11. The patient probably cannot write to dictation.

12. The patient can copy only by tracing.

2, 3, 5, 7, 8, and 9 are answered in the affirmative; 6, 10, 11, and 12, in the negative.

I was a little doubtful as to whether such a case would be able to read aloud or not. It depends on whether the route from the visual centre C passes directly to B, the psycho-motor centre, or indirectly through the auditory centre A; I was inclined to think that the latter route is the correct one, because in lesions of the auditory word centre the patient is not able to read aloud. I have not been able to find a case of this variety in medical literature, but recently I have had under my care a case which is only explicable under the hypothesis that the route C—A was interrupted. In him the symptoms were as stated above, and he could read aloud, although he could not understand what he was reading until he heard himself reading. He could also understand what was said to him and what was read to him by others. The case is a unique one, and is given on page 173. There is also some doubt as to whether a patient with this lesion could write either voluntarily or to dictation; the answer to this depends on whether the route from C to D is direct or through the auditory centre, and also as to whether there is a true graphic centre in D or not. The case above noted could not be tested with the right hand as that was paralysed, but it is very interesting to note that he could not even recall the shapes of letters from memory, although he could see and trace lines from copy quite well. These symptoms, however, are discussed later.

XI. *Inter-pictorial Visual-graphic Aphasia.* (Conduction Agraphia of Wernicke.) Lesion in C D.

The course such fibres may take, whether direct (C to D) or indirect (C B D or C A B D), is not known. In writing most of us are conscious not only of the visual images of the letters we write, but also of the auditory and articulatory images, showing that if the route is not through A and B there must be a radiation of nerve influence

from C and D to A and B. The indirect route through A and B is the more probable, but if the course is direct from C to D,
2. The patient can hear words.
3. The patient can understand words spoken.
5. The patient can see words.
6. The patient can understand written words.
7. The patient can speak voluntarily.
8. The patient can repeat words.
9. The patient can read aloud.
10. The patient can write voluntarily.
11. The patient can write to dictation.
12. The patient can copy.

It will be seen that all these questions are answered in the affirmative, although, as in inter-pictorial auditory-motor aphasia (Leitungsaphasie), there would probably be paragraphia, word and letter intoxication in writing, and other writing disturbances. As, however, no case has been described, it is impossible to say definitely what the symptoms of such a lesion might be.

XII. *Supra-pictorial Graphic Aphasia.* (Transcortical Agraphia of Wernicke.)

Probably the route from the ideational mechanism E to the graphic centre D is through B, the psycho-motor speech centre. If the lesion was therefore between E and B, the symptoms would be as in supra-pictorial motor aphasia, Variety V.; if between B and D, the symptoms would be
2. The patient can hear words.
3. The patient can understand words spoken.
5. The patient can see words.
6. The patient can understand words written.

7. The patient can speak voluntarily.

8. The patient can repeat words.

9. The patient can read aloud.

10. The patient cannot write voluntarily.

11. The patient cannot write to dictation.

12. The patient may not be able to copy printed into written words, but can copy by tracing.

2, 3, 5, 6, 7, 8, and 9 are answered in the affirmative; 10, 11, and 12, in the negative.

The route used in writing to dictation is probably through B, the psycho-motor centre, as its destruction, in Broca's type of aphasia, causes agraphia to everything but copying by tracing the design of the letters. I shall describe later a case of supra-pictorial graphic aphasia, and shall show that some cases that have been described as true cortical agraphias and cases of recovered motor aphasias with agraphia persistent belong to this variety.

XIII. *Pictorial Graphic Aphasia.* (Cortical Agraphia of Wernicke.) Lesion of D, the psycho-motor graphic centre.

2. The patient can hear words.

3. The patient can understand words spoken.

5. The patient can see words.

6. The patient can understand words written.

7. The patient can speak voluntarily.

8. The patient can repeat words.

9. The patient can read aloud.

10. The patient cannot write voluntarily.

11. The patient cannot write to dictation.

12. The patient cannot copy printed into written words, but can trace the design of the letters.

2, 3, 5, 6, 7, 8, and 9 are answered in the affirmative; 10, 11, and 12, in the negative.

XIV. *Infra-pictorial Graphic Aphasia.* (Subcortical Agraphia of Wernicke.) Lesion in fibres between D and d^1.

2. The patient can hear words.
3. The patient can understand words spoken.
5. The patient can see words.
6. The patient can understand words written.
7. The patient can speak voluntarily.
8. The patient can repeat words.
9. The patient can read aloud.
10. The patient cannot write voluntarily.
11. The patient cannot write to dictation.
12. The patient cannot copy except by tracing.

2, 3, 5, 6, 7, 8, and 9 are answered in the affirmative; 10, 11, and 12, in the negative.

These results are the same in the last three forms, but the difference in this form would be that the patient would know how to write the words and letters, but would not be able to do it. This form is, however, highly problematical.

The difference between XII. and XIII. would be that, although in neither of them the patient could write voluntarily, write to dictation or to copy correctly, in XII. it would be seen that, when the patient took the pen in his hand to copy, he would be able to do so in a more expert manner than in XIII., where the psycho-motor graphic centre was destroyed. He would also show paragraphia and *letter* and *very familiar word intoxication*, the graphic centre being only able to write, as it were, automatically, and only the letters and words most familiar to it. The signature or even the initials only of the patient would appear frequently in voluntary writing as well as in writing to dictation. These symptoms were seen distinctly in Case XVI.

These results I now put down in a tabular form :—

Table of the Summary of Results of Answers to the Twelve Questions in each of the Fourteen Varieties of Aphasia.

VARIETY.	AFFIRMATIVE.	NEGATIVE.
I.	1, 4, 5, 6, 7, 9, 10, 12	2, 3, 8, 11
II.	1, 4, 5, 7, 10	2, 3, 6, 8, 9, 11, 12
III.	1, 2, 4, 5, 7, 8, 9, 10, 11	3, 6, 12
IV.	1, 2, 3, 4, 5, 6, 7, 8, 9, 10, 11, 12	
V.	1, 2, 3, 4, 5, 6, 8, 9, 11	7, 10, 12
VI.	1, 2, 3, 4, 5, 6	7, 8, 9, 10, 11, 12
VII.	1, 2, 3, 4, 5, 6, 10, 11, 12	7, 8, 9
VIII.	1, 2, 3, 4, 7, 8, 10, 11	5, 6, 9, 12
IX.	1, 2, 3, 4, 7, 8	5, 6, 9, 10, 11, 12
X.	1, 2, 3, 4, 5, 7, 8, 9	6, 10, 11, 12
XI.	1, 2, 3, 4, 5, 6, 7, 8, 9, 10, 11, 12	
XII.	1, 2, 3, 4, 5, 6, 7, 8, 9	10, 11, 12
XIII.	1, 2, 3, 4, 5, 6, 7, 8, 9	10, 11, 12
XIV.	1, 2, 3, 4, 5, 6, 7, 8, 9	10, 11, 12

From these results it will be seen that it is possible to localise every lesion producing a disturbance of speech if that lesion is limited to a particular centre or the connecting fibres between centres. Probably there is no difference between Variety IV. Inter-pictorial auditory-motor and XI. Inter-pictorial visual-graphic, the chief symptom of both being paraphasia and paragraphia. If lesions are to be accurately localised, it will be seen from a study of this table how essential it is that cases should be accurately observed in all their aspects. An answer to each of these twelve questions which I have drawn up, if accurately obtained in each case, would not only increase our knowledge of aphasia cases generally, but enable us to localise almost every one. It will be shown later how important such localising is in cerebral surgery, and I may state here that I look upon aphasia as being quite as much a symptom which ought to be thoroughly studied and understood by the surgeon as by the physician; indeed I think its localisation is much more important in surgery than in medicine. A study of the cases of aphasia which have been recorded in medical literature very soon leads to the conclusion that the accuracy in every detail with which they have been observed is not the distinguishing feature of them. Probably this is to be accounted for by the fact that our knowledge of aphasia has rapidly grown and widened, and no method of accurate observation has been in universal use. To supply this want Wyllie has carefully drawn up a method of case-taking which, if universally adopted, would very soon be the means of adding materially to a better knowledge of all the central affections of speech.

CHAPTER IV.

CLINICAL VARIETIES OF APHASIA.

ALTHOUGH it is possible, if our theory of the mechanism of speech is correct, to have all the preceding varieties of aphasia, and cases of many of them have been recorded, practically the greater number of aphasic lesions involve more than one centre or set of fibres, so that the cases are usually more complex than those varieties described. This results from the fact that such lesions are most commonly of vascular origin, either due to a hæmorrhage or the blocking of a vessel from a thrombus or an embolus. As such vessels supply more than one cortical area, more than one cortical area is usually involved in the pathological process. Of course sometimes we find a small hæmorrhage or an abscess or cerebral tumour which picks out a limited area. In those cases the symptoms may closely resemble one of the varieties of aphasia described. As a rule, however, as I have said, the lesion is not so limited, and therefore the combination of symptoms varies in different cases. It has been found, as I previously stated, that it is possible to divide aphasic cases into five clinical types, which have gradually come to be recognised as the five different types of aphasia. These are :—

1. Auditory Aphasia, comprising Varieties I., II., and III.

2. Motor Aphasia or Aphemia, comprising Varieties V., VI., and VII.

3. Visual Aphasia, comprising Varieties VIII., IX., and X.

4. Graphic Aphasia, comprising Varieties XII., XIII., and XIV.

5. Conduction Aphasia (Leitungsaphasie), comprising Varieties IV. and XI.

The last type is produced by lesions of the fibres connecting the sensory to the motor side. It perhaps most closely resembles the auditory group, and will be considered immediately after that group. I shall therefore take up the consideration of these five types of aphasic lesion, giving cases of my own observation illustrating the different groups.

CHAPTER V.

I. AUDITORY APHASIA.

THIS group includes :—
  1. Infra-pictorial Auditory . . Variety I.
  2. Pictorial Auditory . . . Variety II.
  3. Supra-pictorial Auditory . Variety III.

The chief distinguishing symptom of the auditory group is that the patient, although he may not be deaf to sounds, is deaf to words, *i.e.* he cannot understand words spoken. Amnesia verbalis of more or less pronounced form is also a very frequent symptom in auditory cases. As, however, the following two cases of my own observation are excellent examples of auditory aphasia, perhaps the best description that can be given of the usual symptoms of the auditory type is to give a record of the cases.

The first is one of very great interest, not only from the fact that it was almost a pure pictorial auditory aphasia, but also from the fact that it was one of those cases of rapid recovery which have been referred to by Wernicke. The explanation of such recovery has been sought for in the fact that the function of the left auditory word centre is taken up by the right side. Later on I shall give reasons for supposing that such a theory does not explain some cases such as this, and that one explanation is to be sought for rather in the theory that there are functional sensory aphasias as well as functional motor ones. Several examples of the latter I shall also record later.

CASE IV. (*Personal Observation*).—*Pictorial auditory aphasia; sudden in onset, temporary in duration; quick, almost immediate recovery; some paraphasia; marked amnesia, chiefly of nouns; no motor symptoms; musical faculty affected slightly in a peculiar way.*

S. C., æt. 18, a domestic servant, was admitted to Leith Hospital March 16th, 1895. Her father died of apoplexy; otherwise there is no history in the family of cerebral disease.

When a child she had measles and scarlet fever, the latter being followed by an abscess behind the left ear, which, however, very soon healed up. Since then she had enjoyed good health. Two months before admission she complained of pain in the left temple, but was able for her work till Monday, March 11th. This pain was thought to be neuralgic in nature, and was treated with quinine. On March 11th she felt sick and was unable for work, but the pain in her head was no worse. On March 12th the pain shifted to the nape of the neck, and on the night of the 12th patient was very dizzy when she got up. There was no disorder of speech on the 13th. On the 14th at 2 a.m. she spoke to her fellow-servants quite well. Her head was then very painful, and she got up and applied vinegar and water to it. At 6 a.m. it was noticed that she could not use the proper words. The words she used were "snow," "auntie," "egg," and "God," but she could always show where she felt pain and would say, "Sore there" or "Fine." She said she heard a song in her ear and whistled it. It was a song called "Molly Reilly." On Thursday she was seen by a doctor, and ice was applied to her head. She was tried with written words, but she could not understand them. She was admitted to hospital on Friday, March 16th.

Condition on Admission.—She was a bright healthy-looking girl with good colour and well nourished. Examination of the circulatory system showed pulse regular and of fair strength. Heart sounds were quite pure and no murmurs; no enlargement or other abnormality. The respiratory, alimentary, and urinary systems were quite normal.

Nervous System.—Ordinary motor and sensory functions as well as the reflexes were normal. Examination of the speech disturbance according to Wyllie's method showed :—

1. *Spoken Speech.* (a) *How received and interpreted?*—The hearing was good. If any noise was made or word spoken, she at once turned in the direction of the sound.

With regard to interpretation of words?—She seemed to understand only those which had frequently been mentioned to her. Thus she at once put out her tongue when asked, because she had been requested to do so before, and was expecting the question. At first when asked to shut her eyes she was unable to understand; subsequently she did so quite readily. When asked to give her hand she could not understand what was meant and said, "I forget." She was unable to understand such words as "nose," "ear," etc. When asked to touch her nose, ear, eyes, or chin, she shook her head, evidently was distressed, and rubbed her eyes and looked inquiringly at the nurse who was standing near. She was quite unable to understand such words as "smile," "whistle," "shut your eyes."

(*b*) *How was spoken speech produced?*—She spoke quite distinctly; there was no slurring of words.

Some common objects were shown to her. A watch she at first called "an egg," a pencil "a book," and an orange she was unable to name, but when the name was mentioned she smiled and nodded her head. Milk she called "snow." A handkerchief and an umbrella she also called "snow." She recognised her mother and called her by that name. Almost all other people she called "auntie," and sometimes common objects were called "auntie." A candlestick she called "God." The candle and the light were called "snow." When asked her own name she said "Sarah." Asked how she was, she always was "fine." Have you any pain? She pointed to the left temple and said, "Sair there." Sometimes she seemed conscious of having used the wrong word, and looked distressed, saying, "I forget." When the right word was mentioned on these occasions she smiled and nodded her head. Usually, however, she was not conscious of her mistakes. She could not be got to repeat words or phrases.

2. *Written Speech.* (*a*) *How received and interpreted.*—Sight was good. There was no hemianopsia. She was unable to understand requests in writing such as "Put out your tongue." She could make out the letters of the alphabet, but could only understand small and common words, such as "to," "so," and "merry." "Knit" she called "fen," "by" she called "to."

(*b*) *How written speech was produced.*—Her name Sarah she wrote easily. Her surname she wrote with more difficulty and hesitation, but correctly. She was unable to write answers to questions or to dictation, except numerals (for instance, 31 was written correctly). She failed to copy correctly words written on paper. If asked to write down any word she usually began it with a "P"; for instance, for eighteen she wrote "Pe," for snow she wrote "Pno," for auntie she wrote "Pumrain," and for God she wrote "Pumrase." She understood gesture language well. She understood the use of some common objects, such as a watch. She was shown one at 7.50, and after examining it closely said, "Ten to three." She then pointed out and named in sequence the various hours 1, 2, 3, 4, 5, up to 12.

Progress.—Her temperature, which was 101 on the day of admission, fell to 99 next day, was 100 on the 18th, and normal on the 19th, after which it remained normal. On the 20th it was noted that her aphasic condition was very much the same, except that she now having repeatedly been asked certain questions understood them better. Thus she always at once put out her tongue and shut her eyes when asked to do so. She had more difficulty when asked to touch the ear or the eye. When asked to touch her ear she said "This?" pointing to her eye. Then she pointed to her ear and smiled and nodded. When asked to shut her eyes she did so at once.

March 31*st.*—Her condition was much the same as on March 20th. On the evening of that day a sudden improvement set in. She asked the night nurse for milk. This she had hitherto called "snow." She now had little difficulty with the names of things, but was easily excited, and when so was apt to use the wrong word, but was at once conscious that she had done so. For instance, she asked if she might be allowed to get up and sit at the window. This she corrected at once, saying, "No, no, I mean the fire." She could read now quite easily.

April 8th.—She seemed now quite recovered. She had no difficulty at all in expressing her wants. She still complained of pain in the left side of the head. She had no recollection of the precise onset of her illness, and had a very vague idea of the difficulties she had experienced with her speech during her illness.

April 20th.—She was discharged quite well.

From these notes, which were very carefully taken by the house-physician, Dr. A. W. Cameron, it will be seen that this patient had all the symptoms of auditory aphasia. There was a little more difficulty with voluntary writing than is usual in most cases of lesion of the auditory word centre pure and simple, but this probably resulted from amnesia verbalis being such a prominent symptom in the case.

Tabulating the answers to the questions I have already drawn out, the results are the following :—

1. The patient could hear sounds.
2. The patient could not hear words.
3. The patient could not understand words spoken.
4. The patient could see objects, etc.
5. The patient could see letters and small words, but not long ones.
6. The patient could not understand words written.
7. The patient could speak voluntarily but showed paraphasia and difficulty in recalling correct words.
8. The patient could not repeat words spoken.
9. The patient could not read aloud.
10. The patient could only write voluntarily a few words, and had paragraphia.
11. The patient could not write to dictation.
12. The patient could not copy perfectly.

1, 4, 5, 7, 10, answered in the affirmative ; 2, 3, 6, 8, 9, 11, 12, in the negative.

Comparing this with the results of our theoretical study of the types of aphasia, we see that there is only one of the forms which precisely corresponds to this case, viz. pictorial auditory aphasia, Variety II. It was thus a very pure case of sensory aphasia, involving chiefly, if not entirely, the cortical area in which is situated the word-hearing centre. In all auditory cases there is a difficulty in saying exactly whether the visual word centre is also involved, because of the fact previously mentioned, that the auditory word centre has to be intact in order to see words intelligently. Other points to notice in this case are the following :—

(1) The very distinct forgetfulness of the names of things, amnesia of nouns, a subject I shall have more to say about later.

(2) The distinct retention of knowledge of, and production of, gesture language.

(3) The retention of the understanding of heard music, as well as the power of reproducing a melody by whistling.

(4) The disturbance of the music-hearing faculty, in so much as the patient had " hallucinations of melody."

(5) It is also to be noted that there was agraphia to dictation, and the patient was not able to copy perfectly, owing to the auditory word centre being involved. It is to be noted, however, that the form of disturbance of voluntary writing she had was not the loss of power of forming the letters, because she could write down letters and words when asked, although they were not necessarily the correct ones.

(6) She had therefore paragraphia as well as paraphasia,

and "word-intoxication," or the tendency to reproduce over and over again the same letter or word in writing and speaking. It will be seen that the word "snow" was used in answer to all sorts of questions, and that in writing the same letter was apt to appear again and again. This is a very common symptom in auditory and conduction aphasias. In pure auditory cases the patient does not know when the wrong word is spoken, whereas in pure conduction cases the patient hears the mistaken word, and is annoyed when the wrong word or the same word is spoken again and again. In the same way with paragraphia: in pure conduction cases the patient sees when he has written the incorrect letter or word, whereas when the auditory word centre is involved the patient is not aware of his mistakes in writing.

(7) That the patient could see letters and figures as well as very small words, although the power of seeing longer ones and understanding a written sentence was almost entirely abolished.

(8) The temporary nature of the case and the sudden and rapid recovery.

The preceding was a case of recovery of a very pure cortical auditory aphasia. The next was an auditory and visual aphasia of seventeen years' duration, and the diagnosis was verified by a post-mortem examination. The case had been observed very carefully at various times during its progress, and notes had been taken. For the notes of the case which had been taken whilst the patient was in Morningside Asylum, I am indebted to the kindness of Dr. Clouston; for those taken whilst under my care in Leith Hospital to Dr. Hill Buchan,

House Physician. The brain of this case was shown to the Edinburgh Medico-Chirurgical Society in January 1896.

CASE V. (*Personal Observation*).—*Auditory and visual aphasia of seventeen years' duration. Hemiplegia at first, but gradually recovered from; sensory aphasia symptoms persistent; marked amnesia, chiefly of nouns; paraphasia; agraphia; insanity; post-mortem.*

Mrs. E. S., æt. 53, was admitted to Leith Hospital on September 26th, 1895, in a semicomatose condition, with the following history of her illness :—

About three weeks before admission she began to vomit after food, and this symptom lasted for a week. She had pain in her head, and after the first week had to keep entirely to her bed. She became gradually more stupid and weaker and less able to recognise her friends, and for about a week before her admission she was unable to recognise any one at all.

The following was her state on admission :—She was lying in a stupid, semicomatose condition, eyes almost closed, face slightly drawn to left, no motor paralysis of arms and legs. Right plantar reflex almost absent, left rather exaggerated, knee reflexes normal. No atrophy of muscles of either side. Pupils "pin-point"; slight external strabismus of both eyes. Patient occasionally gave a deep sigh and an attempt to utter something. She could swallow, though there was considerable difficulty in the act. Pulse 115, no heart murmur; no respiratory change; bladder was distended, and a large quantity of urine was drawn off, which had a specific gravity of 1030 and contained no albumen and no sugar. The following history was got from the friends. Patient is the mother of eight children, of whom one died about three months old. This child was born seventeen years ago on December 8th, the confinement being easy. Fourteen days after, when she had been up and washing clothes, she went to bed all right. At 7 a.m. next day her husband found her lying in bed "stiff and quite unconscious." The right arm and leg were paralysed and the face twisted. Patient began to recover about a month after the onset of the illness (the middle of January). At first she could not speak at all, but gradually slight improvement appeared and went on for six or eight months, and since then her speech had remained *in statu quo*. *Her condition since then is described by her husband as follows :—*

(1) She could speak words, but could not converse. Her vocabulary was very small. She could say "yes" or "no," and some expressions such as "fine laddie," "fine lassie." She was never able to address her friends, even her husband, by their names, but would indicate them by some object connected with them. If wishing to speak of a friend who was a butcher she would nod and point to beef; similarly, if she wanted provisions bought, she pointed to sugar, etc. She could not tell the days of the week, though she knew them quite well. She indicated her various children by pointing to their respective heights. She would sometimes ask, "Are you going out?"

(2) *Understanding of spoken words.*—Such a sentence as "I am" she quite understood, but if one said to her "I am going out to Mrs. Welsh's" (her most intimate friend), she did not understand unless some object connected with Mrs. Welsh was pointed to. Her understanding of spoken words was very limited. The method

of conversing with her on the part of her friends was almost entirely by signs. To indicate her brother, a plumber, they pointed to the gas bracket. Her hearing for sounds was quite acute.

(3) *How did she understand written speech?*—Previous to her illness she was a great reader, but since then she has never been able to read a book, though she frequently tried to. She was, however, able to recognise her husband's and any of her family's names in writing, but if, say, the word "pen" was written, she could not recognise it. Anything, however, in butchers' and bakers' books, if too heavily charged, she challenged at once; for instance, on one occasion a whole loaf had been charged for whilst a half-loaf only had been sent, and she corrected it at once. On the other hand, an error in calculation she could not correct (could not count up). She apparently saw figures, but could not calculate.

(4) *Could she write?*—She was quite unable to write even her own name, after her illness. It is noted in the Morningside report that she could copy. At the end of seven or eight months she had regained almost entirely the complete use of her leg and arm, the paresis of the leg disappearing first. In July she saw an Edinburgh consultant. She then appeared very stupid and complained of pains in her head, making signs as if to indicate that she had a feeling as if something in her head was going round and round, and pointing to her head she would often say, "Noise." Her removal to Morningside Asylum was advised, and accordingly she was taken there.

The following notes were taken at that time in Morningside Asylum:—" Her medical certificate stated that her look was peculiar, fixed, and vacant. When asked questions about her condition she speaks unintelligible nonsense. Appearance indicates chronic organic disease of brain as cause of her insanity. She lost power of one side as result of paralytic shock about nine months ago, and since then has never been of sound mind or able to attend to her duties or behave rationally. Her sister-in-law said that since the shock she has never been of sound mind, been sleepless, refused food, and was totally unable to attend to her duties or children. Her state on admission was:—She was depressed, showed considerable enfeeblement, memory much impaired, coherent at times, generally not. Answered questions generally in an absurd rambling way. Pupils unequal, left larger than right, sluggish. Had partial aphasia. Her sensory nervous system was dulled. Tongue tremulous and pointed to left side. *Disease mania.*"

She did not improve, and after a few weeks was transferred to Larbert Institution, where she remained seven or eight months. On leaving Larbert she was, her husband says, mentally all right, complaining only of dizziness when she stooped.

About five years ago, in July 1890, whilst out walking she took drink and became confused and excited. When she took drink, even one glass of beer or whisky, she became stupid; it was impossible to understand what she said, or get her to understand what was said to her. The result was that she was found wandering by the police, and was again certified as insane and sent to Morningside Asylum, her medical certificate stating that "she had obstinate taciturnity. Quite unable to give any account of herself; does not know her name; talks incoherently."

The following notes were taken in the Asylum:—

"She is slightly depressed. Complains of pain in head. There is slight enfeeblement; confused; memory good; is incoherent; can only answer *some* questions; no delusions. Appearance is not unintelligent looking.

"*Nervous System* (Motor).—*Forehead*, left wrinkles slightly higher than right, left lower eyelid less full. Left upper lid one deep fold; right several folds, none very deep. Eyes Kalmuck. Right nasal groove shallower than left. Tongue on left side of mouth, points to right. Special senses not paralysed on any side. Pain on tapping head, especially on left parietal region. Arm and knee reflexes more marked on left; tongue shaky. *Disease melancholia.*

"Owing to her aphasia patient could not tell her name and address, so that she was here for a few days under the cognomen 'unknown.' The excitement passed off in two or three days, and then she became a case of simple aphasia, but a most interesting one. She suffers from partial amnesic aphasia. She put out her tongue on being asked, but as a rule did not understand what was being said to her. Cannot answer her name. Asked her age said 40 and 3. Makes fair simple reflex replies. After several times pressing told the time (20 to 9). Cannot answer what requires thought. Can't write, but copies writing."

She was only a short time in Morningside Asylum, and was discharged cured of her mental symptoms. About the month of September, three years ago, she suddenly went, as her husband says, "into fits." During the day she had been in her usual health, and in the evening she complained of pains in the head and went to bed. About 8 p.m. she suddenly became unconscious and went into convulsions. No very full account of this can be got from her friends, but they say that "she worked most on the right side," "that her face went to the right," and "that the right eye winked most." She was half an hour in the first attack. At the end of it she lay unconscious and "like a stone for a quarter of an hour," when a second one lasting twenty minutes came on. The convulsions went on with only about minute intervals till 12 p.m., when she fell asleep and did not awake till midday next day. The stupor gradually passed off, and in about twenty-four hours after the attack she was in her usual health again, although weak.

From that date she remained in her usual health till the onset of her present attack, for which she was admitted into the hospital in the semicomatose condition previously described.

Progress.—Her temperature on admission was 101·4, but after an ice cap was applied to her head it gradually fell, and on the morning of the next day it was normal, rising again in the evening to 99·8, falling next morning to normal, and rising again in the evening to 100·4.

She gradually became weaker, and died comatose on September 29th, four days after admission.

The following is the report of the post-mortem examination of the head :—

On removing the skull-cap the dura is seen to be thickened, and vessels in pia-mater congested; membranes are œdematous-looking, and much fluid is found in arachnoid spaces between the convolutions. A large collection of clear fluid in the Sylvian fissure on the left side, where it is seen that the upper two convolutions of the temporo-sphenoidal lobe have almost entirely atrophied, their place being occupied by a large quantity of fluid, the surface vessels being much congested over this area. The atrophic process passed back to the angular gyrus and posterior part of the supramarginal convolution, but the part of these convolutions nearest the Sylvian fissure was also involved in this atrophy. The dura-mater was adherent to cerebrum at various parts of the hemispheres, especially over the vertex. The atrophy was quite evidently due either to an embolus or a thrombus blocking one or more branches of the Sylvian

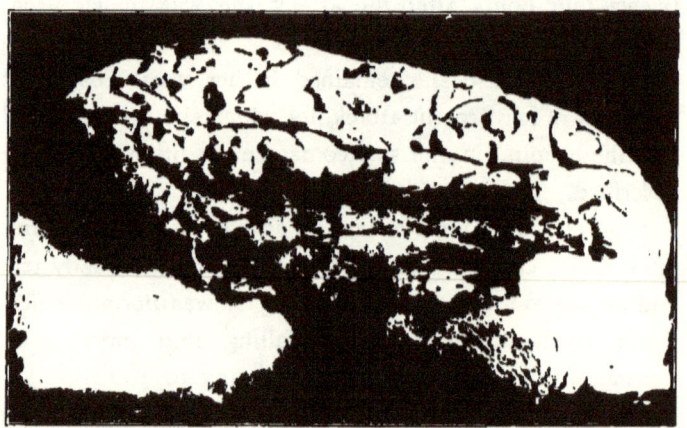

FIG. 16.—COPY OF PHOTOGRAPH OF LEFT CEREBRAL HEMISPHERE OF CASE V. THE TEMPORO-SPHENOIDAL LOBE HAS ALMOST ENTIRELY DISAPPEARED.

artery. The lower half of the third temporo-sphenoidal convolution escaped the atrophic process, as also did the third left frontal and Rolandic areas, but the region of the motor areas, although not visibly atrophied, was not quite so full as the other side. Nothing further was seen on slicing the brain. A copy of a photograph of the left hemisphere is here inserted, which gives a good idea of the precise extent of the disease (Fig. 16). It was taken after the brain had lain some time in spirit, and the third temporo-sphenoidal convolution had contracted relatively a little more than the rest of the specimen.

From the history of this case it will be seen that she had seventeen years ago what was apparently very marked hemiplegia, involving the face, arm, and leg on the right side, along with aphasia.

The attack was probably either thrombotic or embolic in character, more probably the former, for these reasons: 1. There was no cardiac lesion which might have given rise to an embolus. 2. It came on after childbirth, as is not uncommonly seen—one explanation being that, although it is very improbable that an embolus of sufficient size to block a cerebral artery could pass from the venous circulation in the pelvis through the pulmonary circulation to the left side of the heart, and thence into the carotid artery, it is not quite so improbable that a very minute body might do so, or a small piece of clot might become detached from the venous side of a pulmonary apoplexy, and so form the nucleus for the beginning of a thrombosis in a cerebral vessel. She gradually recovered from the hemiplegia, the leg and arm recovering first, and ultimately completely so. On her second admission into Morningside Asylum six years ago, there were very careful notes taken of her motor condition, and it is seen from these that very slight motor impairment could then only be noticed in the face, the arm and leg having completely recovered. Three years ago she had fits, which apparently were more or less of the Jacksonian type, the motor movements being much more marked on the right side. The attack for which she was admitted into Leith Hospital was one of those congestive attacks which so commonly come on in old-standing cerebral cases. There was marked congestion of all the meninges at the post-mortem, together with considerable excess of cerebro-spinal fluid. This attack she did not recover from, and she died a few days after admission. Summarising her symptoms and answering the twelve questions previously considered, we ascertain that—

1. She could hear sounds.
2. She could not hear words.
3. She could not understand words spoken.
4. She could see objects, etc.
5. She could not see words, but could see figures.
6. She could not understand words written.
7. She could speak voluntarily, but used incorrect words.
8. She could not repeat words spoken.
9. She could not read aloud.
10. She could not write voluntarily.
11. She could not write to dictation.
12. She could copy (?).

1, 4, 7, and 12 are thus answered in the affirmative; 2, 3, 5, 6, 8, 9, 10, 11, in the negative.

Comparing these answers with the results we have already arrived at, it will be seen that this case corresponds in the answers given to the last case we have considered, viz. a pictorial auditory, and in addition she had the symptoms of visual aphasia, except that in this case the patient could copy, whereas in the other one the patient could not copy. It is not noted in this case, however, how the patient was tested. In the previous case the patient could not copy perfectly. It has been found that some patients, although they are not able to copy printed words into written words, are still able to print words from copy, just as they would trace a map, a drawing, or a design. Whether this patient copied in that way or not the record taken at Morningside does not say. Later I shall describe a case of word-blindness with agraphia, that was able to copy in this way. That is, he printed from printed copy and wrote from written copy. Amongst some of the most interesting of the facts of this case are the following :—

1. That although the patient lived for seventeen years after the onset of her aphasia, and although her hemiplegic symptoms disappeared, her aphasia remained practically *in statu quo*. This is most interesting for various reasons. It was stated by Wernicke, and the statement has been accepted by most, if not all, writers on aphasia since then, that sensory aphasias often recover more rapidly than motor aphasias, and the explanation of this was sought for in the fact that the right auditory word centre more readily took up the function of the left auditory word centre than the right motor centre took up the function of the left motor centre. It was stated that, as speech was first acquired by the auditory centres, the auditory word memories were not so exclusively confined to the left side as the motor word memories were, and that the uneducated right auditory centre had more word memories stored in it than the right motor speech centre, and more readily acquired a further expansion of its function when called on by a blotting out of the left auditory word memories. Although this may be the explanation in some cases, others such as this rather throw doubt on the theory, because at the end of seventeen years in this case the patient was much in the same condition as at the beginning, although the post-mortem revealed that the

right side of the brain was intact. We have seen also that in the previous case I have recorded, where the symptoms were not very different, and where almost certainly the auditory centre was affected, the patient made a rapid recovery. On reading the literature of aphasia one cannot but be struck with the number of rapid recoveries of all forms of aphasia. There are probably various explanations of such rapid recoveries, such as that the aphasia may have been due to congestion or to anæmia of a cerebral area; to an embolus which had caught in one vessel and then got washed away into an unimportant vessel; to an embolus which, owing to its shape, was able to block a vessel at one time, and, on being changed in its position, failed to block it entirely; to the circulation having recovered by means of anastomosing vessels; to the absorption of exudation or new growths of a syphilitic character, such as endarteritis or pachymeningitis; to the gradual absorption of small hæmorrhages; to some toxic condition such as uræmia, etc., impairing the function of cerebral areas; to a condition of dehydration, as in the case recorded by Chouppe,[1] where a man out of work, and travelling without getting water to satisfy his thirst, fell asleep on the roadside. On being wakened up he was aphasic, but Chouppe found in his pocket an hospital ticket stating that the patient suffered from "polyurie simple." This gave the key to his condition, and on the patient drinking freely of water he recovered his speech in a few minutes.

[1] *Comptes Rend. de la Soc. de Biol.*, 1892, p. 642.

Are there Functional Sensory Aphasias?

Many and various are the causes which have been believed to cause aphasia, and hysterical and functional aphasias have also been described. It has been generally recognised that there are many cases of functional or hysterical motor aphasia and hysterical and functional amnesia of nouns, but true functional auditory aphasia has not, I think, received the attention it probably ought to have done. Wyllie[1] states: "Thus among the phenomena of functional aphasia may, as of occasional occurrence, be reckoned paraphasia, paragraphia, word-blindness, and word-deafness. But the occurrence of these phenomena is rare. The occurrence indeed of word-blindness or of word-deafness ought generally to suggest to the mind of the physician the probability of an organic rather than a functional cause. In common cases of functional aphasia the leading and often the only phenomenon is amnesia verbalis (logamnesia), the loss of the power of calling up words in the memory from within. Commonly the aphasia is purely amnesic; only in a few cases is it also agnostic."

These are the views of an observer of such experience as Wyllie, but nevertheless one is struck on reading many of the cases of sensory aphasia how well a functional cause would explain the rapid recoveries. Case IV. is another of such cases, where the patient without any motor symptoms, and no other symptom but word-deafness, almost in one night recovered the functions of the auditory word centre. The only objection to this

[1] *Disorders of Speech*, p. 408. Edinburgh, 1894.

theory is the fact that for two days there was slight rise of temperature, but even that is not incompatible with hysteria or functional disturbance.

Wernicke's Case 1.[1] may fairly be considered to be one of this sort. The following is a summary of the facts of the case. Susanne Adam was taken ill on March 1st. There was no loss of consciousness. There was complete auditory aphasia, much paraphasia; occasionally correctly expressed herself; became intoxicated with a word, "begraben"; was sent to an asylum. Hearing was equal and good on both sides. Understood absolutely nothing from hearing it. Answered as much to a stranger's as to her own name; named objects rightly at one time, but not at others. Sang a song without a book on hearing it sung by a patient. Had complete alexia. She progressed rapidly, and on April 20th understood almost all that was repeated to her once or twice; speech was a little hesitating; read without stopping; was not able to write to dictation, but could copy pretty well the separate letters of the alphabet. Agraphia was then almost her only disturbance of speech.

I have selected this case of Wernicke's because it is a very well recorded one as well as being well known, and was one of the cases that Wernicke drew his conclusions from as to the temporary nature of sensory aphasias and the reasons of their temporary nature.

His conclusions on this point are stated at page 33, and are briefly :—

(1) Motor aphasia cases show more general symptoms to begin with, which hinder diagnosis; but, on the other

[1] *Der Aphasische Symptomen Complex*, 1874.

hand, the right side is not so ready to take on the function of the left side.

(2) In sensory aphasia, on the other hand, there is early compensation by the other side and only slight general symptoms.

Now, whatever the explanation of these rapid recoveries in sensory aphasia, I cannot believe that cases such as this one of Wernicke's (Susanne Adam) and my case (Case IV.) recover by the right hemisphere taking on the function of the left as regards word hearing and word seeing. The cases were very like each other, but recovery in my case was more rapid and more immediate than in Wernicke's. Of course it is possible that the left auditory area may have recovered from the organic lesion, if it was organic, but such organic lesions are not often so completely and especially so suddenly recovered from as in my case. We know, moreover, that functional motor aphasias (hysterical mutism) often recover quite as suddenly as they begin, but in others are more gradual in their recovery. Later I shall describe an excellent example of functional motor aphasia which gradually recovered, as well as some others which recovered almost suddenly. Another argument against the right side taking on the functions of the left so rapidly in sensory aphasia is furnished by this my second sensory aphasia case (Case V.), which remained *in statu quo* for seventeen years, and the satisfactory fact in the case was that the organic nature of the disease and the precise situation of the lesion, viz. in the auditory and visual word centres on the left side, were verified by the post-mortem examination.

I do not wish, of course, to deny that the right side

may and does take up the function of the left through time and by a process of slow education. Such cases have been recorded, and notably one by Wyllie, and the well-known case of Barlow,[1] where a boy with heart disease had aphasia with right-sided hemiplegia, and after gradually recovering his speech had another attack, which completely deprived him of speech as well as producing paralysis on the left side. At the post-mortem of this case two lesions were found: the first, the old lesion in Broca's convolution on the left side, and the more recent one in the corresponding part of the right hemisphere. This case is usually taken as conclusive evidence of the right hemisphere taking up the function of the left. But what I wish to state just now is that the process is probably almost always a slow one, and that those rapid sensory aphasia recoveries are probably due to some other causes, one of which is that some of the cases are originally functional and not organic in origin.

Passing, however, from this subject, I shall take up a few of the other interesting points in the case (Case V.).

2. *The patient was twice confined in an asylum.*—It was stated by Wernicke that cases of sensory aphasia, especially when there are no general symptoms, are often considered to be insane and are sent to asylums. There is little doubt about the insanity in this case, but it is interesting to note, from a medico-legal point of view, that the medical certificate stated the following facts as being evidence of her insanity on the second occasion on which she was admitted: "She had obstinate taciturnity. Quite unable to give any account of herself. Does not know her name. Talks incoherently." These symptoms—

[1] *Brit. Med. Journ.*, Vol. I., 1877.

without being too critical as to how a person could have obstinate taciturnity and talk incoherently at the same time—are quite what might be expected of any one who was affected with sensory aphasia, but the patient need not necessarily have been insane.

3. *The patient, although she could speak voluntarily, had a very small correct vocabulary.*—This is a point that has to be carefully investigated in all aphasia cases, because one is very apt to suppose that the cause of this difficulty in speaking correctly must be due to some impairment of Broca's convolution. More careful investigation, however, reveals the fact that the correct vocabulary is small from impairment of the auditory word centre, so that the proper auditory word images cannot be recalled by the "ideational" mechanism. She could not often recall the correct word. She sometimes talked a great deal, but the words were not quite correct; hence one medical certificate stated that "she talked unintelligible nonsense," and the other that "she talked incoherently." This is the symptom called "paraphasia," which is such a marked symptom in conduction aphasias, but is also always present in auditory aphasia proper. Case IV. also showed this symptom markedly, and it will be seen that in the next case I have to record, one of conduction aphasia, the symptom was very marked.

4. *The patient could see figures, but not words.*—She could, however, not calculate ("could not count up"). It is noted that this case on one occasion picked out a mistake in the figures in a baker's bill. When I consider cases of visual aphasia I shall refer again to this difference between word and figure memories.

5. *She possessed intact the language of signs—pantomime*

language.—Her friends used signs in conversing with her, and she used signs in conversing with them. She pointed to the height of her children to distinguish one from another. In referring to her brother, a plumber, she pointed to the gas bracket, etc. Sometimes this language of gesture or signs is lost as well as speech, written and spoken, but often it is not, as in this case, Case V., and also in Case IV. The reception centre for such speech is probably in the occipital lobes, in or near the ordinary seeing centres; the production centre in the centre for that part of the body used to produce the sign—the hand, head, etc.

6. *The very marked forgetfulness of names—amnesia of nouns (amnesia verbalis).*—She forgot almost all proper names, even the names of her husband and children, and could not recall the names of objects and things about her. This is a symptom I have said little about as yet, because I did not wish to complicate the schema which I have already drawn up. Both of these auditory cases I have described had this symptom very markedly, and it will be found on studying the literature of aphasia that there are very few complete sensory aphasias that do not show this symptom in a more or less marked degree, and it is also seen, although to a less extent, in many motor aphasias. It has been recognised for many years that patients were more apt to have forgetfulness for noun substantives than for the other parts of speech. The usual explanation for this has been that, although nouns are of course used in almost every sentence, still the same noun does not recur often in ordinary conversation, whereas the other parts of speech recur again and again. Sentences are simply for the purpose of binding nouns in various

ways to each other, and the binding words are comparatively few in number and often recur. Many well-known observers have adopted this view, but, on the other hand, there are some who hold that there is a special centre for the storing up of the names of objects, etc. Broadbent has written much on this subject, and has published several most interesting examples of it.[1]

From an examination of the anatomical arrangement of the connecting fibres in the cerebrum, he located the naming centre theoretically in the posterior part of the temporal lobe, as he found that a large number of fibres converged to that region from the perceptive centres, the visual, auditory, tactile, etc., centres. Broadbent's papers, however, were written at a time when a word-hearing and a word-seeing centre had not been so generally recognised, and he does not so fully differentiate these centres from the naming centre. His cases, besides being excellent examples of amnesia verbalis, had also lesion of the word-hearing and word-seeing centres. Bastian, Wyllie, etc., believe that in all probability there is no single centre for "concepts or ideas," but that many parts of the cortex are concerned in the elaboration of concepts and ideas. They also believe that there is no special naming centre. They believe that this forgetfulness of nouns may be one of the symptoms of all aphasias, and that motor aphasias also often show it; that as the stimulus from within, in the recalling of names, is less than that from without, when there is any affection depressing the higher cerebral centres the stimulus from within is not sufficient to

---

[1] "Cerebral Mechanism of Speech and Thought," in *Med. Chir. Trans.*, 1872; *Med. Chir. Trans.*, 1878; *Med. Chir. Trans.*, Vol. LXVII., 1884.

raise the name memory. Broadbent (*loc. cit.*), Charcot,[1] Kussmaul,[2] and Mills,[3] however, hold that there is a special naming centre, but they do not differentiate this centre distinctly from the higher or ideational mechanism. That the ideational mechanism is not one centre, but that probably many parts of the cerebral cortex act together so as to produce concepts or ideas, and so act as one centre, seems the most feasible theory. The term "ideational mechanism" is thus a convenient one, and more correct than "ideational centre," as I have previously pointed out. I think, however, that if speech be theoretically as well as clinically studied, it will be seen that the probability is that there is a special naming mechanism apart from the ideational mechanism. The fact that we have some cases where apparently all the higher intellectual centres are intact, where the patient can think and act rationally, can form ideas of objects, recalling their form, appearance, and other characteristics, but on speaking cannot recall their names, shows, I think, that the ideational mechanism is distinct from the naming mechanism. And again, the fact that we have cases with no affection of the auditory word centre and no affection of the higher intellectual centres, but very distinct amnesia of nouns, shows that the mechanism concerned in the recalling of names is not quite the same as the auditory word centre. Such cases are to be found in medical literature, and recently there has come under my own observation a case of this sort. It was a case of

[1] *Lect. on Diseases of the Nervous System*, Vol. III., New Syd. Soc.

[2] Ziemssen, *Cycl. of Pract. Med.*, Amer. edition, Vol. XIV.

[3] *Nervous Diseases*, by American Authors. Edited by Dercum, 1895.

abscess in the temporo-sphenoidal lobe, where amnesia of nouns was the most marked symptom, there being little or no impairment of the word-hearing centre and there being no motor aphasia. It has been also shown, for instance, that there are some cases where nouns could not be produced by the patient either voluntarily or by imitation, all other parts of speech being used freely. Such a case is recorded by Broadbent[1]: "During the whole of his illness (five years) he was scarcely ever known to utter a noun substantive, and if he did, it was so to speak, inadvertently and erroneously. Other words he said unhesitatingly, and he would employ fairly long phrases, speaking them smoothly and naturally so long as a noun did not come in his way." Every one knows how, when the nervous system is tired and worn out, either from fatigue or as the result of debilitating disease, the memory for nouns (proper names, etc.) is apt to fail, even although the binding words (verbs, adjectives, etc.) in the sentence may be recalled quite easily. Of course the explanation of this, according to some, is as previously stated, that the binding words are much more familiar, having been used much oftener than nouns, and that, when the nervous system is depressed, the stimulus from within is too weak to recall the nouns which are the least familiar. This theory does not satisfactorily explain such a case as Broadbent's, where every noun substantive seemed to have been blotted out. A more satisfactory theory, in my opinion, would be one in which a special naming or noun-substantive mechanism found a place. Such a mechanism must be very closely associated with the auditory word centre and the ideational mechan-

[1] *Med. Chir. Trans.*, Vol. LXVII., 1884.

ism, and on the receptive side must be connected with all the primary perceptive centres. The primary perceptive centres from which it could receive impressions would be the following: the centres for

    Tactile Sensations,
    Muscular Sense,
    Olfactory Sense,
    Taste Sense,
    Seeing Sense, including form, colour, etc.,

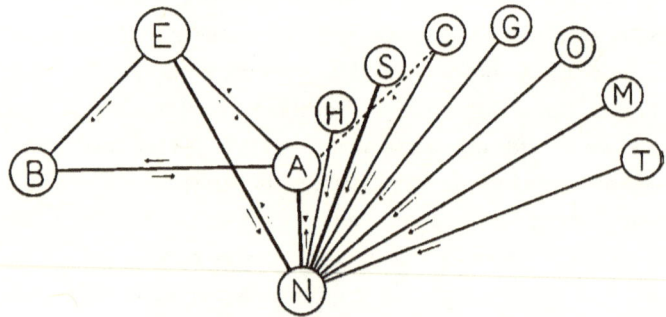

FIG. 17.—DIAGRAMMATIC REPRESENTATION OF THE SENSORY CONNECTIONS OF THE NAMING MECHANISM.

E. Ideational mechanism; B. Psycho-motor speech centre; A. Auditory word centre; N. Naming mechanism where are associated impressions from A. Auditory word centre, H. Hearing centres, S. Centres for sight, C. Word-seeing centre, G. Taste, O. Olfactory, M. Muscular, and T. Tactile senses.

    Word-seeing,
    Hearing,
    Word-hearing.

Fig. 17 is a diagrammatic representation of the connections of the naming mechanism.

In order to produce a complete schema of speech, therefore, this diagram (Fig. 17) would require to be added to the one I have previously drawn out, and the result is seen in Fig. 18.

Most objects receive their distinguishing name probably chiefly on account of the impressions of their form, colour, etc., which we receive through the visual perceptive centres. I have therefore drawn the line connecting the visual centres to the naming mechanism broader and heavier than the others; but for some objects most of the other perceptive centres send impressions to the naming mechanism, for others not so many. Take a violin, for instance. The cerebrum receives impressions of a violin through the

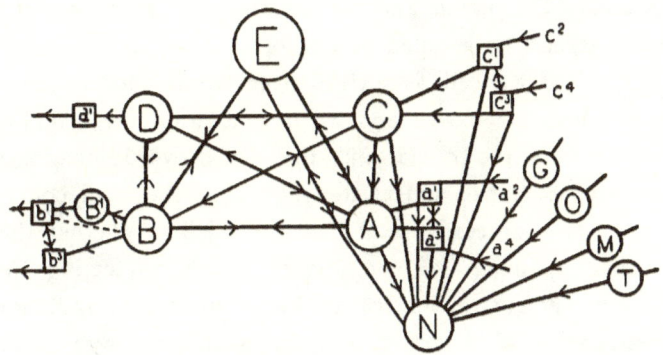

FIG. 18.—DIAGRAMMATIC REPRESENTATION OF CONNECTIONS OF NAMING MECHANISM ON THE RECEPTIVE SIDE.

E. Ideational mechanism. B. Psycho-motor articulatory speech centre; B^1. Corresponding centre on right side; b^1 and b^2. Articulatory motor centres on both sides. D. Graphic centre; d^1. Centres for the right hand. A. Auditory word centre; a^1 and a^2. Auditory sound centres on the two sides. C. Visual word centre; c^1 and c^2. Visual perceptive centres on the two sides. G. Gustatory, O. Olfactory, M. Muscular, and T. Tactile senses. N. Naming mechanism by which the different percepts are associated with the name.

nerves of sight (form, colour, etc.), through the nerve of hearing (recalling its sound, etc.), and through tactile and muscular sensations. All these impressions are received from the primary centres (which, it is to be noted, are in both hemispheres), are associated in what I have called the naming mechanism with the auditory word image, or sound of the name of the object, received from the auditory word centre, in the left hemisphere only, and in educated persons probably also associated with the visual word image of the name, received from the visual word centre in the left hemisphere only; and the complete knowledge of the object—that is, all we know of it from the sensory impressions, including its name and the visual image of the name—can be transmitted to the ideational mechanism, or can be revived in the memory by the ideational mechanism. The name and the other sensory impressions, however, can be recalled by one or more of these sensory impressions as well as revived from within; for instance, if our eyes are closed and we hear a violin, the sound at once recalls the name and the visual word image in educated persons; and at the same time the form, colour, and other characteristics of it are recalled. Whether this is done by means of commissural fibres connecting the various perceptive centres, or by a process of radiation from one naming centre, it is impossible to say; in all probability the various centres are linked in a most complete and complicated manner. For a full appreciation, therefore, of the *object* "violin," the naming mechanism must receive impressions from the visual, tactile, muscular, auditory, and word-seeing centres, and these impressions are associated with the impression received from the word-hearing centre—that is, the *word-sound* "violin"—which we call the *name* of the object. On this theory the naming mechanism is lower than the ideational mechanism, but higher than, although probably very closely associated with, the word-hearing centre, and receiving impressions from probably all the other perceptive centres. For some noun substantives impressions may be received from one perceptive centre only, for others from two, for others from three, and so on; but from however few or many perceptive centres, impressions may be received for a particular noun substantive, these impressions are associated in the naming mechanism with the name sound of the object, the image of which name sound is received from the auditory word centre. From this naming mechanism these associated impressions can, as I said, be transmitted to the ideational mechanism or revived by the ideational mechanism. How do noun substantives differ from other words, as, for instance, verbs, adjectives, etc., the binding words in a sentence? It will be seen that it is not necessary to receive any sensory impressions other than the ordinary word image—and in educated persons, the visual word image—of the binding words in the sentence, in order to use these words in forming sentences. Such words are revived almost, if not entirely, from within—that is, by the ideational mechanism—and probably the word is revived, if not in all, in some persons at least, by a direct route from the auditory word centre to the ideational mechanism, or *vice versa*, without the intermediary of a naming mechanism by which the name is associated with the other sensory impressions of an object. From this argument it will be seen that I have, to avoid confusion, omitted all mention of impressions received from the word production centres, as they are common to all words, nouns as well as binding words. These impressions, however, are of very great importance indeed in the reviving of words in the memory, the psycho-motor articulatory images being almost if not quite as important as the auditory word images in enabling the individual to have the complete "word percept," a fact which has been very distinctly emphasised by Wyllie, who has named centres A and B the "primary couple." As I have previously mentioned, probably the most decided sensory impressions of most objects are received from the visual perceptive centres, and therefore there must be many connecting fibres between the occipital lobes and the naming mechanism. Theoretically, therefore, we would expect that the chief part of the naming mechanism would be in the posterior part of the temporo-sphenoidal lobe—that is, in a near neighbourhood to both the word-hearing centre and the general visual perceptive centres in the occipital lobes.

On studying carefully many of the recorded cases of amnesia verbalis, where post-mortems have taken place, the lesions have usually involved one or more than one of the centres for speech, but the auditory word centre and the visual word centre, or one of them, have been most frequently involved, so that it is very difficult getting sufficient evidence to localise exactly the naming mechanism. Broadbent's cases proved quite distinctly that there was amnesia of nouns if the greater part of the temporo-sphenoidal lobe was destroyed, and they tended to show that, in all probability, lesion of the posterior part of that lobe produced the symptom.

Recently, Mills[1] has recorded a case where at the post-mortem there was found a lesion limited to the third temporo-sphenoidal convolution. The case goes a long way, I think, to settle the precise position of the lesion which causes amnesia of nouns. I give an abridged note of the case here. The patient—a woman, aged about forty—had had cerebral symptoms for five years before her death, showing

[1] *Nervous Diseases*, by American Authors. Edited by Dercum, 1895.

gradual cerebral impairment, amongst the symptoms being a convulsion fit, word-blindness, and verbal amnesia. She was first seen by Mills in consultation in July 1894. In April of that year she had had vertigo, and from this time on "it had become almost impossible for her to name objects." In July there was no anæsthesia or paralysis. She had an irregular left lateral homonymous hemianopsia. She was word-blind, but not letter-blind; she could name single letters slowly. She could not name objects either from sight or touch. When a pencil, pen, scissors, or purse was held before her, or when she was allowed to touch them, she could not give their names, although she understood what they were. On one occasion she called the scissors "what I sew with," and the purse "what I buy with." When such objects were named to her she would promptly indicate that the names were correct, and she could also as a rule repeat the names spoken in her hearing, but not always quickly, and occasionally she had considerable difficulty in repeating them. She used "yes" and "no" properly, and knew the uses of objects, but could not give their names. She talked spontaneously, but not freely, not using concrete nouns, or but rarely, and sometimes misplacing words. She became gradually more stupid, and died in September 1894.

At the post-mortem a small nodulated, half-disintegrated mass about the size of a hickory nut was pulled out of the brain substance at a position which corresponded to the posterior fourth of the third temporal convolution. The surface of the third temporal in its posterior half, and to a much less extent of the second temporal in the same region, and of the fourth temporal, presented a granular, slightly disintegrated appearance. On cutting into the temporal lobe, a tumour, hard and yellowish brown in colour, was revealed. Its hardest and apparently oldest part was about the middle of the third temporal, and passing slightly into the second temporal. The mass extended cephalad and caudad a short distance almost entirely in the white matter of the third temporal gyre, but a soft nodulated more or less hæmorrhagic condition reached caudad as far as the white matter of the middle of the occipital lobe, and cephalad to the junction of the first and middle thirds of the second and third temporal convolutions.

The parts chiefly destroyed were the white matter of the third, to a less extent of the second, and to a still less extent of the fourth, temporal convolution. Internally the roof of the posterior horn presented a slightly granular appearance. The disease almost certainly started in the third temporal convolution at a point in a line with the posterior extremity of the horizontal branch of the Sylvian fissure.

A diagrammatic representation of the area of the cortex involved is seen in the accompanying figure (Fig. 19).

Here we have a very distinct localisation of the naming mechanism, and the position is near to the place where we have theoretically supposed it would be, and where Broadbent long ago supposed it to be from a minute study of the connecting fibres in the cerebrum. On examining carefully the records of many of the post-mortems of cases of amnesia of nouns, such as those recorded by Wyllie and by Broadbent, I find that this region was more or less involved in most if not all of them. In my case (Case V.), where amnesia of nouns was such a prominent symptom, this region was certainly also involved in the lesion (see photograph, Fig. 15).

Recently a case of amnesia of nouns has come under my observation. It was under the care of Mr. Miles at Leith Hospital, and has not yet been published. The interesting symptom in the case from an aphasic point of view was the very marked amnesia without word-deafness. He had great difficulty in recalling names from within, and he also named objects at sight very incorrectly. Mr. Miles trephined over the temporo-sphenoidal lobe, and evacuated

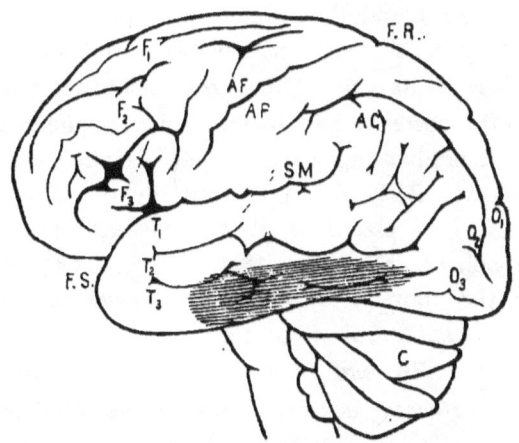

FIG. 19.—LOCALISATION OF THE LESION IN MILLS' CASE.
The shaded portion shows the position of the lesion.

pus from that lobe. The case, after temporary improvement, ultimately died, and at the post-mortem the abscess was seen to have been in the lower part of the temporo-sphenoidal lobe.

It is of course well known that lesions of the temporo-sphenoidal lobe are more apt to cause amnesia than lesions of any other part of the brain, but I think the time has come when the precise locality of lesions in amnesic cases should be accurately noted, in order to enable the surgeon and physician to diagnose exactly the site of the disease which causes the amnesia, whether we grant a special naming mechanism or not. The following case of my own observation was one where slight amnesia of nouns was the only aphasic symptom. The patient died, and the post-mortem revealed the site of the lesion. During life I stated that there was only impairment of the mechanism concerned in recalling nouns, either from within or from without, and that if there is a noun centre it was not destroyed, but its functions were impaired from a lesion close to its site. I diagnosed acute softening, probably in the posterior part of the temporo-sphenoidal lobe and the neighbouring part of the occipital lobe. The diagnosis was fairly well borne out by the post-mortem examination. I placed it at the posterior part of the temporo-sphenoidal lobe, rather than the anterior part, because the most marked amnesic symptom was his inability to name objects at sight.

CASE VI. (*Personal Observation*).—*Amnesia of nouns; no word-deafness; acute softening in occipital lobe and posterior part of temporo-sphenoidal lobe.*

P. B., æt. 66, a labourer, admitted to Leith Hospital May 7th, 1896, complaining of pains in right side of abdomen, speech disturbance, and sleeplessness.

History.—The patient was a strong healthy man until beginning of this year, and had always been temperate in his habits. On the Saturday before new year his "speech and memory failed." This took place gradually in the course of the day, and there appears to have been no sudden shock, and no paralysis or unconsciousness. The power of producing sounds was never lost, but for two or three days it was impossible to make out even the words in his attempts at speech. Although he appeared to see what was going on around him, his intelligence seemed not to be retained. (This is the account as given by his friends.) His condition improved gradually, and in a few weeks he regained his full intelligence and was able to talk distinctly and sensibly. He had, however, a constant difficulty in getting the words that he wanted, especially in regard to nouns, and more particularly names of persons and places, and would frequently substitute quite irrelevant ones. Until five weeks before admission he was able to go out to his work, but complained a good deal of spasmodic pains across the upper part of his abdomen. These attacks had occurred at intervals since the new year, sometimes coming on when he was at work, and causing him to feel sick and giddy, and occasionally to vomit. At first he was able to go about, and went several times to see Dr. George Elder at the New Town Dispensary. He conversed easily and correctly with Dr. Elder, and nothing peculiar was observed in his speech, except on one occasion when he spoke about having " a roller drawn over his back." Five weeks before admission, from the increased severity of the pains, he took to bed. Since then his condition has become worse. He has complained much of the pain in his abdomen, has become rather incoherent in his talk, and latterly sleepless and noisy at nights.

On admission it was noted that he was a strong, well-developed looking man.

Circulatory System.—Pulse rate 80 per minute, irregular both in rhythm and force; tension low and not well sustained between beats; vessel walls thickened, but not markedly atheromatous. Heart sounds are faint in all the areas, but no definite murmur.

Respiratory System.—Bronchitis with considerable congestion of bases of both lungs.

Abdomen is normal, with the exception of the subjective attacks of pain which come in paroxysms. Urine acid; sp. gr. 1018; no albumen and no sugar.

Nervous System.—No convulsions or other seizures. No paresis or paralysis can be made out. No interference with co-ordination or muscular power. Reflexes normal.

Face.—Can close both eyes perfectly. Left corner of mouth drooping very slightly; no difficulty with whistling; tongue protruded in middle line. Rapid twitching or quivering movements about the angle of the nose and mouth, most marked on speaking, but also observed occasionally when at rest.

Sensory Functions.—From condition of patient no accurate tests could be applied; no alteration in cutaneous sensibility could be made out.

Vision apparently unimpaired, but could not be tested satisfactorily; pupils react to light and accommodation slightly unequal.

Hearing apparently good. Taste and smell could not be tested.

His general intelligence is dulled, but—

1. He hears and understands what is said to him.

2. He sees apparently all right, but could not be tested as to reading.

3. He speaks quite well—that is to say, he forms and pronounces the words all right—but he makes mistakes in the words which he uses.

He sometimes has difficulty in recalling the word he wants to use, and the nouns and names are found to be the words he has difficulty with. Sometimes he cannot tell his own name. When shown objects he has difficulty in naming them. Sometimes he names them quite easily, either by recalling them from within or on seeing them, but at other times he has greater difficulty. He can repeat words, nouns as well as other words. There is thus no auditory aphasia, no visual aphasia, and no motor aphasia, but slight logamnesia, if anything more marked for nouns requiring to be recalled from sight than from within.

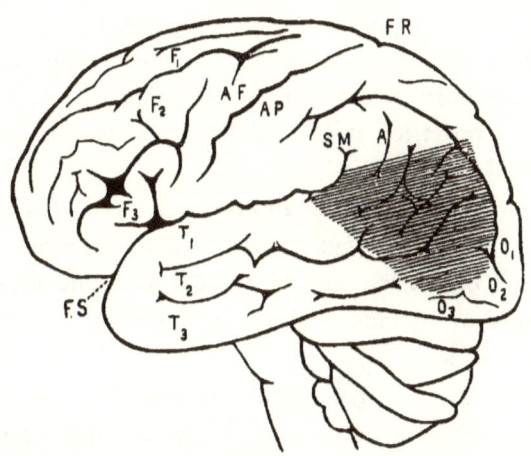

FIG. 20.—LATERAL SURFACE LEFT HEMISPHERE.
The shaded portion shows the position of the area of the cortex affected in Case VI.

He gradually became more restless and sleepiess, and then became comatose, and died May 14th. The following is the post-mortem report of the examination of the brain made by Dr. Shennan, Pathologist to Leith Hospital:—

There was a large quantity of fluid on removing the dura-mater, also thickening of the arachnoid.

Left Hemisphere.—At posterior end of first temporo-sphenoidal convolution there is an area of softening which extends backwards, becoming wider as it goes into the occipital lobe. There is destruction of the grey matter, and the softening extends on an average three-eighths of an inch inwards. The area of the softening is seen in the diagram (Fig. 20).

The Cause of Death.—Acute softening of the cerebrum, with, in addition, a fairly acute cerebral meningitis.

If, therefore, there is a naming mechanism separate from the auditory word centre, then the clinical and pathological evidence points to an important part of that mechanism being situated in the near neighbourhood of the auditory word centre, but probably lower down, viz. in the posterior half of the third and second temporo-sphenoidal convolution.

The objection to this localisation is the fact that amnesia probably is often a symptom of motor aphasia, with a lesion not in the temporo-sphenoidal lobe, but anterior to the fissure of Sylvius. There are probably two explanations of this :—

1. That some of the cases that have been recorded as having amnesia verbalis have in reality not been cases which could strictly be considered to be cases of amnesia of nouns. The patient may have been able to recall the auditory and visual images as well as the other associations of the words, whether nouns or binding words, in the sentences, but owing to the affection of Broca's convolution the psycho-motor speech images could not have been recalled. Such cases of complete motor aphasia would have equal difficulty with all words, except the very familiar ones which had been imprinted on the right side.

It is, therefore, very essential to distinguish between true forgetfulness of names and want of knowledge as to how words are to be produced. The former is a fault in the reception and psychical mechanism, the latter in the psychical and production mechanism. As previously pointed out, it is to be remembered that the psycho-motor articulatory images of words play a very important part in the revival of words in the memory, names as well as other words.

2. That it is possible that a lesion in Broca's convolution may interrupt the fibres which pass from the higher centres in the frontal lobe to the naming mechanism and auditory centre in the temporo-sphenoidal lobe. The temporo-sphenoidal lobe is probably connected with the frontal lobe by fibres, and these fibres, if they pass in the subcortical substance anywhere near Broca's convolution, must sometimes at least be involved in a lesion of any great size in Broca's convolution. If part of the ideational mechanism is situated in the frontal lobes, it is easy seeing, therefore, how a lesion in the neighbourhood of the third left frontal may give rise to difficulty in recalling a word, whether we consider that there is a special naming mechanism, or an auditory word centre pure and simple.

These two explanations, therefore, might account for most, if not all, of the cases of amnesia verbalis in motor aphasia.

The post-mortem examination in Case V. was also confirmatory of the position of the lesion that produces amnesia verbalis as well as of the position of the word-hearing and the word-seeing centres. If, therefore, we admit a naming mechanism, it will be seen that it is possible to have various lesions involving that mechanism, or the fibres connecting that mechanism with other centres, and these lesions might give rise to various symptoms according to the position of the lesion. This fact would account, I think, for the varieties we find of amnesia of nouns. We might have:—

1. *An infra-pictorial or subcortical naming lesion* (an infra-pictorial or subcortical logamnesia) —that is, a lesion cutting off the naming mechanism from the incoming impressions, chiefly, as I have shown, from the visual centres. Such a patient would not be able to name objects at sight, although, if the chief part of the mechanism itself was intact and not cut off from its connection with the ideational mechanism and the auditory word centre, the patient might be able to use nouns voluntarily or repeat nouns heard.

The lesion is a subcortical lesion, and Broadbent's first case[1] showed a lesion, viz. in the white substance immediately external to the descending cornu of the lateral ventricle, just exactly where one would expect the course of the fibres from the visual centres to the naming mechanism to lie. A marked symptom in Broadbent's case was the inability to name objects at sight.

2. *A pictorial or cortical naming lesion* (cortical or pictorial logamnesia), which probably is the most common. The patient would not be able to name objects, or to recall names from within. Mill's case and Case VI. may be considered to belong to this group. Most verbal amnesia cases show this symptom.

3. *A supra-pictorial naming lesion* (supra-pictorial or transcortical logamnesia), where the fibres between the

[1] "Cerebral Mechanism of Speech and Thought," *Med. Chir. Trans.*, 1872.

ideational and naming mechanisms are involved. Such a patient might be able to repeat names if the naming mechanism was intact, but would not be able to name objects at sight, nor recall names in conversation.

From what I have previously stated some of the cases of motor aphasia which have amnesia verbalis as a symptom probably belong to this group.

The conclusions we are now able to arrive at from a consideration of the subject of amnesia verbalis are these :—

1. That amnesia verbalis may be a symptom both of sensory and motor aphasia, but that the most marked amnesic symptoms are found in sensory aphasias.

2. That amnesia verbalis, and especially the form where there is amnesia of nouns, such as proper names and concrete nouns, may occur without there being any word-deafness or motor aphasia.

3. That auditory aphasias show almost if not always amnesia verbalis.

4. That lesion in the temporo-sphenoidal lobe, especially if towards the posterior part of the lobe, produces amnesia verbalis ; if in the second and third temporo-sphenoidal convolution amnesia verbalis occurs without word-deafness, but if the first temporo-sphenoidal is also involved the patient is word-deaf.

5. That these facts tend to show that an important part of the mechanism concerned in the recalling of words and names is situated in the temporo-sphenoidal lobe towards the posterior part of the lobe, and that this part of the mechanism is very closely associated and probably continuous with the word-hearing centre, although not identical with it.

The whole subject, however, of the naming mechanism as apart from the word-hearing centre and the ideational mechanism is still involved in doubt, but I believe that a true solution to the question is to be found on the lines of the theories I have endeavoured to indicate.

CHAPTER VI.

II. CONDUCTION APHASIA.

PASSING from Auditory Aphasias proper, I shall now consider *Conduction Aphasias, Leitungsaphasie of Wernicke,* comprising

1. Inter-pictorial Auditory-motor . . Variety IV.
2. Inter-pictorial Visual-graphic . . Variety XI.

Probably the symptoms of these two are the same, and indeed it is doubtful whether Variety XI. occurs clinically. There are very few absolutely pure cases of conduction aphasia. Usually they present some disturbance either of the auditory or visual word centres. The following case is a good example, although it shows also some word-deafness.

CASE VII. (*Personal Observation*).—*Conduction aphasia; some word-deafness; marked paraphasia and paragraphia; marked gibberish speech; marked word-intoxication; marked amnesia of nouns; no motor aphasia; no involvement of the music-hearing centre.*

E. N., æt. 60, consulted me on July 19th, 1893, complaining of loss of memory for proper names, and a peculiar flushed feeling coming on him occasionally. The first feeling of this sort had occurred about a fortnight before at a railway station. He lost his memory for a few seconds, so that he could scarcely speak. He was going to the country at the time, and he remained in the country for a few days, and had one or two attacks of the same kind each day.

This continued till I saw him. He had the last attack of this sort in my presence on the first occasion on which I saw him. During all this time he had more or less difficulty in recalling proper names, even the names of his nearest and most intimate friends. His memory for proper names was worst during and immediately after these attacks. The attack I saw him in was a short one, but of the usual character. He was speaking, giving an account of his illness, when he suddenly stopped for about half a minute, and then said, " That was one of my attacks." I noticed that for a few minutes afterwards he hesitated often in speaking, especially at the nouns, and more especially when he wanted to use some special noun or proper name. His friends stated that he had been failing in health for a year or so, and his present illness had really begun before he himself confessed to its having commenced. He was an exceedingly temperate and regular man in every respect.

Examination of his organs revealed nothing but slight impurity of the first sound of the heart. The only symptom apparent at that time in his nervous system was the slight difficulty he had in recalling proper names and nouns. He could read and write quite well. About a week afterwards he began to complain of a severe pain in his head, and he showed a tendency to get worse in his memory. He was put to bed for a few days and not allowed to see any one. He now rapidly became worse, and on August 2nd the following was his condition :—

He could read aloud comparatively well, making very few mistakes.

He could not write a correct note voluntarily. He put in wrong words, and repeated the same word over and over again. He made also a great many mistakes when asked to write to dictation, often putting down wrong words and repeating the same word. He could copy a paragraph perfectly. When asked to repeat such a phrase as "West Register Street," he said something that sounded like it, such as "Westminster Street."

When shown a watch he said it was "a watch." When shown a pencil he said it was "a watch." When shown a watch-chain he said it was "a watch." When shown a button he said it was "a watch." In conversation he showed the same tendency to repeat the same word. He said, for instance, that he had difficulty in getting a full breath on going upstairs, and then proceeded to talk about taking his dinner, and instead of "food" or "dinner" he always used the word "breath." He sometimes did and sometimes did not know he had used the wrong word. He always knew he had difficulty in finding the word, but after getting one he often seemed satisfied. Often he used the word that sounded like the one he wanted, and often he used a sound like the word wanted, but not a word at all in reality. He had difficulty in counting (addition, subtraction, multiplication, etc.); but this apparently was not so much from difficulty in knowing how much, for instance, six and five were, as the difficulty in recalling the word "eleven." He understood and used gesture language well. There was no disturbance of motion or sensation.

A specimen of his writing to dictation, voluntarily, and to copy is seen in Figs. 21 and 21A. His voluntary writing was an attempt to write an account of his illness; paragraphia was the most marked symptom of it, as well as word-intoxication. The words "about fortnight" were written twice in the first three lines, and appeared again

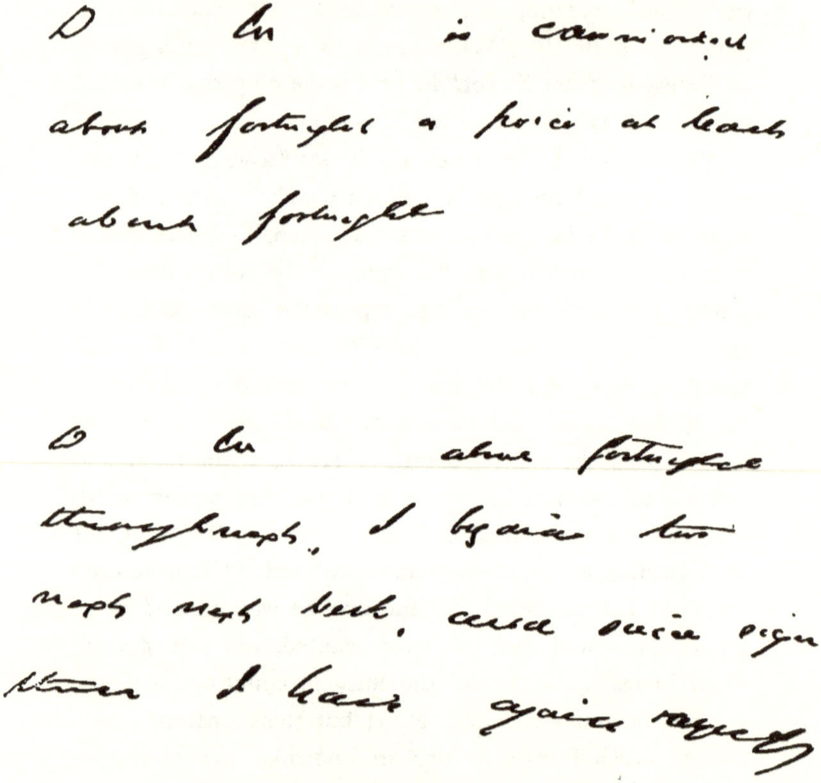

FIG. 21.—VOLITIONAL WRITING OF CASE VII.

Note the paragraphia and word-intoxication. He probably wrote the same word as he would have spoken—that is to say, he wrote correctly the paraphasic word.

in the fourth line when he made another attempt to write. In the fifth and sixth lines the word "next" appears

Written to Dictation.

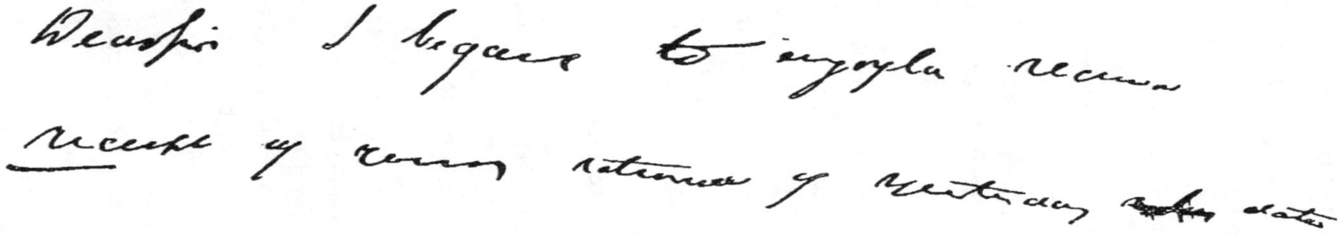

Copied from print.

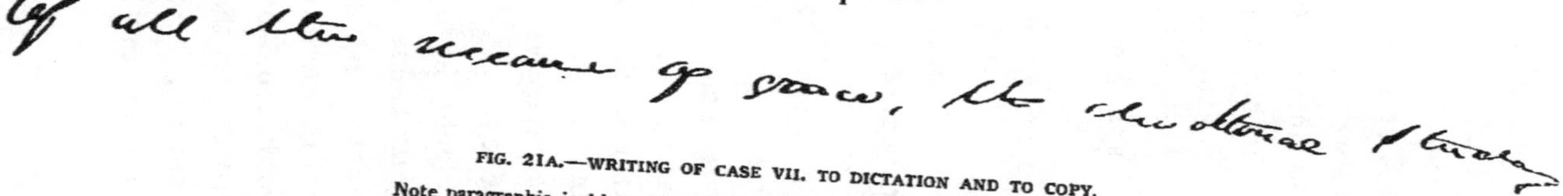

FIG. 21A.—WRITING OF CASE VII. TO DICTATION AND TO COPY.
Note paragraphia in his writing to dictation, and retention of his powers of copying.

three times. Some of his attempts at writing were not words at all, although they probably all could have been pronounced, and the grammatical arrangement of the sentences as they stand is very incorrect.

In his writing to dictation (Fig. 21A) some of the words are also incorrectly written. The sentence that was dictated to him was, "Dear Sir, I beg to acknowledge receipt of your letter of yesterday's date." The words "beg," "acknowledge," and "letter" are incorrectly written, and his first attempt at "receipt" was also incorrect.

In copying he could both copy written writing and also could copy print into writing, a fact which shows that his word-seeing centre was intact. The words seen reached his intelligence, and he was able to convert the printed letters into written letters. This is very important, because it showed that there could not have been much impairment of his auditory word centre, as the path from the visual word centre to the intelligence is supposed to pass through the auditory.

Later I shall describe a case where the patient could copy, but only by tracing, so that he always copied printed letters as they were printed and written letters as written (see Fig. 23).

The faults in writing, therefore, in this patient were entirely faults due to the interruptions between the auditory word centre and the centres for the hand. The visual image of the word could be correctly raised, and the letters and words could be formed all right, but the word that was written was the paraphasic word, showing, as I shall point out when considering agraphia, that there was no interruption in the fibres between Broca's convolution and the graphic centre. He had thus the commonest form of paragraphia.

E. N. gradually but very slowly got worse; his memory became more impaired; he used wrong words more frequently, so that in about three weeks he could scarcely make himself understood, only being able to answer a question " yes " or " no," or short sentences, such as " very much," " very bad," etc. He often gave practically the same answer to many different questions, becoming often intoxicated with a word and using it over and over again.

It was noticed also that there was a very slight dragging of the right foot, as if he had not quite so much power in that leg. His right hand had also a little less power than the left, and there was slight drawing of the face and angle of the mouth to the left.

August 25*th.*—He was much the same as at the last report. He could scarcely make himself understood, beginning sentences apparently all right, but ending in a " mixture of words," the same word often appearing in many sentences.

September 1*st.*—Much the same, but generally a little weaker and more staggery. The right side was slightly weaker, the right side of his face flatter. There was slight increase of knee reflexes on the right side. On being asked he gave his name all right.

What do you do?—(A.) Do I mean? I can't tell any more.

Are you forty?—(A.) Fifteen—fifty pounds—fifteen shillings.

Were you out for a walk yesterday?—(A.) No, I don't think so.

What had you for breakfast to-day?—He muttered a lot of words, amongst which "fifteen" was recognised.

What had you for dinner?—(A.) Crystal, good-a-look, good-a-look, and other gibberish.

What is two times five?—(A.) Three times to the right.

When asked to touch his nose he opened his mouth, but did touch it after some time.

When asked to touch the doctor's ear he said, "Yes," and a lot of gibberish.

Say "grocer." Answer, "Yes." Put out your tongue. Answer, "Yes."

Opthalmoscopic examination of the eyes was very unsatisfactory on account of the difficulty in getting him to look steadily at anything. It was seen, however, that there was optic neuritis of the right eye. The following particulars are supplied by one of his relatives :—

"On two successive Mondays he has asked that the list of newly published books should be read to him from the *Scotsman* newspaper, the day of the week never having been told him nor that part of the paper near him. On Thursday, August 31st, on being asked if there was anything in the newspaper of that date he wished read to him, he took hold of the paper and pointed to a biographical sketch of an old friend who had just died. He has always been fond of music, and during his illness especially so. For hours he will listen and never wish to move. Whenever he hears a wrong note played he winces. He was tested as to this, a wrong note being intentionally introduced, and he detected it at once. Every Sunday he has asked that hymns should be played, and on two different Sundays when

'Lead, kindly Light,' was begun he became emotional and broke down."

On September 11th I noted that he talked even more gibberish, and that it was very difficult getting any intelligible answer to any question. He got gradually weaker from this date, and duller intellectually, and died on October 8th, 1893. No post-mortem was obtained. Dr. Wyllie, Edinburgh, kindly saw the case on two occasions with me.

From a careful study of this case it will be seen that the answers to the twelve questions I have previously drawn out are all in the affirmative, although there were great imperfections in the performance of many of the acts to which the questions refer. The only centre, in addition to the naming or noun-substantive mechanism, that was partly involved from the beginning was the word-hearing centre. The disease in all probability began subcortically in the connecting fibres between the auditory word centre and the motor word centres, but nearer the former, which was also partly involved at the beginning, and ultimately almost entirely so. The most marked symptoms in the case were paraphasia and paragraphia, which are such distinguishing features of conduction aphasia cases. "Word-intoxication" and "gibberish" speech were also very prominent symptoms in the case, as well as marked amnesia of nouns, whilst the visual word centre seemed to have escaped altogether. He knew the uses of objects, but could not usually name them. Lastly, a very marked feature of the case was the retention of the power of hearing melody and of appreciating and understanding heard music.

One cannot in the absence of a post-mortem be definite

as to the precise cause of the disease, but the slow and gradual onset and progress rather pointed to some form of new growth, although the symptoms are not incompatible with acute softening or atrophy from a thrombus or an embolus. Towards the end of the life of the patient the motor tract passing from the fissure of Rolando on the left side became slightly affected, probably from a spreading forward of the disease. The position of the lesion causing conduction aphasia is supposed to be usually in the floor of the Sylvian fissure and in the island of Reil; probably the disease primarily began a little farther back in this case, viz. in the substance of the temporo-sphenoidal lobe, subcortically to the auditory word centre and naming mechanism; hence the early symptoms of slight word-deafness and amnesia verbalis. In addition to being a conduction aphasia it was therefore an example of what I have called the first form of logamnesia, the symptoms of which I have previously indicated when I was considering the noun-substantive mechanism. The distinguishing feature of this first form is the symptom of want of ability to name objects at sight, from a subcortical lesion cutting off the naming mechanism from the perceptive centres.

CHAPTER VII.

III. VISUAL APHASIA, WORD-BLINDNESS, OR CÉCITÉ VERBALE.

THIS type of aphasia has within the last few years been very carefully investigated and the two principal forms of it described by several well-known French authors, chief amongst whom are Déjerine and Sérieux. In a series of papers read before the Biological Society of Paris in 1891-92[1] they brought forward cases which conclusively proved the separate existence not only of visual aphasia (*cécité verbale*), but also the existence of two distinct clinical and pathological forms of it. Little, however, had been done in this country on the subject until Wyllie[2] showed the position of our knowledge up to date. Recently (December 1895), in an article contributed to the *Lancet*, Hinshelwood gave an excellent *résumé* of the work that had been done on visual memory and word-blindness, and he contributed some clinical observations on the subject. From what I have already indicated in a former part of this work, it will be seen that there are two principal forms of word-blindness (*cécité verbale*), and the distinguishing symptom between

[1] *Compt. Rendus de la Soc. de Biolog.*, 1891 and 1892.
[2] *Disorders of Speech.* Edinburgh, 1894.

them is the presence or absence of agraphia. Déjerine in his able contribution on the different varieties of *cécité verbale* divides the cases into two forms :—

1. *Cécité verbale avec agraphie ou troubles très marqués de l'écriture.*

2. *Cécité verbale pure avec intégrité de l'écriture spontanée et sous dictée.*

These two forms are two of those we have theoretically presumed to exist when we were considering the mechanism of speech.

1. Cortical alexia or pictorial word-blindness, due to lesion of the word-seeing centre (visual word centre) in the angular gyrus and supra-marginal convolution. In addition to not being able to see words, patients with this form have also very marked disturbances of writing. They are not able to raise the visual image of the word in their memory, as such image has been blotted out, and so are not able to write voluntarily or to dictation. This is Variety IX., lesion of C in schema (Fig. 13).

2. Subcortical alexia or infra-pictorial word-blindness, where the word-seeing centre itself is intact, but the centre is cut off from the visual perceptive centres in the posterior and internal part of the occipital lobes by a lesion involving the fibres passing from these centres to the word-seeing centre. Such a patient, although he cannot read, can still write spontaneously and to dictation, owing to the fact that he is still able to raise the visual images of the word and letters in his memory. His ability to copy, however, is much disturbed. He copies letters written or printed just as he would copy a design, a map, or any drawing. He copies printing as printing and writing as writing. He does not copy printing into

writing. This is Variety VIII., lesion of c_1—C and c_3—C in the schema (Fig. 13).

No case of the other theoretical form of visual aphasia, Variety X. Supra-pictorial Visual (Transcortical Alexia of Wernicke), apart from Varieties II. and III. Pictorial Auditory and Supra-pictorial Auditory, has, as far as I am aware, been yet described. Later, however, I shall describe a case (Case X.) which I believe was one of this variety.

Before proceeding to give clinical examples of these types of visual aphasia, it will be necessary to consider briefly the bearing of what we have already learned with regard to the visual receptive tract on the production of disturbances in speech due to lesion in that tract. We have already found—

1. That each retina is bilaterally represented in the hemispheres; that the visual perceptive centres for the left half of the left retina and the left half of the right retina are situated in the left hemisphere; and the visual perceptive centres for the right half of the right retina and the right half of the left retina are situated in the right hemisphere.

2. That the visual perceptive centres are situated in the occipital lobes in the cortical region on the internal surface of these lobes in the neighbourhood of the calcarine fissure. The centres for colour, although not exactly in the same region, are close to it. The lingual lobule and the cuneus may be taken as including the visual centres.

3. That the course of the optic tract from the anterior quadrigeminal body to these visual centres is in the radiations of Gratiolet.

4. That these visual perceptive centres are probably

connected with each other by commissural fibres, seeing that both halves of each retina require to act together. These fibres probably pass in the posterior part of the corpus callosum from one hemisphere to the other, but they have not definitely been made out.

5. That there has been specialised a centre for the perception of written words, which, like the other speech centres, is situated in the left hemisphere only, in the angular gyrus and posterior part of the supra-marginal convolution.

It will be seen why it is necessary to have such a centre when one considers that the ordinary visual centres in all probability, besides enabling us to see the colour, etc., enable us to perceive also the form, shape, etc., of objects, but this form or shape is simply as we would perceive a drawing, an object, or the letters of a language unfamiliar to us such as Chinese. It is necessary for reading to have stored in the cerebral cortex the visual memories of special shapes and forms—that is, letters—and combinations of shapes and forms—that is, combinations of letters or words previously perceived. And in order that these visual memories may be associated with the auditory memories of the letters and words, it will easily be seen that it is more convenient and economical for nature to store them in the *zone of speech* in the left hemisphere. The visual memories of words are therefore situated in the angular gyrus and the posterior part of the inferior parietal lobule or supra-marginal convolution. On this theory the most specialised part of this word-seeing centre, viz. the memories of the longest and least common combinations of letters, is situated probably farthest forward, or at least not *exactly* in the same place as the less specialised part, viz. the visual memories of the more familiar words and single letters. If such be so, it would explain the fact that some patients who may not be able to read long and unfamiliar words are able to read letters and small familiar words, words that they apparently perceive as one object or form, just as they would a letter. It will be found that, although a word-blind patient is not able to read words, he may be able to read figures. The explanation of this is, as I have said, probably because all the visual memories are stored not precisely in the same region, although it is probable that some of the more familiar and common visual memories may be imprinted also in the corresponding uneducated centre on the right side. Whether the visual perceptive centres alone—both angular gyri being destroyed—could enable an individual to see a letter, a figure, or small and familiar word such as "the" as a letter, a figure, or "the," we do not at present possess sufficient knowledge to say definitely, but in all probability it will be found that the visual word centre can be divided into various areas each having its own special memories stored in it. Such is the most feasible explanation of the clinical facts. As I have said, some patients, although word-blind, can read figures. Case V. showed this symptom quite distinctly, and there are others in medical literature. Granted therefore that we have the two visual perceptive centres and one specialised centre for letters, figures, and words, both visual centres must be connected with the word-seeing centre by fibres, the left visual centres directly, the right visual centres either directly or indirectly through the left visual centres. The accompanying. diagram, which is modified from the one in Déjerine's paper, shows the course of these different fibres (Fig. 22).

C is the word-seeing centre in the angular gyrus; C^1 is the left visual perceptive centre region in the occipital lobe, and C^3 the corresponding region on the right side.

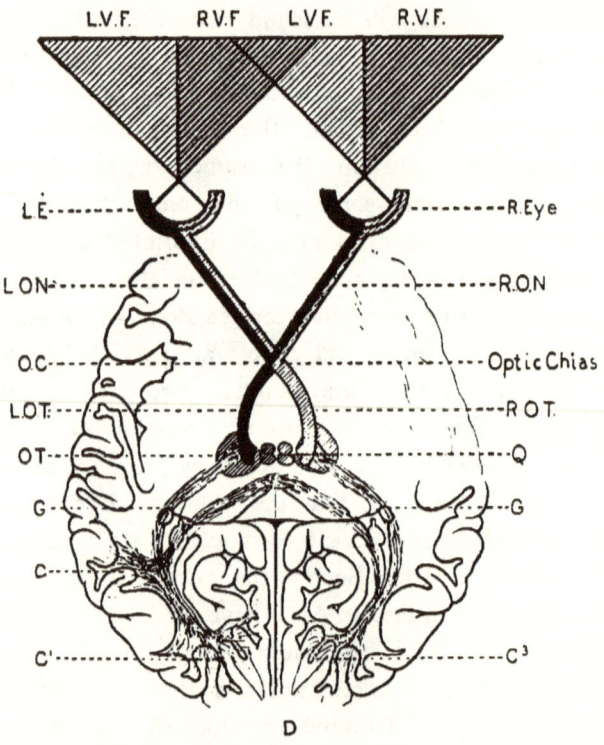

FIG. 22.—DIAGRAMMATIC REPRESENTATION OF THE COURSE OF THE OPTIC FIBRES, MODIFIED FROM DÉJERINE.

D, the commissural fibres connecting these two centres.

G and G, the radiations of Gratiolet passing down from the occipital lobes.

Q, the corpora quadrigemina.

O T, the optic thalamus.

L O T, the left optic tract.

R O T, the right optic tract, semidecussating at O C, the optic commissure.

L O N, the left optic nerve.

R O N, the right optic nerve.

L E, the left eye, and R E, the right eye.

L V F, the left visual field, and R V F, the right visual field.

From a study of this diagram it will be seen how lesion of the fibres between O C, the optic commissure, and C^1, the visual perceptive centres on the left side, produces blindness on the left side of the retina of each eye (hemianopia), and in the right field of vision (right lateral homonymous hemianopsia and hemiachromatopsia); and lesion in the corresponding fibres on the right side produces left lateral homonymous hemianopsia and hemiachromatopsia.

Lesion of the radiations of Gratiolet, G, thus produces those symptoms, and lesion of the centres C^1 or C^3 also the same symptoms.

Lesion of the fibres passing between the visual perceptive centres C^1, C^3, to C would not produce hemianopsia if they only were involved in a lesion, but the radiations of Gratiolet would also be very apt to be involved, so that right lateral homonymous hemianopsia and hemiachromatopsia is a very common lesion along with infra-pictorial or subcortical word-blindness, as well as with pictorial or cortical word-blindness, if the lesion extends deep enough into the white substance of the occipital lobe.

Hinshelwood [1] has collected eleven such cases, which,

[1] *Lancet*, December 21, 1895.

with two others recorded by himself, make thirteen cases, having all this symptom along with word-blindness. As, however, cases of word-blindness can occur without this symptom, it proves that the word-seeing centre is separate from the ordinary visual centres. Of the four cases of word-blindness of my own observation, three had not hemianopsia. One of these latter had auditory aphasia as well as visual aphasia, and has already been described in an earlier part of this work (Case V.). The second was a case of cortical visual aphasia; the third was a supra-pictorial visual aphasia, and the fourth case was not tested as to her visual fields. These cases are described later.

I shall now give clinical examples of the three forms of visual aphasia, taking them in the order in which we theoretically considered them.

I. INFRA-PICTORIAL VISUAL APHASIA *(Wyllie)*; SUB-CORTICAL ALEXIA *(Wernicke)*; CÉCITÉ VERBALE PURE *(Déjerine)*.

CASE VIII. *(Personal Observation.)*—*Infra-pictorial visual aphasia; word-blindness, but not blindness to letters or figures; ability to write spontaneously, but inability to read what she had written; very slight and temporary disturbance of the object-seeing faculty (mind-blindness); rapid and complete recovery.*

M. P., æt. 67, was engaged one day in March 1892 writing a letter to a friend when she suddenly discovered that she could not see the words distinctly and that after she wrote a sentence she could not see what she had written. She thought that she was losing her eyesight, and consulted me about it. Her only other complaint was that she had difficulty in recalling proper names and nouns, as well as slight impairment of her memory for events. The friend to whom she had written, on receiving her letter, wrote back and asked her what was wrong with her, as she had repeated some sentences and words in the letter over again. Shortly before writing this letter, on her servant, who had been with her for some time, coming into the room, she turned to a friend and asked "what strange woman that was." In a few minutes, however, she was able to recognise the servant and every other object about her, and never had a return of this. On testing her eyesight I found that she could see objects quite well, that she saw letters well and could name them slowly, but that she could not put them into words. When, however, I spelled short words aloud for her she could pronounce the word from the sound, but often in a slow and disjointed manner. She herself could read in this way, viz. by reading the letters aloud and pronouncing the word from the sound of the letters, but this could only be done with the smaller words. She could write voluntarily, but she could not read what she had written, although she could make out the letters and figures. She was not tested as to copying or writing to dictation, but probably the latter faculty was quite retained, as she had no word-deafness. She could hear quite well and could converse quite well, so that there was no impairment of her auditory and motor word centres. These symptoms persisted for two or three days, and then they gradually passed off, so that in three weeks she had quite recovered, except that her memory was slightly impaired for a little longer period. She is now (four years afterwards) in good health, and has had no return of her complaint.

Answering the twelve questions I have previously drawn up,—

1. She could hear sounds.
2. She could hear words spoken.
3. She could understand words spoken.
4. She could see objects, etc.
5. She could not see words written or printed.
6. She could not understand words written or printed.
7. She could speak voluntarily.
8. She could repeat words spoken.
9. She could not read aloud.
10. She could write voluntarily.
11. Probably she could write to dictation (but not tested).
12. She could probably copy as from a design.

It will be seen that the answers correspond to Variety VIII., and it was therefore a very typical case of infra-pictorial visual aphasia or *cécité verbale* (but not *littérale*) *pure*.

It is interesting to note that she had her power of writing so well retained that she had actually been writing a letter when she noticed she could not read what she had written. There is little doubt about the fact that her trouble had come on before she started to write this letter, as she had shown a very slight form of *cécité psychique*, or mind-blindness, before it. This is a form of disturbance allied to aphasia which I shall have a little to say about later.

Another interesting fact in the case is that the patient had retained the power of reading letters and was able to read short words; by pronouncing each letter she heard the sounds, and repeated them combined into a word. I have not seen this power taken note of in any of the recorded cases.

The patient made a very rapid and complete recovery, and in this respect her case is very like Case IV., an auditory aphasia case, and the remarks I made about functional and temporary aphasias in connection with that case are equally applicable to this. Alongside of this case of my own observation let me now place a note of the case of *cécité verbale pure* recorded by Déjerine in a paper [1] which I have referred to on several occasions previously. It was the case that definitely settled the question as to whether there were separate pathological lesions corresponding to the two clinical forms of *cécité verbale*. The paper is a masterful exposition of the whole subject as well as a model record of a clinical observation.

Déjerine's Case.—The patient, a man aged sixty-eight, was under observation for four years, first by Landolt, who recorded the case in the work published in Utrecht in 1888, on the occasion of the Jubilee of Donders, and dedicated to him. The case was sent to Déjerine in 1887, and between then and 1892 he was seen frequently. The patient was a highly cultivated and intelligent man, and during these four years he was incapable of reading manuscript or printing. He wrote papers without being able to read what he had written. The word-blindness was total (*cécité littérale et verbale*), and was accompanied by right lateral homonymous hemianopsia and hemiachromatopsia. He also had complete blindness for the notes of music, although he had had a good knowledge of music previously. But although he could not decipher a single

[1] *Compt. Rendus de la Soc. de Biolog.*, 1891 and 1892.

note of music, he sang himself and listened frequently to his wife playing or singing opera music to him. Spontaneous writing and writing to dictation were perfect and easily performed, although the letters were a little larger than before, just as any of us would write if our eyes were closed. On the contrary, the act of copying was defective; he could only copy with each letter distinctly before his eyes and traced simply as a design. The letters were badly formed, and it was difficult believing that the same man wrote the specimens from copy as wrote those to dictation and spontaneously. He copied printed letters differently from written letters—in other words, he printed in copying printing.

He had preserved intact the power of reading figures, and was able to calculate both mentally and on paper. He never had the least symptom of word-deafness (*surdité verbale*), and never, except during the ten days preceding his death, did he show the least trouble in speaking. His interior language was normal. He thought in spoken speech and heard mentally the words sounding in his ear; when he wished to write spontaneously he heard the word and then saw it mentally. The visual images of the letters were intact in his interior language; the integrity of writing spontaneously and to dictation showed this. When one took his right or his left hand or his foot and traced passively in the air the form of letters he recognised and named them. He was able actually to read letters by tracing them with his fingers in this fashion by means of his muscular sense. In January 1892 he was seized suddenly with very pronounced paraphasia and complete agraphia. He was incapable of writing the smallest word or a letter, and could only scratch lines without distinct form. He died ten days afterwards, having preserved up to the end all his intelligence and the perfect knowledge of spoken speech, having not the least word-deafness (*surdité verbale*). From the clinical history Déjerine draws the following conclusions.

The clinical history is made up of two stages. During the first stage, which lasted four years, the patient presented a clinical picture, the purest that one could imagine, of the second variety of *cécité verbale*, viz. *cécité verbale pure*, without any alteration of spontaneous writing or writing to dictation. During the second stage, which lasted about a dozen days, he had complete agraphia with paraphasia along with the *cécité verbale*. In this second stage the clinical picture coincided with that of the first variety of *cécité verbale*, *cécité verbale* with marked alteration of writing. (It is to be noted that Déjerine's first variety is my second variety and *vice versa*.)

At the post-mortem examination pathological changes were found which accounted for these two different stages.

The first, an old lesion, occupied the occipital lobe, and more particularly the convolutions at the extremity of the occipital lobe, the base of the cuneus, and also the lingual and the fusiform lobules. The convolutions of this region were small and atrophied. The lesion was continued into the white substance subjacent, and penetrated in the form of a wedge, reaching the occipital horn of the ventricle. The optic radiations were degenerated and atrophied, and the patch had destroyed the grey substance of the convolutions which lie alongside of the posterior part of the internal temporo-occipital fissure.

This lesion was therefore situated in the visual cortical areas. The other lesion of recent date occupied the angular gyrus and inferior parietal lobule, and thus accounted for the word-blindness with agraphia which came on during the last few days of the patient's life.

This case of Déjerine's, besides giving an excellent clinical picture of both of the more common forms of visual aphasia, is quite conclusive as to the position of a lesion producing each of these forms.

From this case it will be seen that the word "subcortical," as used by Wernicke, is a confusing term, and that the word "infra-pictorial," as suggested by Wyllie, is a much more suitable one, because, although the patient had subcortical word-blindness, the post-mortem revealed a very extensive cortical lesion in the visual perceptive centres. No doubt the effect of this lesion was the same as if the lesion had alone been limited to the white matter underlying the cortex at the angular gyrus. All that is necessary to produce Wernicke's subcortical word-blindness, or Wyllie's infra-pictorial visual aphasia, or Déjerine's *cécité verbale pure*, is that the angular gyrus be cut off from receiving impressions from the perceptive visual centres on the same and the opposite sides. It matters not whether that lesion is in the cortex so long as the effect is the cutting off of the angular gyrus from receiving incoming impressions from the nerves of sight. The same objections, however, do not apply to the term "cortical," because in cortical word-blindness the cortex at the angular gyrus must be involved in the lesion.

The following case is an example of the second variety of visual aphasia, the variety which Déjerine's case had during the last ten days of life.

II. PICTORIAL VISUAL APHASIA (*Wyllie*); CORTICAL ALEXIA (*Wernicke*); CÉCITÉ VERBALE AVEC AGRAPHIE (*Déjerine*).

Variety IX. Lesion in C (Fig. 13).

CASE IX. (*Personal Observation*).—*Word-blindness with agraphia in voluntary writing and writing to dictation; able to copy, but only by tracing the letters; no word-deafness; no motor aphasia; considerable motor enfeeblement, and increase of reflexes.*

The following are the notes of the case taken by Dr. Hill Buchan, House Physician:—

R. R., æt. 24, a worker in a biscuit factory, was admitted to Leith Hospital on March 31st, 1896, complaining of weakness, difficulty in walking, and general shakiness.

His parents are alive and healthy. Two brothers are alive and apparently healthy in body and mind. Eight of his brothers and sisters died when quite young—one from consumption when quite a lad, who had taken fits up to the age of fourteen, and could never speak properly.

Personal History.—The patient's mother says that he could never speak very distinctly. He knew what he was going to say, but his pronunciation was defective. Till he reached the age of five he was always delicate. A doctor is reported as having said that he had consumption of the bowls. He never had fits, never had scarlet fever or rheumatism. He was five years old before he began to walk. He went to school at the age of eight. He was quite bright and sharp mentally, and used to play about with other children, and could do everything like them, but was a bad speaker. According to the statement of his teacher he could read, but looked always a little "queer."

When fourteen he went to work in a biscuit factory, and was five years at this occupation, after which he became a painter in a shipbuilding yard. He was two years there when he took a fit. The day before he had got accidentally shut into a confined place exposed to vapours of turpentine and naphtha, and when he was got out he was very dazed and sick. He was better next day, but on coming home from his work he took a fit. He fell down and became unconscious, and kept moving his arms and hands about in a " waving " manner. He did not bite his tongue. This moving his hands and arms continued for a day, as also did the unconsciousness. He did not recognise his mother and did not take any food. For three days he could not move his legs at all. After this the power gradually came back, but he was unable to walk for a fortnight, and then only with difficulty. He remained dazed and stupid for some time. About three months ago, after a wetting, he began to be troubled with pains shooting up from the ankles to the knees. These attacks since then have come on occasionally, and when they do come he says the legs become quite stiff for five minutes, after which the pain passes away.

State on Admission.—He was a lad of rather poor muscular development. His general expression of face was rather stupid-looking. His palate was fairly high-arched.

Nervous System, Sensory.—There was very slight tenderness on percussion in upper part of the spine. The patient did not complain of pain, but said that he occasionally was seized with pain shooting up from ankles to knees. There was no paræsthesia. General tactile sensibility and temperature sense were unimpaired. His muscular sense was not only not lost, but it was probably exaggerated. When he was asked to touch his nose he did so correctly, but the movement was rather sudden.

Special Senses.—His hearing was quite acute, taste good. Vision for objects, etc., was good, but he was word-blind. Nothing abnormal revealed on ophthalmoscopic examination; no nystagmus.

Reflexes.—Plantar, cremasteric, and abdominal, all exaggerated. On tapping forehead marked reflex of eyelid obtained. Pupils reacted to light and accommodation. Deep reflexes were also much exaggerated, both ankle and knee clonus being easily obtained. No disturbance of organic reflexes.

Motor.—No paralysis, but weakness of muscles. The grasp of both hands diminished, but the right more than the left. Dynamometer gave 25 K. with left and 15 with the right hand. Muscular power in right leg less than the left. On making him twitch his face the muscular action was much more marked at the right angle of the mouth than the left, which was scarcely twitched at all. No marked difference on asking him to show his teeth. He put out his tongue straight and it was slightly tremulous. His walking was very defective. He planted his heels down almost like an ataxic person, but all the time the limbs were in a sort of spastic condition, and clonic spasm readily appeared if he stood on front part of his foot. He could turn round fairly quickly. There was no nystagmus.

Speech, Motor.—Patient spoke in an indistinct slurring manner; no "staccato." There was a trace of fine trembling movements at the angles of his mouth at times. Test sentences were badly pronounced.

Graphic.—A specimen of his writing, voluntarily, to dictation, and to copy, is seen in Figs. 23 and 23A.

It will be seen that there is almost complete agraphia in his voluntary writing and writing to dictation. The

Dictation of words "To & Man."

Voluntary writing of name.

Dictation of letter "O."

Dictation of Figures "1, 2, 3, 4, 5."

FIG. 23.—COPY OF SPECIMENS OF ATTEMPTS AT WRITING BY CASE IX.

only letters that can be detected in his name are *R*, *s*, and *l*. He can write some figures, although very imperfectly. In copying he simply traces each line. He copies writing as writing and printing as printing, putting in every peculiarity of the letter he is copying from. He was tested by writing frequently, and always the same result was obtained. He was always more able to copy plain printed letters than letters as written. This is a point I will refer to when I consider agraphia.

Sensory.—(*a*) He could hear and understand spoken

Voluntary writing " 1 to 5."

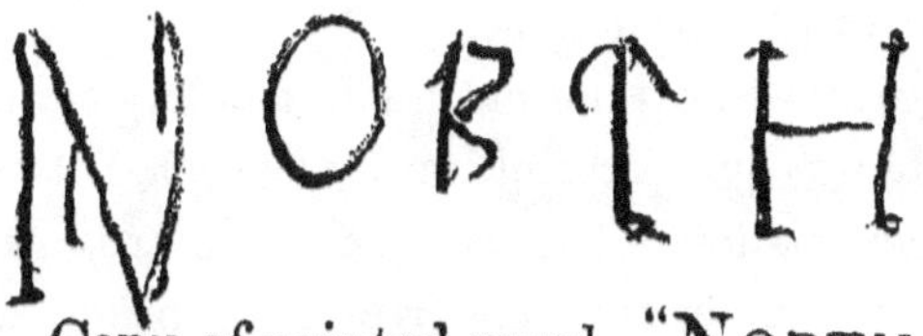

Copy of printed word "NORTH"

Copy of the word North as written above.

FIG. 23A.—COPY OF SPECIMENS OF ATTEMPTS AT WRITING BY CASE IX.

words perfectly, there being not the slightest trace of auditory aphasia.

(*b*) Vision for words. He was quite unable to read words. He could sometimes make out letters, and very occasionally a small word. He could read figures more easily.

He was tested with the following :—

1, 2, 3, 8, 12, 10 ; he said 1, 2, 3, 8, 12, 10.
100 ; he said 100.
1,500 ; he said 105.
10,000,000 ; he said 1,000.

He said he understood what he read, although he could not read aloud, but on practically testing him it was found that this was not so. For instance, the following sentence was printed and shown to him : " Put out your tongue." He said it was his own name.

Intelligence.—Below normal. His memory seemed fairly good. He was quite sensible in his speech, but he seldom began conversation. He had no delusions, was shy in manner and somewhat sensitive as to being examined. There was neither depression, nor exaltation, nor ideas of grandeur.

His other systems seemed all normal. He was treated by rest in bed and given iodide of potash internally in ten-grain doses. He showed signs of improving in his powers of reading and writing, and it was noted on April 24th, 1896, that the improvement was well marked. He was much brighter-looking, could now read small words, and knew all the letters. He could also write a few letters, but the improvement in his powers of reading was greater than in those of writing. He remained in hospital for some time longer, and ultimately went home much in the same condition as he was on April 24th.

Remarks.—This case was one of very considerable difficulty as to diagnosis, and at the stage of the disease it was very difficult being definite as to the precise nature of the lesion causing the symptoms. He presented many of the symptoms of multiple cerebro-spinal sclerosis, but there are two symptoms commonly present which were absent in this case, viz. nystagmus and "staccato" speech. What also was rather against it being a case of multiple sclerosis was the symptom of most importance to us here— namely, word-blindness, and the fact that that word-blindness was due to a cortical lesion. The cortex is not very frequently involved in the early stages of multiple sclerosis, the sclerotic patches being more limited to the white substance, and involving the conduction fibres rather than the nerve cells. We are enabled therefore to say in this case, from our study of aphasia, that the lesion producing some of the symptoms was situated in the cortex, and as most, if not all, of the other symptoms could be produced by involvement of some of the other, and notably the motor areas in the cerebral cortex, probably the same kind of lesion produced all the symptoms. This lesion I believe to have been of the nature of pachymeningitis of a chronic nature, with probably adherence of the meninges to the cortex. The patient also showed some of the symptoms of general paralysis, but the distinct involvement of a limited cortical area was rather against this view also.

Into the whole question of the diagnosis in this case I have no intention of entering, as all we have to deal with here are the speech symptoms, and these symptoms, as I have said, helped very much in the localisation of the lesion. He was an imperfect speaker, but he had always been so, although probably he had not quite so complete control over the movements of his articulating apparatus as he used to, owing to the excessive irritability of his motor apparatus from increased reflexes, due probably to motor enfeeblement of his cerebral motor areas and perhaps also due to patches of descending sclerosis as a result. Still there was nothing in the least of the nature of motor aphasia. He had no auditory aphasia, but had distinct, almost complete, word-blindness, *cécité littérale et verbale*, with agraphia.

Answering our twelve questions,—

1. He could hear sounds.
2. He could hear words spoken.
3. He could understand words spoken.
4. He could see objects.
5. He could not see words written or printed.
6. He could not understand words written or printed
7. He could speak voluntarily.
8. He could repeat words.
9. He could not read aloud.
10. He could not write voluntarily.
11. He could not write to dictation.
12. He could copy very imperfectly, and only by tracing lines.

This, as will be seen, exactly corresponds to Variety IX. *Pictorial or Cortical Visual Aphasia*, the patient being exactly in the same condition as Déjerine's case was during the last ten days of life; except that there was no trace of paraphasia in this case, the cortical area having been apparently very neatly picked out by the lesion. It is very rarely that a lesion is found so limited, as in a large number of cases the auditory word centre is also involved, and word-deafness therefore often accompanies word-blindness. Case V. is an example of this, and it is almost as typical a case of cortical word-blindness as it is of cortical word-deafness. In it, as we saw from the description and the photograph, the post-mortem revealed that the lesion had just reached to and involved the angular gyrus and supra-marginal convolution, so that that case supports the theory that these areas are the seat of the word-seeing centre.

The following case is one of supra-pictorial visual aphasia, and presents several very interesting features.

III. SUPRA-PICTORIAL VISUAL APHASIA; TRANS-CORTICAL ALEXIA (*Wernicke*).

Variety X. Lesion in C A (Fig. 13).

CASE X. (*Personal Observation*).—*Hemiplegia; supra-pictorial visual aphasia; agraphia.*

E. H., æt. 67, was seized in the summer of 1896 with slight difficulty in speaking and weakness of the right arm and leg. For some months previously he had been treated for weak and irregular action of the heart. The hemiplegic symptoms, although they began suddenly, progressed slowly for a month or six weeks, when he had lost almost entirely the use of his right arm and leg. His difficulty in speaking, however, rather improved. He had no true motor aphasia, the difficulty in speaking being due to dysarthria. His intelligence, which was slightly dulled at first, gradually improved, and about two months after the onset he was perfectly intelligent, and took a great interest in his business and all around him. He found, however, that, whilst he could understand perfectly what was read and spoken to him, he himself could not intelligently read a book. He said to his wife one day: "It is very curious that, whilst I can understand what you read and can remember it well, I cannot understand what I read myself. I see everything quite well, and can see the words, and can pronounce the words aloud, but I cannot connect them into sentences."

On being tested it was found that practically his statement was correct. He could read letters, figures, and words, although he spoke them a little more slowly than one usually reads. Occasionally with a long word he would make a mistake in a syllable, substituting some other syllable in the middle for the proper one; but he usually could correct himself. For instance, he was asked to read aloud the following sentence from a paper: "Shires and Clydesdales. Some few weeks ago, in commenting——" He first read, "Shires—and—Clydesdales. Some—few—weeks—ago—in—commuting——"; then he looked at the last word again, and, after two attempts, he said "commenting." In reading he heard what he himself said, and understood it. He could thus read slowly and understand what he read, but the understanding of sentences was done entirely through his ears. He could spell words when asked to with the greatest ease, and when a word was spelt over to him he could tell what it was at once. He had very slight dysarthria in speaking.

On testing his powers of writing it was found that he was absolutely agraphic. His right hand was paralysed, and so it could not be tested; but when asked to write his name with his left hand he took the pencil and was about to begin doing so, when he suddenly found that he could not, and said so. He could not write a single letter of the alphabet. He was then asked to trace an "A" in the air with his left fore-finger or hand, and he could not do so, to his great surprise. Similarly with other letters, apparently he could not recall their shapes. At this date (November 1896) he is practically in the same condition.

The case is one of very unusual interest. I am very

strongly of opinion that this was a case of supra-pictorial visual aphasia, lesion between C and A in diagram. This is a form of aphasia of which I have not been able to find a case in medical literature. In this form the patient, although he would be able to see words, would not be able to understand them. One would not have thought, however, that such a patient would be able to read aloud as this patient could. The greatest objection to the lesion, however, being in this situation seemed to me the fact that he was so absolutely agraphic; he could not even raise the outline of letters in his visual memory. Such a fact points strongly to the visual word centre being involved. There are, however, facts which decidedly point to the visual word centre not being so completely involved as so complete agraphia would indicate. He could read letters, figures, and words, although a little slower than usual, showing that if the visual word centre was not perfect in its action, it was far from being completely obliterated. Again, the presence of complete agraphia might be accounted for in a supra-pictorial visual aphasia by not only the incoming fibres from the visual word centre to the intelligence mechanism being involved, but also the outgoing fibres from the intelligence to the visual word centre, fibres which convey impressions to the visual word centre for revival of the visual images of letters in order to write them. It is also possible that the connecting fibres between the visual word centre and the centres for the hand in both hemispheres might also have been interrupted.

The case is therefore a difficult one to localise exactly, but the symptoms as a whole point strongly to its being a case of supra-pictorial visual aphasia, Variety X.

Before leaving the subject of visual aphasia it is necessary to refer to a few cases that have shown symptoms which have been described under the name of

Object-blindness, Mind-blindness, or Cécité Psychique.

Not many cases have been described, and we do not as yet know a great deal about it. Charcot[1] described one very interesting case; Sérieux[2] another, in which he had a post-mortem examination; Gogal a third, also followed by a post-mortem examination; and Hinshelwood[3] a fourth.

Personally I have not seen a typical case of this, but Case VIII. apparently had *cécité psychique* slightly for a short time, as "on seeing her servant come into the room she asked what strange woman that was." In object or mind blindness the patient is not able to recognise objects, persons, etc., which used to be familiar to him. The room seems strange; the streets and roads which he ought to know are quite strange. He does not know the uses of objects, etc.

In Gogal's case (quoted by Wernicke) the patient bit into the soap, micturated into the wash-hand basin, looked on jugs, thermometers, etc., as strange objects. In an earlier stage he could neither speak nor understand what was said. At the post-mortem there was found a lesion in the posterior part of the first temporal convolution and behind the fissure of Sylvius, and a similar condition in

[1] *Lect. on Diseases of the Nervous System*, Vol. III., New Syd. Soc.
[2] *Compt. Rendus de la Soc. de Biolog.*, 1891 and 1892.
[3] *Lancet*, December 21, 1895.

the third left frontal, the operculum shrivelled up, and the island of Reil exposed. On the outer part of the surface of the occipital lobe on the right side and exactly on the tip there was a yellow patch of indrawn cicatrix with superficial softening. In Sérieux' case there was word-blindness and agraphia, and also word-deafness and paraphasia, as well as object-blindness. She could not recognise her relatives and friends; their faces seemed changed just as if they wore masks; objects also she did not recognise, although not to so marked a degree as faces. At the post-mortem, on the left side there was a patch of softening in the supra-marginal convolution and a limited patch in the first temporal; on the right side there was a patch of softening involving the supra-marginal convolution and angular gyrus and posterior part of first and second temporal convolutions. These are the only two post-mortems of cases of *cécité psychique* which I have been able to find in medical literature, and in each of these cases it will be seen that there was a bilateral lesion, viz. a lesion both in the right and in the left hemispheres; and it is therefore supposed that, although the visual memories for words, etc., are stored in the left hemisphere, the less specialised visual memories are stored in both hemispheres. In order, therefore, to produce mind-blindness it is necessary to have a lesion in both occipital lobes, probably in the neighbourhood of the angular gyrus, or the cortex more posteriorly; hence the rarity of this form of blindness, and the few cases of it that have been recorded.

CHAPTER VIII.

IV. APHEMIA, MOTOR APHASIA, BROCA'S APHASIA.

WE now pass from lesion of the receptive speech centres and conducting fibres, to lesions of the production speech centres. Motor aphasia includes three of the varieties I have previously sketched, Varieties V., VI., and VII.

1. Variety V. Supra-pictorial Motor Aphasia (Wyllie); Transcortical Motor Aphasia (Wernicke). Lesion of E B in schema (Fig. 13).

2. Variety VI. Pictorial Motor Aphasia (Wyllie); Cortical Motor Aphasia (Wernicke). Lesion of B in schema.

3. Variety VII. Infra-pictorial Motor Aphasia (Wyllie); Subcortical Motor Aphasia (Wernicke). Lesion of B—b^1 and B—b^3 in schema.

I. SUPRA-PICTORIAL MOTOR APHASIA, VARIETY V.

Of the supra-pictorial form there are one or two cases recorded in medical literature, notably one by Lichtheim[1] and one by Hammond.[2]

In this form the answers to our twelve questions are

1. The patient can hear sounds.
2. The patient can hear words spoken.

[1] *Brain*, January 1885.
[2] *Diseases of the Nervous System*, 7th Edition, Chap. VII. (quoted by Lichtheim).

3. The patient can understand words spoken.
4. The patient can see objects, etc.
5. The patient can see words written.
6. The patient can understand words written or printed.
7. The patient cannot speak voluntarily.
8. The patient can repeat words.
9. The patient can read aloud.
10. The patient cannot write voluntarily.
11. The patient can write to dictation.
12. The patient can copy by tracing, but it is doubtful if he can copy perfectly.

As will be seen by consulting the answers to the twelve questions, this variety differs from the usual Broca's form of motor aphasia in that the patient can repeat words, can read aloud, and can write to dictation. The only symptoms present are the loss of power to speak voluntarily and to write voluntarily, which are symptoms of all motor aphasias. I have not had any cases of this variety under my care.

II. Pictorial Motor Aphasia, Variety VI.

This form is probably the best known of all the varieties of aphasia. It was the form described by Broca, and his cases were excellent examples of it.

1. The patient can hear sounds.
2. The patient can hear words.
3. The patient can understand words spoken.
4. The patient can see objects, etc.
5. The patient can see words, etc., written or printed.
6. The patient can understand words written or printed.
7. The patient cannot speak voluntarily.
8. The patient cannot repeat words.

9. The patient cannot read aloud.
10. The patient cannot write voluntarily.
11. The patient cannot write to dictation.
12. The patient can copy by tracing.

The lesion producing this variety has been proved by many cases to be situated in the posterior part of the third left frontal convolution (the psycho-motor speech area of Broca). The following three cases are examples of this variety. The first was an organic lesion; the second a most interesting case of a very temporary nature due to toxæmia in a case where albumen was present in the urine; the third also a very temporary form, probably due to a functional cause.

CASE XI. (*Personal Observation*).—*Motor aphasia; hemiplegia; gibberish speech for four years before death.*

M. R., æt. 91, was seen by me on November 12th, 1895, four years after having had a shock of paralysis. During that attack she was also seen by me, and the following was her condition :—She had complete paralysis of the right arm, very marked right facial paralysis, involving most decidedly the angle of the mouth, the lips, and the tongue. There was also distinct paralysis of the right leg. She had also complete motor aphasia. She could not speak more than one or two familiar or common words, although she gave utterance to one or two sounds which were not words She saw and heard quite well, and understood what was being said to her.

Four years afterwards (1895) the following was her condition :—The movements of the right leg were slightly impaired; there was also distinct impairment of the movements of the right arm and hand, and there was distinct contracture of the same. Right facial movements were very slightly impaired. She could put out her tongue and it did not point distinctly to either side. During these four years she had been able to say very few words, occasionally "yesey," "aye," "no." She articulated quite well, but the word she articulated had usually no meaning, as, for instance, "bitty, bitty, bitty," when she evidently wanted to say a few words. When asked a question she answered at once, but the sounds used were not intelligible words. Her hearing was very acute, and she saw and understood everything that was going on. On account of the paralysis of her arm it was impossible to ascertain whether she could write or not. She died shortly afterwards from bronchitis. No post-mortem was obtained.

This case was one of a common form.

It was the usual right-sided hemiplegia with aphasia. She had also a slight degree of paraphasia, and "gibberish" speech. It is interesting to note that during four years, although there was considerable improvement of the motor power on the right side, the aphasic symptoms remained practically the same. The right psycho-motor speech centre had not taken up any of the functions of the left side; there had been no education of the "uneducated" centre of the opposite side. Probably the age of the patient (87) had a determining influence on this, but, as I have indicated in a previous part of this work, it has generally been believed that motor aphasias do not so readily recover by the education of the right uneducated centre as sensory aphasias do. In marked contrast to this case in respect to the duration of the aphasic symptoms were the two following cases.

CASE XII. *(Personal Observation).—Pictorial motor*

aphasia, temporary in duration and recurring on two occasions in a patient with albuminuria; complete loss of the power of producing words and even sounds of any kind except groans; complete agraphia; no auditory aphasia; no visual aphasia.

T. P., æt. 28, whilst recovering from a dysenteric attack as result of malaria, was seized with aphasia. He had had dysentery for several weeks and was gradually getting better, being able to be up and out, when one day (April 3rd, 1895) he partook very freely of food, a large quantity of which was of a nitrogenous kind. He drank a large quantity of strong tea, and then went to bed. In the morning, about seven o'clock, on his friends going to his room, they found him lying in bed in a rather stupid-looking condition, with his jaws clenched. He understood what they said to him, but he did not speak. He pushed his finger into his mouth and tried to make himself sick, as he appeared to think that would relieve him. I saw him about 9.30 a.m. and found him in bed, slightly stupid-looking, with jaws clenched. When asked he moved his arms and legs about as requested, and pressed my hand with his when I tested his grasping power, which I found to be normal. His arms showed a tendency to remain in the position in which they were put (catalepsy). On asking him to put out his tongue he indicated that he could not open his mouth. On attempting to put the handle of a spoon between his teeth I found he forcibly resisted the opening of his mouth. Occasionally he gave expression to a very slight groan, but never made the slightest attempt at a word. He heard and understood words quite well, and indicated that he could understand writing and printing when given a pen and paper. He held the pen as if he was going to write, but never used it in any way, even to draw a line. Mustard was applied to the back of the neck, and over the epigastric region, where he complained of some pain. About 1 p.m. of the same day he took what was apparently a mild form of fit. He moved his arms and hands about, but did not clench the hands, except once or twice spasmodically. For the greater part of this fit the hands were quite open. There was distinct twitching of the face more

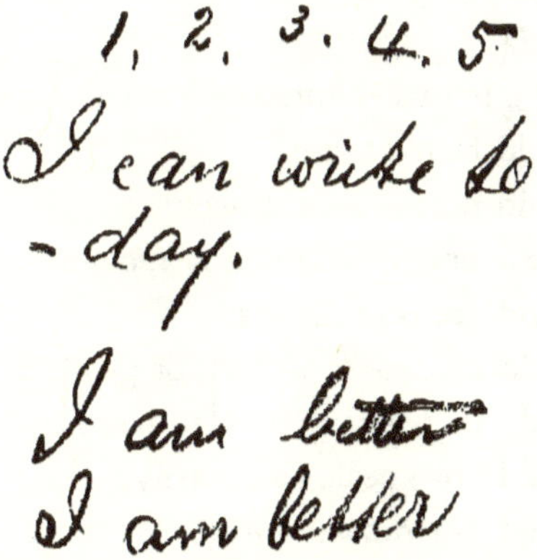

I. *1, 2, 3, 4, 5*

II. *I can write to-day.*

III. *I am better*

IV. *I am better*

FIG. 24.—WRITING OF CASE XII., SHOWING COMPLETE RECOVERY FROM AGRAPHIA.

I. Dictation of figures; II. Dictation of sentence; IV. Patient's copy of III.

to the right than to the left side. He did not bite his tongue. His legs were moved up and down, bending at the knee and then straightening. This fit passed off in a few minutes, and he immediately started to speak just as usual. He had two other similar fits during the afternoon, and when I saw him in the evening he had recovered. He could speak quite well. Next day about 1 p.m. when I saw him he was going on well. There was no aphasia, and I procured a specimen of his writing spontaneously, to dictation, and to copy, from which it will be seen that he had quite recovered from his agraphia as well as his aphasia (see Fig. 24).

About 2 p.m. he suddenly was seized with aphasia just as before. His jaws were clenched; he could not speak; he had no paralysis of any kind. This condition lasted till 3 a.m. (thirteen hours), when he again quite recovered, and he remained in a weak state, but free from aphasic symptoms, till towards the end of April he had an attack of uræmic asthma, became comatose, and died in uræmia.

Answering our twelve questions it will be seen that
1. He could hear sounds.
2. He could hear words spoken.
3. He could understand words spoken.
4. He could see objects, etc.
5. He could see words written or printed.
6. He could understand written words.
7. He could not speak voluntarily.
8. He could not repeat words.
9. He could not read aloud.
10. He could not write voluntarily.
11. He could not write to dictation.
12. He could not copy.

It was therefore a very complete case of cortical motor aphasia. The most interesting fact about the case is its temporary character and complete and sudden recovery. The first attack lasted at least six hours, the second thirteen hours. He had albuminuria, and there was a distinct history of his having partaken freely the night before of nitrogenous food, but I must say that at that date I had my doubts as to his being a case of uræmia.

It is well known that there are some cases of aphasia produced by some forms of toxæmia, and uræmic aphasias have been described by various authors. In the *Lancet* for April 11th, 1896, a case is quoted which Dr. Rendu, physician to the Hôpital Necker, Paris, reported to the Association Médicale des Hôpitaux on March 27th, 1896, in which the patient had been seized with an apoplectiform attack. After regaining consciousness three symptoms remained, viz. aphasia, right brachial monoplegia, and a systolic bruit at the base of the heart. Embolus was diagnosed, but a few days later the patient was seized with intense dyspnœa, going quickly into "Cheyne-Stokes respiration." The urine was scanty and albuminous. Phlebotomy was practised, the blood revealing the presence of 75 centigrammes of urea per litre. Evidently it was uræmia. The blood-letting improved his condition; the dyspnœa disappeared and the somnolence gradually diminished, whilst the vocabulary became more extensive. A month later no trace of either aphasia or monoplegia remained.

The case of diabetis insipidus, recorded by Chouppe[1] and quoted in an earlier part of this book, where a dehydration of the blood produced aphasia, may also be referred to in this connection. Whilst therefore Case XII., in all probability, was a case of uræmic aphasia very complete and sudden in onset and rapid and sudden in recovery, analogous to some cases of uræmic amblyopia which are sudden and complete in character and temporary in duration, still a theory which might be advanced is that it was functional or hysterical in its causation. The patient's appearance did not suggest uræmia; the

[1] *Comptes Rend. de la Soc. de Biol.*, 1892, p. 642.

fits were not uræmic, but more like hysterical fits in character.

Hysterical motor aphasias due to loss of function in a cortical area are, I believe, rare, if they ever occur. All hysterical mute cases conform to the subcortical or infra-pictorial motor type. We know that this case was cortical in type from the presence of agraphia. Taking all the evidence therefore, and especially the fact that the patient ultimately died from undoubted uræmia, in all probability it was a case of aphasia due to uræmia.

The following short note of a very temporary aphasia case may also be inserted here :—

CASE XIII. (*Personal Observation*).—*Pictorial motor aphasia, temporary in duration, recurring on several occasions.*

M. F., æt. about 78, on three different occasions had been seized with sudden and temporary aphasia. On at least one occasion it had come on in the middle of a sentence. She stopped speaking, looked dazed, and remained unable to speak for three or four minutes.

On one or two other occasions she found herself unable to speak. She had a peculiar dazed feeling, could see and hear sounds and words quite well, but could not utter any word. She had been troubled with weak action of the heart, otherwise she was in good health. I did not see her in one of these attacks, but was summoned to her immediately after one. Recently she had one attack one evening and another attack on the following evening. The most feasible explanation of a case like this is, I believe, that there is a temporary disturbance of the circulation or interference with the nourishment of the cortex in Broca's convolution, so as to interfere with the function of the cortical area, and to produce temporary suspension of function. Of course this case also might be classified under hysterical cases, but in all probability there was some physical interference with the function of the psycho-motor centre.

These three cases of pictorial motor aphasia give a good clinical picture of the symptoms of this variety of motor aphasia, the second one being the only one whose case was thoroughly investigated in all its aspects, so as to ascertain the answer to each of the twelve questions, although I have indicated sufficiently the symptoms in the other two cases to classify them in this group.

Passing now from cases of the pictorial or cortical motor group to cases of

III. INFRA-PICTORIAL OR SUBCORTICAL MOTOR APHASIA,

We shall see that this form is distinguished from the pictorial form, as I have previously indicated, by the fact that the patient with this variety knows how a word ought to be articulated, that is, he knows how many syllables it contains. He is also able to write voluntarily, write to dictation, and to copy. Cases of this variety are not common as organic lesions; indeed Pitres, at the Medical Congress at Lyons in 1894, doubted whether this variety of aphasia exists apart from cases of anarthria or pseudo-bulbar paralysis. There is, however, a functional form of speech disturbance, viz. hysterical mutism, which I believe conforms entirely to this variety. Charcot[1] and others have described cases of hysterical mutism. Bastian, in his able work on *Hysterical and Functional Paralysis*, endeavours to locate many functional and hysterical paralyses to particular parts of

[1] *Lectures on Diseases of the Nervous System*, Vol. III., New Syd. Soc.

the nervous system. Amongst others, he locates hysterical mutism, or the functional form of complete aphemia. He says (page 50): " It must be due to functional degradation occurring in the course of the internuncial fibres that pass between the glosso-kinæsthetic centre in the posterior part of the third frontal convolution and the motor centres for articulation situated in the bulb. In this class of cases patients are absolutely dumb, that is, they are voiceless as well as speechless, but they understand everything that is said to them, and can express their thoughts perfectly and with unimpaired facility by means of writing. Their intellectual faculties are, moreover, quite unimpaired." Again later (page 53) he says: " I may repeat, then, my belief that this form of speech defect may be produced by damage to efferent internuncial fibres in any part of their course from the left glosso-kinæsthetic centre to the articulatory centres in the bulb." These views of Bastian, although propounded by such an able observer as well as clear writer, I cannot altogether agree to, because, as I think I have proved in an earlier part of this work (pages 27 to 52), the vocal articulatory centres are not in the posterior part of the third frontal, but in an area farther back, viz. in the lower part of the ascending frontal and ascending parietal convolutions. Case I., as also the case I quoted from Mills,[1] proved distinctly that this was so, and that the psycho-motor speech centre was in the posterior part of the third left frontal; whilst besides the centres for the movements of the tongue, there were also in the lower part of ascending frontal and ascending parietal convolutions centres for adduc-

[1] *Nervous Diseases*, by American Authors. Edited by Dercum, 1895.

tion and abduction of the vocal cords, and centres for the movements of the lips, cheeks, and lower part of the face. Mills' case and mine proved that lesion of these areas, the executory motor centres, or centres for the vocal and oral articulative mechanism produced paresis, not paralysis, of the muscles of vocal and oral articulation on the opposite side. This is a dysarthria, and not an aphasia at all. Lesion of the fibres from these centres to the bulb would produce the same symptoms. If the lesion was on both sides, then of course there would be aphasia, but there would also be pseudo-bulbar paralysis, that is, paralysis of the oral articulative muscles. But in hysterical mutism there is no such paralysis. The patient can move his tongue, lips, cheeks, jaws, etc., and I believe also the vocal cords, as usual, although he cannot do so to produce words. What is wanting is the proper cell-grouping in the vocal and oral articulative centres, and, as I have shown, this arranging, co-ordinating, or cell-grouping in these centres, so that the correct movements in the muscles may be produced, is brought about by the psycho-motor speech centre in the foot of the third left frontal. The position of a lesion, either functional or organic, which produces a complete infra-pictorial motor aphasia, must be therefore so that it cuts off the psycho-motor centre from the vocal and oral articulative centres on the same and the opposite sides. Instead, therefore, of the interference being, as Bastian says, in the efferent internuncial fibres in any part of their course from the left glosso-kinæsthetic centre to the articulatory centres in the bulb, the interference must be in the fibres passing from the psycho-motor speech centre (B, Figs. 12, 13) in the posterior part of the third frontal to the vocal and oral articulative centres of the same (b^3) and the opposite sides (b^1).

The following are two cases of hysterical mutism, which is, as I have said, the functional form of *infra-pictorial motor aphasia.*

CASE XIV. *(Personal Observation).*—*Complete motor aphasia, sudden in onset, gradual in recovery, able to read, to write, and to understand spoken speech perfectly, in a highly intelligent working man, whose intellectual faculties were not in the least affected by the attack.*

J. S., æt. 37, married, admitted to Leith Hospital November 5th, 1895.

History.—Five years ago, whilst in a passion, patient fell down and lay insensible for about twenty minutes. When he wakened up he could only speak imperfectly. He could just use words, but could not join his sentences. Within an hour the speech returned completely. His wife thinks that during that attack he could hear and understand quite well.

About a year ago he was kicked on the thorax and head by a horse, and lay unconscious for some time according to his wife's story, but according to his own he was not insensible at all. Since then till the present attack he has been healthy.

On November 5th, 1895, patient went out to work apparently in his usual health. In the forenoon he had had some sort of vague feeling of illness; he felt out of sorts, had no pain, but felt cold and shaky. He told the manager that he would have to go home as he did not feel well. He was "all out of sorts" and unable to take charge of horses. He loaded his lorry at one street and delivered it at another. The last thing he remembers was asking a man to give him a lift with some casing. He was seen to drop down suddenly beside his horse. He lay unconscious for ten minutes; apparently there were no convulsions. Dr. Langwill, Leith, saw him, and sent him to Leith Hospital. When Dr. Langwill saw him he had regained consciousness, and had no motor paralysis, but was unable to speak.

State on Admission.—Patient was brought in on a stretcher, but had quite the use of his limbs. He was a man of fairly good muscularity, and had no obvious morbid appearance.

Nervous System.—There was no paralysis, sensory or motor, of the extremities. Knee jerks normal; no ankle clonus. Pupils were equal and reacted to light. Organic reflexes were normal. His intellectual functions appeared normal, but when he attempted to speak he seemed to get excited.

Speech, Motor.—He was quite unable to speak, to answer questions, or to repeat words. On attempting to do so it was seen that his face gradually became flushed; the right side of his face moved; then first his right hand, and then his left hand, were moved gently, and then rather forcibly, so that sometimes he could be described as "striking out." His legs moved restlessly in bed; he raised himself a little off the pillow, and then fell back exhausted with a deeply flushed face and taking deep breaths. This process was gone through whenever he made an attempt to speak, and it continued, although in a gradually lessening degree, as he gained more power in speaking. It seemed to be an overflow of energy from the motor speech centre to the other motor centres, and brought to one's mind the efforts that a very bad case of stammering makes in his attempts to get out the proper pronunciation.

He was able to write without the slightest difficulty. In writing he moved his hand in a rapid, excited manner. Asked his name, he wrote it quite well as well as his address. He then wrote of his own accord, "I know well enough what you say; I am sensible." Later he wrote, "I cannot articulate." Shown a watch and asked what it was, he wrote "watch." Questioned as to the time, he wrote correctly 4.25.

Sensory Speech.—There was no apparent impairment. He seemed to understand without any difficulty all that was said. He copied writing and print quite correctly. He wrote to dictation quite correctly, wrote figures to dictation, and could count them up correctly :—

$$\begin{array}{r} 156 \\ 459 \\ 346 \\ \hline 961 \end{array}$$

He wrote down the answer correctly. He could tell the number of syllables in a word. Ophthalmoscopic examination revealed no abnormality. There was no albuminuria, nor glycosuria; there were a few uric acid crystals in urine.

November 6th.—Asked, "How are you to-day," he answered with great effort, "Better." Then he wrote, "I am all right if I could only get my speech." He answered "Yes" and "No" with great difficulty to some questions. He wrote, "I can hear everything that goes on." On being questioned about his musical faculty he wrote, "I am no musician." He could not tell his own name in speech, nor repeat it after one, but he could repeat "yes" and "no" and "better," with great difficulty. When he did get a word out it came "with a great explosion" and in a loud voice.

November 7th.—The following was the result of his attempts at naming the letters of the alphabet. A + means he was able, an o he was unable, to pronounce the particular letter below which it is placed.

a b c d e f g h i j k l m n o p q r s t u v w x y z
o o + o + o + o + o o o + + + + + + + + + + + + +

g was pronounced with very great difficulty and with a violent explosion; *w* also with great difficulty.

It will be seen that the first letters of the alphabet he did not produce so easily as the later ones; the further he went on, the better he spoke.

To-day patient said "Quin," the name of the nurse in the ward, and learnt since his illness.

When asked to say 1, 2, 3, 4, 5, he said 1 and 2.

November 8th.—He said, "Good morning."

" Do you like that book?"—(A.) "No"; and wrote, "It is childish."

" Say 'childish.'"—(A.) "Child."

" Say 'childish.'"—(A.) "ish."

" Say it again."—(A.) "Child - ish."

" How many syllables are there in 'childish'?"—(A.) "Two."

When asked how he knew the number of syllables, he wrote, "I know how it should be articulated." Asked what he felt in trying to say for instance "Quin," he wrote, "Exhaustion and a slight pain," pointing to left side of head just over Broca's convolution. "How do you think the words get out?" He wrote, "Some of them are coming away naturally." (Q.) "And the difficult ones?"—(A. in writing) "I have to force the articulation; the articulation is there."

The following was the result of his attempts to name the letters of the alphabet:—

a b c d e f g h i j k l m n o p q r s t u v w x y z
+ + + o + + + o + + + + + + + + + + + + + + + + + +

g, *w*, and *z* with great effort.

November 9th.—Asked, "How are you feeling to-day?"—(A.) "Well."

"How did you sleep?"—(A.) "Rested well. I dreamt—that—I—was—preaching—t-to—the—whole—ward.'

"What were you preaching about?"—(A.) "The l-o-o-ost lamb."

"Can you tell me your name?"—(A.) "No."

"Can you say it after me?" He did so after great effort.

Asked to name the alphabet, the following was the result:—

a b c d e f g h i j k l m n o p q r s t u v w x y z
+ +

g, *w*, and *z* with great effort.

Asked to read out of a book, he read correctly: "The—door—flew—open—as—doors—al-ways—do—when—there's—a—boy—at—the—other—s-s-side."

There was a good long pause between the words. By the time he had reached *do* he put down the book exhausted. In a minute or two he continued, "And T-To (= Tom) S-s-s-sidy—rushed—in—almost—*breathless*" (last word with great effort). "I—am—strug-ger." "What? Struggling?"—(A.) "No." "Stronger?"—(A.) "Yes." He then wrote, "The articulation and words do not seem so far away to-day."

On November 10th he was speaking still better—could use the whole alphabet, and could speak sentences, but words separated by a pause. On the 12th it was noted that he had now only difficulty with difficult test sentences, such as "British Constitution" and "My mother munches mushrooms."

On November 13th he was dismissed with speech quite returned, exactly ten days after admission. Dr. John Wyllie, Edinburgh, kindly saw the case with me on November 10th.

The notes of the case were taken by Dr. Hill Buchan, House Physician, to whom I am indebted for them.

The notes of the case are so explicit that it is hardly necessary to say much about them. The patient was a very intelligent man, and as he was able to write, we were able to ascertain his own opinion as to the cause of his mutism, and his feelings in attempting to speak. On several occasions he wrote, "I cannot articulate"; "The articulation cannot get out"; "I know how I should articulate a word, but I cannot get it out." When recovering he wrote that "the words he could speak came away naturally," but "the difficult ones he had to force the articulation"; "the articulation is there." He also wrote that speaking a word gave him a feeling of exhaustion, and a pain over the left side of the head (pointing to Broca's convolution).

These opinions and feelings of the patient are so much in accord with the opinions I have expressed with regard to the position of the functional derangement in hysterical mutism, viz. in the same region as an organic lesion which produces an infra-pictorial motor aphasia, that I have recorded the notes of the case in full.

The extent of nerve fibres whose function is deranged is short, especially on the left side, where they pass only from the posterior part of the third left frontal to the lower part of the ascending frontal and ascending parietal convolutions; the fibres passing from the third left frontal to the vocal and oral articulative mechanism of the right side have, however, a greater length. As there was no paralysis of the muscles of the tongue, lips, etc., there could not have been functional derangement of the fibres passing from the vocal and oral articulative centres in the lower parts of the ascending frontal and ascending parietal convolutions on both sides to the centres in the bulb, which fact, as I have said, is contrary to the theory and opinion of Bastian.

The answers to the twelve questions in this case were :—

1. He could hear sounds, etc.
2. He could hear words spoken.
3. He could understand words spoken.
4. He could see objects, etc.
5. He could see words written and printed.
6. He could understand words written and printed.
7. He could not speak voluntarily.
8. He could not repeat words.
9. He could not read aloud.
10. He could write voluntarily.
11. He could write to dictation.
12. He could copy.

Although he could not speak voluntarily, repeat words, nor read aloud, he knew how the words should be articulated, that is, the number of syllables, etc., the word contained. This, as will be seen, is exactly what we have found to be the case in infra-pictorial motor aphasia.

The next case is one of the same kind, viz. a case of hysterical mutism. It was seen by my brother, Dr. George Elder, whilst assisting me, and to him I am indebted for the notes of it.

CASE XV.—*Hysterical mutism for eighteen hours.*

C. D., a girl aged 15, employed in a dressmaker's shop, was seen in Leith in February 1895. She was said to have fallen down in a fit about six hours previously, and had not been able to speak since.

Family History.—Her father had tubercular joint disease, but none of the other children, seven in number, had any hereditary disease. There was no epilepsy or other nervous affection in the family. All her mother's family menstruated early, at about twelve years.

Previous Health.—Very good. Began to menstruate before thirteen. Had recently worked very hard.

Present Illness.—Came on quite suddenly when standing by the fireside speaking to others. She fell down on the floor, and her arms and body were thrown about freely for a few minutes, and then these movements ceased, but patient could not speak. It was impossible to make out from the history whether the patient was conscious during the fit.

State on Examination.—She was seen about 12 p.m. She was lying quite still in bed and quite conscious; she followed every movement with her eyes, and understood evidently everything that was being said, but when she tried to speak, although the lips moved, absolutely no sound was emitted. Temperature was normal; pulse steady and normal; free perspiration. No sign of any weakness or paralysis anywhere. Heart sounds were quite good, and absolutely nothing else abnormal could be made out on examination. The mother was told not to alarm herself, and not to make much to-do about the patient, or to show her too much attention.

She was seen again next day about noon. She had slept well and taken her food, and was quite sharp in every way, but had never uttered a sound. It was then explained to her that the voice was produced by two bands in the throat, and that these had got suddenly affected so that they could not be tightened, but that if they were tightened she would be able to speak as before. The fingers were then firmly pressed over the thyroid cartilage, the wings being pressed inwards, and she was told that she would then be able to speak. On being asked if she could she said "Yes" in a clear tone, and she was able to answer quite clearly all the questions asked, and to speak quite freely. So far as known there has been no return of the mutism.

This case, besides being a very typical one of hysterical mutism, is interesting from the method of treatment which was adopted in its cure. It is a method that I have very frequently adopted for the cure of hysterical and functional aphonia, whether that aphonia was due to a previous laryngitis or came on in a hysterical subject.

I don't know who originally suggested this method, but it is one which I know to be practised by several physicians.

The patient is told that pressing the wings of the thyroid cartilage will enable her to produce voice, and she is asked to say ā or ē or ō, whilst the fingers press the cartilage. The result frequently is that voice is at the moment produced, and after the fingers are withdrawn she still continues to use her voice.

Hysterical mutism differs, however, from hysterical aphonia, in that in the former there is no voice or sound whatever produced by the larynx, or muscles of oral articulation, whereas in aphonia the patient can speak in a whisper or a very low broken voice.

I have no intention of entering into a discussion as to whether in hysterical mutism the oral articulative or the vocal mechanism is at fault. I believe that in all cases both are as would be supposed if my theory as to the localisation of the functional derangement is correct.

CHAPTER IX.

AGRAPHIA (GRAPHIC APHASIA) AND THE QUESTION OF THE EXISTENCE OF A SPECIAL GRAPHIC CENTRE.[1]

AGRAPHIA has been known for many years to be a frequent symptom in all the types of aphasia, but the question as to whether there is a type of aphasia which could be strictly called graphic aphasia without any other lesion has been one that has been much discussed in recent years.

I shall shortly summarise what are the graphic symptoms which are usually found in each of the varieties of aphasia.

I. *In Auditory Aphasia* the patient is usually able to write voluntarily, although, if the lesion is cortical, that is pictorial auditory, there is usually paragraphia in his voluntary writing as there is paraphasia in his voluntary speaking. Paragraphia is the term applied to writing the incorrect word, and paraphasia to speaking the incorrect word. Th retically there are two forms of paragraphia: first, the form due to paraphasia, where the incorrect word memory is raised in the psycho-motor speech centre (that is, the centre of Broca). The patient

[1] An abstract of this chapter was read at the meeting of the Medico-Chirurgical Society, Edinburgh, on January 13th, 1897, and was published in *The Scottish Medical and Surgical Journal* for February and March 1897.

in that case writes correctly the paraphasic word; but in the other theoretical form it is possible for the patient to write incorrectly the letters of a word which would be correctly spoken, or he might write a different word from the word he spoke, or he might trace incorrect lines in writing the letters. These would be all different forms of paragraphia, and the specimens of writing in Figs. 21, 23, 25, 26, 27, 28, and 29 show these characteristics. As there is more or less amnesia verbalis and articulative amnesia in auditory aphasia cases, the patient shows these symptoms also in his writing. He fails to recall the word he requires, and sometimes makes mistakes in the syllables in writing as in speaking.

Auditory aphasia cases have agraphia to dictation, except the supra-pictorial form, where the patient may be able to write letters and short words, but not long words nor sentences to dictation. This is because in the pictorial and infra-pictorial form the patient cannot hear words, whereas in the supra-pictorial form his word-hearing centre is intact, although the word sounds do not reach his intelligence, the writing to dictation being almost what might be called a reflex act. The patient is usually able to copy when he suffers from auditory aphasia, but only as a tracing in the pictorial and supra-pictorial form, whereas he can copy intelligently in the infra-pictorial form. This is because the auditory centre requires to be intact in order that the visual images of words may reach the intelligence.

II. *In Visual Aphasia*, or word-blindness, if the lesion is infra-pictorial (the *cécité verbale pure* of Déjerine) the patient is able to write voluntarily and to dictation, but there are great disturbances in his powers of copying;

he cannot copy intelligently; he may be able to trace as a drawing.

A case of word-blindness of this sort (Case VIII.), as previously stated, actually wrote a letter whilst in this condition, but was not able to read what she had written; and it was noticed in the letter that some of the sentences were repeated over again, as she could not intelligently see what she had written, although her sight was quite good.

In pictorial or cortical visual aphasia, on the other hand, as was so distinctly proved by Déjerine by a post-mortem of his case, the patient is not able to write spontaneously nor to dictation, and if he can copy at all it is only very imperfectly by tracing as a drawing. These symptoms are due to the visual images of words and letters being blotted out.

A good specimen of the writing of a case of pictorial visual aphasia is seen in Fig. 23. He was for some time in Leith Hospital, and his case is fully reported in an earlier part of this work (Case IX.).

He was a young man whom I believed to have pachymeningitis of a chronic nature, and the aphasic symptoms enabled me to state pretty definitely that the lesion was cortical and not in the substance of the cerebrum.

He could hear and understand words perfectly, could speak, but could not read either aloud or in silence. His voluntary writing was very imperfect. He could not write to dictation, and he copied very imperfectly and only by tracing the shape of the letters, those of simple form being better traced than the more complicated. This is shown very distinctly in his attempts at copying the word "North" as printed and written; he tried to imitate the shape of the letters. He could copy printed type better than manuscript and could not copy print into written letters. This is a point I shall refer to later.

In supra-pictorial visual aphasia the patient is probably not able to write voluntarily nor to dictation, and may not be able to trace as a drawing. This is a form of which, however, no uncomplicated cases have yet been described in medical literature, but, as previously stated, Case X. was, I believe, one of this sort, and he was so agraphic that he could not even trace the outlines of letters with his fingers, although he could read letters and words aloud without understanding them.

III. *In Motor Aphasia*, if the lesion is infra-pictorial or subcortical, there is no disturbance of writing. Probably very few, if any, organic lesions of this variety have been recorded, most of those claimed to belong to this group being purely dysarthrias and not aphasias at all, but the functional form is well known under the name of hysterical mutism. Hysterical mutes conform to this variety of aphasia, as I have previously pointed out, and it is well known that, whilst they can't speak, they can write voluntarily, to dictation, and to copy.

In pictorial or cortical motor aphasia (Broca's aphasia) the patient has agraphia in voluntary writing and also to dictation. He can only copy by tracing. These cases are often met with, and the agraphia has been long known as a symptom of Broca's aphasia. A few exceptional cases are alluded to later. In supra-pictorial motor aphasia the patient has agraphia in voluntary writing, but not to dictation, and can copy.

IV. *In Conduction Aphasias* (Leitungsaphasie of Wernicke) the patient can usually write, that is, form the words, letters, etc., voluntarily and to dictation, but he shows paragraphia—he writes the wrong word and letters, and often repeats the same word or letter in writing, just as he uses the incorrect word and repeats the same word over and over again in speaking.

This tendency to repeat words is sometimes called "word-intoxication." In this form the patient usually copies perfectly.

Case VII. showed these symptoms very markedly.

He was a man who was gradually attacked by aphasic symptoms. At first his chief symptoms were paraphasia; paragraphia; amnesia verbalis or logamnesia, or the loss of memory for names and substantives; and articulative amnesia, or the tendency to put incorrect syllables and letters into words. He could speak, but used the wrong words sometimes, occasionally a wrong syllable or letter in the proper word, and repeated the same word over and over again. He could read and understand what he read, and he could hear and understand what was said to him. Towards the end of his life, however, the auditory word centre became involved, probably from a spreading of the disease, which was believed to be either of the nature of acute softening or a cerebral tumour. His writing was frequently tested, and copies of some specimens of it are seen in Fig. 21. It will be seen that paragraphia and word-intoxication in writing were the most marked symptoms of his voluntary writing, and also his writing to dictation. He was asked to give an account of his illness in writing, and the two copies under volitional writing were his two attempts. As will be seen, incorrect words were written and the same words appear several times. "About fortnight" appears twice in the first attempt and once in the second. The word "next" appears three times in the second attempt. He was asked to write to dictation: "Dear Sir, I beg to acknowledge receipt of your letter of yesterday's date." Several of the words were incorrectly written. He could, on the other hand, copy perfectly from print.

Is there any evidence to show that there have been cases of agraphia other than those due to lesions of the speech centres and fibres already considered? No convincing evidence can be found in medical literature.

Exner[1] in 1881 produced what he believed to be some evidence to prove that there was a special graphic centre in the posterior part of the second left frontal convolution, and this had been pretty generally accepted till, in recent years, Déjerine[2] has done much to show that all the cases that have been recorded in favour of a special graphic centre could be explained in some other way than admitting the existence of that centre. He showed, for instance, that the well-known case of Henschen (Margarita Andersen),[3] besides having agraphia, had also word-blindness and hemianopsia, and at the post-mortem, besides having a lesion in the posterior part of the second left frontal convolution, there was another lesion in the angular gyrus, the latter lesion being quite sufficient to account for the agraphia independently of the other.

The case of Bar[4] can be explained in a similar way. There had been a motor aphasia along with the agraphia.

[1] *Untersuchungen über die Localisation der Functionen in der Grosshirnrinde des Menschen*, 1881.
[2] *Comptes Rendus de la Soc. de Biol.*, Paris, 1891-92.
[3] *Klinis. und Anat. Beitrage zur Pathol. des Gehirns*, p. 273. Upsala, 1890.
[4] *France Médicale*, p. 609, 1876.

The case reported by J. B. Charcot and Dutil[1] had also multiple lesions, although one of these lesions occupied the foot of the second left frontal convolution. She had neither word-blindness nor word-deafness, although there was complete agraphia for over twenty years. She had, however, embarrassment of speech, and therefore motor aphasia cannot be excluded in this case. Similarly the cases of Balzar[2] and A. Schaw[3] had multiple lesions. These are the only post-mortems which I can find that might be produced as evidence of a special localisation of a graphic centre. There are, however, a good many cases where patients have only shown the symptoms of agraphia clinically, but most of these cases had also shown symptoms of the other forms of aphasia at some time or other. Such are the cases of Charcot and of Pitres,[4] quoted by Déjerine[5] and Wyllie.[6] In Charcot's case there had been motor aphasia some time previously, and in Pitres' case[7] there was hemiplegia and right homonymous hemianopsia, but no word-blindness nor motor aphasia. Although he had almost complete agraphia with the right hand, he had trained himself to write with the left.

There was no post-mortem in either case, but the history shows that other parts than the graphic centre must have been at one time involved, so that they are not at all conclusive as to the separate existence of a graphic centre.

[1] *Comptes Rendus de la Soc. de Biol.*, p. 129, July 1893.
[2] *Gazette Médicale de Paris*, p. 97, 1881.
[3] *Brit. Med. Journ.*, February 1892, and *Brain*, 1893, p. 449.
[4] *Revue de Médecine*, 1884, p. 864.
[5] *Comptes Rendus de la Soc. de Biol.*, Paris, 1891-92.
[6] *Disorders of Speech*, p. 357.
[7] *Congrès Française de Médecine*, 1894.

Very recently (September 1896) Gombault and Philippe,[1] in a careful analysis of the evidence on this subject as well as on motor aphasia, produced in three groups a few cases which have been published by various authors tending to show that a special graphic centre exists. These groups are :—

1st. Cases showing preservation of the power of writing spontaneously with loss of the verbal articulatory images (cortical motor aphasia without agraphia). In this group they include the case of Kostenitsche[2] and the case of Guido Banti.[3] The post-mortem in both cases showed that Broca's convolution was destroyed, although the patients had not had agraphia. The one patient wrote well with the left hand, but not with the right, the significance of which I shall refer to later; the other wrote well with the right hand. We may dismiss the case that wrote with the left hand for reasons stated later, but it is very difficult explaining the other case, because it is generally believed that pictorial motor aphasias always show agraphia. If the lesion had been subcortical, one could have understood the symptoms which corresponded so markedly to the symptoms of infra-pictorial motor aphasia. The most feasible explanation of the case appears to me to be that the patient was very decidedly *auditive*, and was enabled to write by means of the auditory images without the motor images of the syllables and words.

2nd. Cases showing preservation of spontaneous writing when there was loss of the visual verbal images. One of

---

[1] *Archiv Physiol. et Experimental Medicin*, 1896.
[2] *Deutsche Zeitschrift für Nervenheilkunde*, Bd. IV.
[3] *Afasia e sue forme. Lo Sperimentale*, 1886, p. 270.

Wernicke's cases[1] is cited as an example of this. It, however, had transitory agraphia. The post-mortem showed destruction of the angular gyrus.

3rd. Cases showing preservation of spontaneous writing along with the loss of the auditory images of words. A case of Pick[2] is cited as belonging to this group. The case conformed to the infra-pictorial or subcortical auditory variety, but the post-mortem showed a destruction of the auditory centres in both hemispheres. It is just possible, therefore, that the patient had word-deafness on account of the loss of his common auditory centres, and the word-hearing centre may have partially escaped.

Although, therefore, it is difficult explaining these exceptional cases brought forward by Gombault and Philippe, still they cannot be taken as conclusive that there is a special graphic centre. We must take it, therefore, that no conclusive evidence can be got as to the existence of a graphic centre from a study of cases of agraphia that have been recorded. That being so, what evidence can be got from a theoretical study of the subject of writing? In learning to write the individual simply traces the lines as he sees them before him in the copy, but through practice he becomes more expert in the particular movements necessary to form the letters and their combinations into words. When writing is done from memory voluntarily and to dictation, the visual images of the letters are raised in the visual memory, and to a great extent the writing is traced from the copy perceived in the visual memory, just as it would be if the copy were placed before the eyes. On this theory,

[1] *Der Aphasische Symptomen Complex.*
[2] *Archiv f. Psych.*, Bd. XXIII., 1892.

then, the movements of the hand in writing are directed or guided by the word-seeing centre—in other words, the cell-grouping in the centres for the hand and fingers is directed or co-ordinated from the word-seeing centre in the left angular gyrus. But whilst this may be so for the ordinary outlines of letters, there is, however, something more than this in the individual who has been trained to write. Where are stored the memories for the fine movements and delicate touches which produce the peculiar shapes and flourishes in the letters of the expert writer? Why are letters formed so differently by different individuals? Why are little peculiarities in an individual's writing reproduced over and over again, so that there is no mistaking one person's writing for that of another, although we have all learned to write from the same or very similar copy, and raise always much the same visual letter images in our word-seeing centres? We not only are not conscious of raising in the visual memory the particular images of the letters as written by ourselves, but many of us, if asked to say how we usually wrote a particular letter, would not be able to tell until we had practically done so by writing it. Where then are the movements which produce these delicate lines, etc., guided from? Are they guided from the visual word centre, or from a special centre in the immediate neighbourhood of the centres for the movements of the hand? I believe that at first writing is done entirely from copy, but that the memories of the muscular movements for writing are stored in the neighbourhood of the motor centres for the hand, what Bastian would call the kinæsthetic centres. Writing, it must be remembered, is only one of the many different accomplishments for which the hand can become specialised, and the same muscles are used for all of them, although in different combinations. Take, for instance, the very delicate movements of the musician playing such a musical instrument as a piano, a mandolin, or a violin; or let us take the movements necessary for expert typewriting; the movements necessary for painting; the movements necessary for the handling of a club by a golfer or the cue by a billiard-player; or the movements necessary for the doing of any work by a skilled workman: are not impressions of these skilled movements conveyed by the tactile nerves, and the nerves of the muscular sense, to the nerve cells in the cortex, to be there stored in the memory, and reproduced again when necessary? Is it not reasonable to suppose that certain cells get specialised for the storing up of the memories of these special movements, so that they can be reproduced at will, and is it not reasonable to suppose that these cells act by bringing about the necessary cell-grouping in the motor centres for the particular part of the body where the particular muscular movements are produced? On this theory then there are certain specialised centres in the neighbourhood of the motor centres for the hand, and one of these specialised centres is that for writing.

If for a moment one considers all the movements necessary for writing, and if it be granted that a nerve centre varies in size in direct ratio to the number of combinations necessary to produce the movements for which it has become specialised, then the graphic centre need not necessarily be a large one in order to produce all the letters and figures, and all their combinations. It is not necessary to have stored in a graphic centre the memories of the graphic images of *words*, because we do not write words as words. We write letters, and combine them so that words are produced. All that is necessary, therefore, is to have the graphic images of all the letters in their capital and small form, and all the figures and other signs used in writing, and the graphic images of the appendages to the letters and figures, such as the lines connecting them, special flourishes, etc. The graphic centre is enabled to combine these letters into words by means of the psycho-motor speech centre and the auditory word centre, because, as we can easily test on ourselves, when we write there is a process of silent articulation always going on, the articulatory image as well as probably the sound image of the letters and words being raised in the cerebrum. Hence the necessity of having both the psycho-motor and probably also the auditory sound centre unaffected if correct writing is to be produced. This is why a cortical motor aphasia almost, if not always, produces agraphia.

I do not intend here to enter fully into a discussion of the question as to which of the speech centres takes the foremost place in the act of spelling correctly, although it has a very distinct bearing on this question of writing Some hold that the visual centres are chiefly concerned in spelling correctly; but, whilst this may be so in some individuals, I think in most cases the most necessary centres for correct spelling are the articulatory motor and the auditory centres. When we are asked to spell a word, such as "picture," we at once raise first the syllable sound memories in the auditory word centre, and then are able to pronounce in succession and in their proper sequence the letters which compose the syllables and the word as a whole. This is why a child when learning to spell articulates the letters in their proper sequence over and over again. The psycho-motor letter memories are raised at once in the cerebrum, whilst, although the visual memories of the letters and words may also be raised, in many cases they are very imperfectly raised. I think this is very clearly shown by the fact that it is with difficulty we can spell words backwards. If the visual memories were first and distinctly raised, we would be able to spell words and syllables easily backwards as we would mentally see them. I am aware that the visual memory is often used in order to correct words if badly spelt. Many people, if in doubt as to the spelling of a word, write it down to see how it looks. If one considers, therefore, that only the letter graphic memories, and probably also the graphic memories of very familiar small words and syllables, or familiar words such as the signature, can be stored in the graphic centre, the spelling and combining into words being accomplished by the other centres, and chiefly by the psycho-motor articulatory centre, it will at once be seen that there are not very many graphic image memories required altogether. We are all in the habit of writing each letter in a particular form, and if we wish to change that form we at once call in the help of the visual centre in a very decided manner, and trace the new form of the letter as we would from a copy. Take even our attempt to print with a pen or pencil all the letters of the alphabet, or our attempts to write the letters of a language whose letters are unfamiliar to us: we simply trace them as we would a map or design. If we have not the form of the letters in a copy before our eyes, we raise them in the visual memory and we mentally see them. And not only can we write letters of any language or any shape by simply tracing them in this way with the right hand, but we can do the same thing by means of the left hand, although not quite so well as with the right.

The only difference is that our right hand is used for almost every action, and the movements of the right hand are more under the control of the will and better co-ordinated than those of the left, from more constant use, and from the fact that it is trained to hold a pen and to draw lines, curves, etc., although not the exact form of the strange letter it is attempting to write. Although such letter as a whole is strange, parts of it are familiar, so that the right hand, which is accustomed to draw lines, etc., is more expert at the new letter than the left, but the expertness with which the letter is written is a long way behind the expertness with which a familiar letter is written.

Not only can letters be traced as from a copy by the left hand, but the same thing can be done by a pen between the teeth, by one attached to the leg or the elbow. This, I believe, is brought about by the guidance or direction of the visual centres where are stored the memories of the forms, shapes, etc., of objects.

But how different is this from writing! Is there much resemblance between the writing as written by the right hand and that written by the left?

If one knew a man's handwriting, as, for instance, his signature, would it be possible to tell his signature if he wrote with his left hand instead of his right hand? and yet he has got the same muscles in the left hand as in the right, and has got the same visual centres to guide it. There would probably be slight resemblances, but this would result merely from having the form and shape of the letters of his signature in his visual memory when he was tracing it.

About this question of left-hand writing I think there has been a considerable amount of misconception and false reasoning. When Wernicke pointed out that the left hand could be used for writing as well as many other parts of the body (in fact any part which could be moved and to which a pen could be attached), and that such writing was undoubtedly guided or directed from the visual centres, too much importance, I think, was put on those facts. As I have pointed out, such writing is only tracing, and not writing in the true sense of the word; and not only so, but if the question be carefully considered, it will be seen that if we take for granted that there is a true special graphic centre in the left cerebral cortex which co-ordinates or guides the movements necessary for writing with the right hand, and we now consider how such a centre would act if it was suddenly called on to co-ordinate or guide the movements of the left hand in writing, it will be seen that the left hand would not write in the same way as the right. The left hand would write in the peculiar way known as

"Mirror Writing."

Mirror writing, as is well known, is writing that can be read in a mirror. It is written from right to left instead of from left to right.

The left hand, I hold, would write from right to left if guided entirely by the writing centre in the left hemisphere. And why? Because if the same muscles (that is, the homologous muscles) were acted on in the same manner in the left hand as they would have been if the impulses had passed to the motor centres for the movements of the right hand, then the left hand would move in the opposite direction to the right, in its relation to the mesial line of the body—that is, all movements from side to side would be in an opposite direction, whilst antero-posterior movements would be in the same. In other words, adduction movements on the right side are in the opposite direction to adduction movements on the left, and abduction on the right to abduction on the left. One can easily test on oneself how much more easy it is to move the different parts of the two hands by acting on the homologous muscles in the same manner than it is to act on heterologous muscles. Take the mere act of twirling the thumbs in the same direction—an easy performance when twirled either in one direction or the other, provided they both go in the same direction—and the much more difficult feat of twirling the thumbs in opposite directions. The fact is, although the two hands act quite independently of each other, and are as near to unilateral representation in the cortex as any part of the body is, it is easier for them to act in the same way (more especially in movements very similar to each other) than to act against each other. This fact I take to be slightly analogous to the complete bilateral representation which we find for some muscles, as the masseter muscles and the adductors of the vocal cords, which act always together, and which can only be completely paralysed by central lesions when they are in both hemispheres. The muscles of the face take a place midway between such muscles as those of the vocal cords and muscles such as those of the hand, and therefore are partially bilaterally represented, and are only paresed by a single lesion in their cortical centres or tracts from the centres.

This bilateral representation is brought about, it is

believed, by commissural fibres joining the centres through the corpus callosum. In all probability, therefore, there are commissural fibres joining the centres for the hand; and although these fibres are not sufficient to innervate both sides, they probably act sufficiently to make it easier to move homologous muscles in the same than in the opposite direction. I repeat, therefore, that one would expect mirror writing if the left hand was used for writing and was guided by a special graphic centre on the left side.

Patients who when they get paralysed on the right side learn to write with the left hand require to call in the visual centres to guide the left hand in writing, and therefore left-handed writing in the usual form is directed at first by the visual centres. Through practice, however, the left hand gets more expert at writing, and a special graphic centre gets specialised on the right side for expert left-hand writing, just in the same way as on the left for expert right-hand writing.

It has been noticed that mirror writing is sometimes shown by some patients who have to write with the left hand, and some, it is said, have not been aware of their peculiarity.

This of course must have been due to some want of intelligence in the patient, although I must say, however, that I have been struck with the fact that some mirror writers did not perceive that they had written the wrong way until they had finished their signature for instance. With the view of testing the question as to whether some people would naturally write in the mirror fashion if asked to write with the left hand, I asked those whom I came in contact with, in hospital and elsewhere, to write their names with their left hand, and I very soon found that a certain proportion of people wrote in the mirror fashion. Some of these cases, when being tested, were very interesting in the way they went about it. Several took the pen in the left hand, put it down to the paper near the left edge, commenced to write, and very soon found that they went over the edge of the paper. One girl after doing this hesitated for a few seconds, shook her head, and then began at the right side of the sheet. None of the cases, I may say, knew what they were being tested for. I have only noted as being mirror writers those who commenced of their own free will to write in the mirror fashion. Many, however, could write as well in the one way as the other.[1]

Results of Tests of Writing with the Left Hand.

	Total number.	Female.	Male.	Ordinary writers.			Mirror writers.			Percentage of		
				Total.	Female.	Male.	Total.	Female.	Male.	Mirror writers.	Female do.	Male do.
Over 15 years of age.	154	95	59	138	81	57	16	14	2	10·39	14·73	3·39
Under 15 years of age.	297	242	55	290	237	53	7	5	2	2·35	2·06	3·63
Total .	451	337	114	428	318	110	23	19	4	5·1	5·63	3·5

The figures bring out some remarkable results, some of which, I must say, I quite expected. As will be seen, I have separated those tested into two divisions: 1st, those

[1] For help in testing many of these cases I am indebted to Nurses Duckworth, Vass, and Burnet, Leith Hospital, and for many of the others to the kindness of Miss McIntosh and Mr. Porteous.

above fifteen years of age, and 2nd, those below fifteen years of age. Each of these groups is again divided into females and males. I quite expected that, if my theory as to mirror writing was correct, there would be found a larger number of mirror writers amongst persons over fifteen years of age than amongst those under fifteen, for the simple reason that those over fifteen years have had more practice in writing, and do not call in the help of the visual centres so markedly as boys and girls under fifteen, who are at the stage of their education when they use the visual centres to trace the outlines of letters and to improve their writing. They have their ideal of what writing ought to be like much more prominently in their mind than older people, who have acquired more proficiency in writing and may be said to have a permanent form of handwriting. Those under fifteen have, as a rule, not yet acquired the free and easy style of the adult; in other words, the special graphic centre has not yet been sufficiently developed to write mirror writing with the left hand *in spite of* the visual centre, as it is to be remembered that the visual centre would naturally lead a person to write in the usual way with the left hand.

Out of 154 over fifteen years of age, 16, or 10·39 per cent., were found to be mirror writers; whereas out of 297 under fifteen years of age, 7, or 2·35, were mirror writers.

Those under fifteen years of age were tested for me by teachers in schools, and the teachers noted as to several of these seven that they were specially clever boys and girls. The grouping of those tested into females and males brought out a very remarkable result, for which I have no satisfactory explanation. It was found that whilst out of 95 females over fifteen years of age,

14, or 14·73 per cent., were mirror writers, out of 59 males over fifteen years of age, only 2, or 3·39 per cent., were mirror writers. There was, however, not the same difference between the sexes in those under fifteen years of age, because out of 242 girls, 5, or 2·06 per cent., were mirror writers, and out of 55 boys, 2, or 3·63 per cent., were mirror writers.

The total number of all ages tested was 451, of whom 337 were females and 114 males.

The total number of mirror writers was 23, or 5·1 per cent., of whom 19 were females and 4 males; 5·63 per cent. of the total females were mirror writers, whilst 3·5 per cent. of the total males were mirror writers.

These facts show, to my mind, that there is a certain proportion of mirror writers, and I believe that the reason of it is to be found in the theories I have propounded. What lends support to this is the fact that, whilst it can't be said that the most expert and best writers were mirror writers, still only those were mirror writers who had been fairly well educated. I found none of the poor hospital patients who had had little education and less practice in writing mirror writers; their visual centres probably took too prominent a part in the guiding of the hand in writing. Some of the nurses and some of the well educated and better class patients were the mirror writers, and only those were found to be mirror writers who had had considerable practice in writing.

Other evidence in support of the theory that mirror writing with the left hand is guided from the same centre as ordinary writing with the right hand is supplied by a comparison of left-hand mirror writing with the writing of the same individual with the right hand

If the mirror writing is held before a mirror or read through the paper so as to compare it with the same individual's right-hand writing, it will be seen that there is no mistaking that the handwriting is the same. Every detail of the handwriting is reproduced in the mirror writing, and the resemblance is so great that one at once must admit that such resemblance must be brought about by the two hands being guided from the same centre (see Fig. 24A). I believe that the centre that guides the two hands is a graphic centre in the left cerebral cortex, and I cannot possibly imagine that that centre is the visual centre, seeing that the natural tendency of the visual centre would be to reproduce the writing in the usual shape and not in the mirror fashion.

As this question of mirror writing is of considerable importance, I here insert the notes of a case of mirror writing I had under my care recently. She was often tested, and could write long sentences with the left hand in the mirror fashion. As she recovered the use of her right hand later, it was possible to compare the writing of the left with that of the right hand. A specimen of it is seen in Fig. 24A, where the mirror writing is on one side of the page and the ordinary right-hand writing on the other. If the page is held up to the light, and the two compared, it is seen at once what a remarkable resemblance there is.

For the notes of the case I am indebted to Dr. Eason, House Physician.

CASE XVA. (*Personal Observation*).—*Right-sided hemiplegia, temporary in duration; mirror writer with left hand.*

R. D., æt. 22, married, admitted to Leith Hospital December 21st, 1896, complaining of loss of power of right arm and right leg of one day's duration. She has always been naturally left-handed, but always wrote with the right hand.

Present Illness.—Has had no previous illness. She had returned from a Maternity Hospital two days before she took ill. There she had had her second child—an easy labour and a normal puerperium, getting up on the ninth day and walking home on the tenth. She felt perfectly well till two days later. She had just washed and was in the act of drying herself when her right hand dropped useless by her side, her right leg got powerless, and she only saved herself from falling by leaning against the door. She was assisted to bed, when she found that she could move neither her arm, her leg, her fingers, nor her toes, but she felt the clothes being taken off them and they were quite warm. Soon after being in bed she began to regain the power of moving her leg so far as to be able to pull it up in bed, and she describes a sort of "thick feeling" coming over her arm, and in the morning she could pull up the arm and move the fingers a little. Her friends noticed no change in her face or speech. She walked up to hospital, with the assistance of a friend and a stick.

On Admission. Sensation.—Touch, temperature sense, and sense of pain normal on both sides.

Reflexes.—Plantar and patellar normal.

Voluntary Motion. Right Leg.—Limited flexion, extension, and adduction at the hip. Slight flexion and extension at knee. No movement at the ankle or toes.

Right Arm.—No movement whatever, even at shoulder.

Face.—Muscles of right side of mouth and nose are weakened, the lower part of the face being drawn to the left with movements. Tongue is pushed out slightly to the right side. No change observable in muscles of eye or forehead.

Progress of Case. December 21*st.*—Had an attack of speechlessness lasting for several minutes. Some movement of the paralysed arm during this fit is reported to have taken place.

December 22*nd.*—Movements at thigh and knee freer. No movement of toes. Frequent slight involuntary movement of right fingers.

December 23*rd.*—7 a.m. Epileptiform attack. 11.15 a.m. Another fit lasting for about three minutes. Muscles of face—mouth, nose, eyes, and forehead—twitched on both sides, apparently equally, about every second. Coincidently muscles of both arms, the right grasping firmly at each twitch. Both legs were twitching, and in fact all the muscles of the body shared in the spasm.

December 26*th.*—Has had no more convulsive seizures since 23rd, when Pot. Bromid gr. xv. every four hours was begun. Also having Pot. Iodid gr. x. four times daily. Yesterday began to feel as if her arm was "working," and could move the right arm slightly at night. This morning can move arm very freely, and also can grasp fairly strongly with hand. Began to bend knee last night, and this morning began to move foot. Very slight movement also in great toe.

December 27*th.*—Exaggerated knee jerk on right side, and ankle clonus well marked.

December 28*th.*—Her writing was tested to-day with the left hand, and found to be mirror writing. It was frequently tested after this, and found to be always the same. A day or two before her discharge she was asked to write with both hands, the right having recovered sufficiently, and the result is seen in Fig. 24A.

January 6th, 1897.—Now going about the ward. No lameness. Doing now the finer movements with the fingers of right hand.

January 7th.—Discharged to-day almost recovered.

Into the details of this case it is not my intention to enter, although it presents many interesting features. The question naturally arises whether this was a functional or an organic hemiplegia. Much might be said for both sides of the question. If it was functional, and if my theory as to mirror writing is correct, then the lesion was not cortical, but in the fibres passing from the cortex to the bulb.

The symptoms were exactly like an ordinary hemiplegia due to a lesion in the internal capsule. If in a case one has any doubt whether a lesion is cortical or subcortical, and mirror writing is exhibited by the patient with the left hand, I believe it is quite justifiable to conclude that the lesion is not cortical. This, I believe, was a case where, the graphic centre being suddenly cut off from innervating the right hand, was still capable when the patient tried to write with the left hand of guiding the left hand, so that mirror writing was produced, and that mirror writing, when read in a mirror, exactly resembled her ordinary right-hand writing. She was enabled to write so well from the fact that she was naturally a left-handed person, and had trained her left hand to do fine actions. She had never, however, trained her left hand to write in the mirror fashion.

Recently J. J. Allan[1] has recorded his own sensations and views as a mirror writer. He was a mirror writer

[1] *Brain*, 1896.

from the age of thirteen, and could nearly write as well backwards with the left hand as he could write forwards with the right. The assistance of sight is not necessary, and may even impede it. He says "that the sensations accompanying all kinds of writing, whether right-hand or left-hand, right-foot or left-foot, are so similar as to suggest that in all cases the messages start from the same region of the brain, but it seems as if a series of commutators existed at a lower level whereby the impulses could be turned into different channels leading to an analogous but sometimes heteronymous group of muscles. This supports the view that the true graphic centre is not coincident with either of the motor centres, but superior to all of them."

The fact is, we are forced to the conclusion that there must be stored in or in the neighbourhood of the cortical centres, for the movements of the right hand, special cells whose function it is to do the cell-grouping or co-ordinating of the movements necessary for writing in the true sense of the word. These cells form, therefore, the psycho-motor graphic or the special graphic centre, but the area where they are need not necessarily be anatomically separable from the centres for the hand, so that it is quite possible that no pathological lesion could blot out those cells and at the same time leave the ordinary motor centres for the hand intact. The fact that no really well authenticated case has been produced where it could be said with certainty that the psycho-motor graphic cells were alone involved shows that, in all probability, these cells are not pathologically separable from the centres for the movements of the hand in the middle of the ascending frontal and ascending parietal convolutions. The position the graphic centre has usually been considered to be located in is a little farther forward, viz. in the adjoining part of the second left frontal convolution.

It will be well, however, for clinical observers to remember that, if this graphic centre was alone involved, without the movements of the hand being involved, and without the visual word centre being involved, *there would not be loss of the power of writing*. Writing could still be performed, just as we are able to write with the left hand, or with our foot; in other words, the patient would be able to trace letters and words, but what would be lost would be the power to write in his usual handwriting, and in a rapid and expert manner.

This fact has not been sufficiently borne in mind by clinical observers, so that we constantly see notes taken as to whether a patient was able to write or not, without paying particular attention to whether he wrote in his usual handwriting or not. It also disposes of those cases which have been recorded as not being agraphic because they could still write with the left hand, such writing, as I have stated, being simply tracing. The presence of real mirror writing, on the other hand, is almost conclusive as to the graphic centre being intact.

A practical test as to whether a patient is simply tracing or not would be to ask him first to print a sentence and then to write a sentence. It would be found that probably he would be able to print the letters quicker and better than he could write them. This results from the fact that letters as used in print are more distinct in their outlines, more easily raised in the visual memory, and more easily copied as one would a drawing, than letters as written. The movements necessary for their production are not so intricate and complicated as those for writing, the lines being straighter. I refer here to plain Roman printing type.

This fact I have noticed very distinctly in cases with agraphia due to word-blindness, as in Case IX., where there was a very considerable difference in the facility with which he copied plain printing from the difficulty with which he copied manuscript, especially if the letters had any appendages, flourishes, or any little peculiarity of form. In attempting to copy the word "North" as written, he looked long at the loop on the N, and then made several attempts to write it. He seemed in great difficulty as to how it was to be added to the rest of the N.

This, I think, is brought out by a study of his writing (Fig. 23). Normally we all write manuscript letters more easily and better than we draw printed letters, whilst in graphic disturbances, whether from lesion of the visual word centre or graphic centre, we draw printed more easily and better than manuscript letters. Pitres says that visual aphasia cases cannot copy at all, whilst true agraphias can. I think, however, that many visual aphasias see sufficient of the forms of letters to be able to trace them.

In a former part of this work I theoretically sketched three different forms of each type of aphasia, viz. infra-pictorial, pictorial, and supra-pictorial. As I have now stated, no true authenticated case of graphic aphasia verified by a post-mortem has been published, but many cases have been claimed as pure graphic aphasias. Granted that there is a special graphic centre, theoretically we might have :—

1. Supra-pictorial graphic aphasia.
2. Pictorial graphic aphasia.
3. Infra-pictorial graphic aphasia.

No case has ever been claimed to belong to any but the second group. There is little doubt that a lesion which destroys all the centres for the movements of the hand, the specialised as well as the ordinary motor centres, that is, a cortical lesion producing paralysis of the right hand, can be scientifically considered to be a case of graphic aphasia. Although all the movements of the hand as well as the movements necessary for writing are rendered impossible, still the patient, looked at from the aphasic point of view, suffers from agraphia. If the lesion existed independently of the true graphic centre he would have infra-pictorial agraphia; if the true graphic centre was also destroyed, he would have pictorial agraphia. He is probably able to write with the left hand, but the writing is simply by tracing or copying until he gradually educates the right hemisphere and specialises another centre there. There are therefore many such cases of agraphia if these cases be accepted as agraphias, but, as I have said, there are none in medical literature where the centres for the ordinary movements of the hands escaped, and the graphic centre alone or the connecting fibres from it to the centres for the hand were involved in a lesion. But there is another class of case which I believe belongs to the first group, and of this class the case of Pitres,[1] which I have previously referred to, may be taken as an example. It was, I believe, a case of

[1] Pitres, *loc. cit.*

supra-pictorial graphic aphasia, that is, a lesion in the fibres between the psycho-motor speech centre and the psycho-motor graphic centre, and not a lesion of the graphic centre alone, as Pitres claimed.

A lesion in this position theoretically must occasionally occur, whether we hold there is a true graphic centre or only a centre for the movements of the hand, and the existence of this lesion probably accounts for those cases of motor aphasia with agraphia in which the latter symptom persists after the patient has recovered from the motor aphasia.

These cases are not considered by Déjerine to be true agraphia cases, but to be simply the remains of the motor aphasia. I think, however, that theoretically as well as clinically they can be truly classed as supra-pictorial graphic aphasias (lesion of B D, Fig. 13). The following is a very interesting case of this sort. He was at first a case of pictorial motor aphasia with agraphia, but the motor aphasia soon disappeared and he remained agraphic.

CASE XVI. (*Personal Observation*).—*Motor aphasia with agraphia; rapid recovery of motor aphasia; agraphia persistent.*

T. D., æt. 59, admitted to Leith Hospital October 15th, 1896, with complete loss of speech. Two or three days before admission he had suddenly lost his speech. On admission he was found to have no paralysis either of the face or of the limbs. Pupils equal, semi-contracted, reacted to light and accommodation. Hearing all right; eyesight hypermetropic. He could scarcely speak a word; occasionally, in answer to questions, he would say "Yes" or "No," "I can't," etc., but with the greatest difficulty and after apparently considerable distress. He could not tell his

1. Voluntary attempts at writing his name.

Fig. XXV. Writing of Case XVI. on 15th October, 1896.

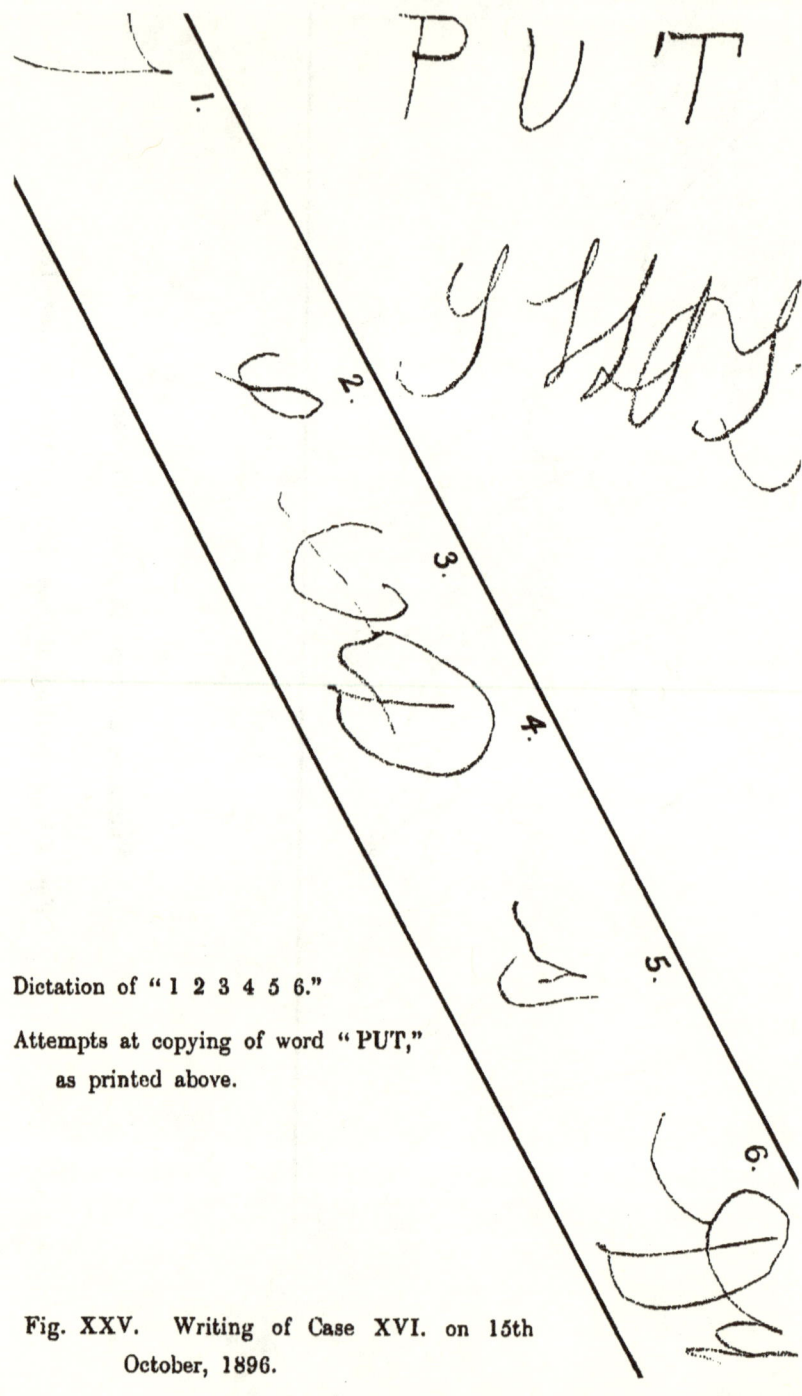

Dictation of "1 2 3 4 5 6."

Attempts at copying of word "PUT," as printed above.

Fig. XXV. Writing of Case XVI. on 15th October, 1896.

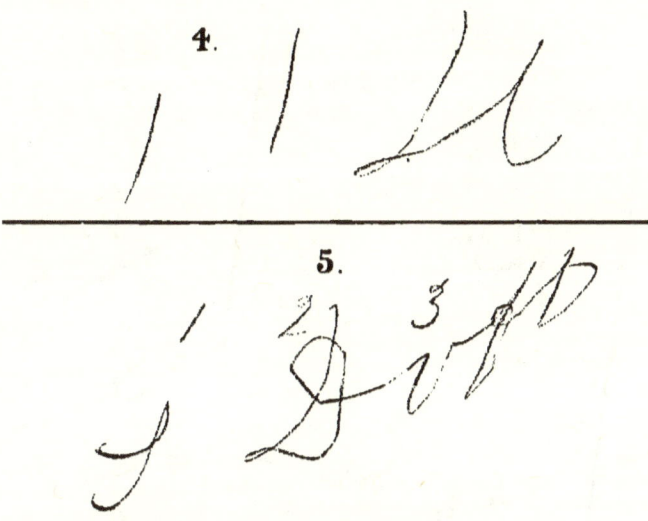

1. Voluntary attempt at writing name.
2. Voluntary attempt at writing his address.
3. Attempt at writing "I am better" to dictation.
4. Attempt at writing "1 2 3" to dictation.
5. Attempt at copying "1 2 3," as printed above.

Fig. XXVI. Writing of Case XVI. on 16th October, 1896.

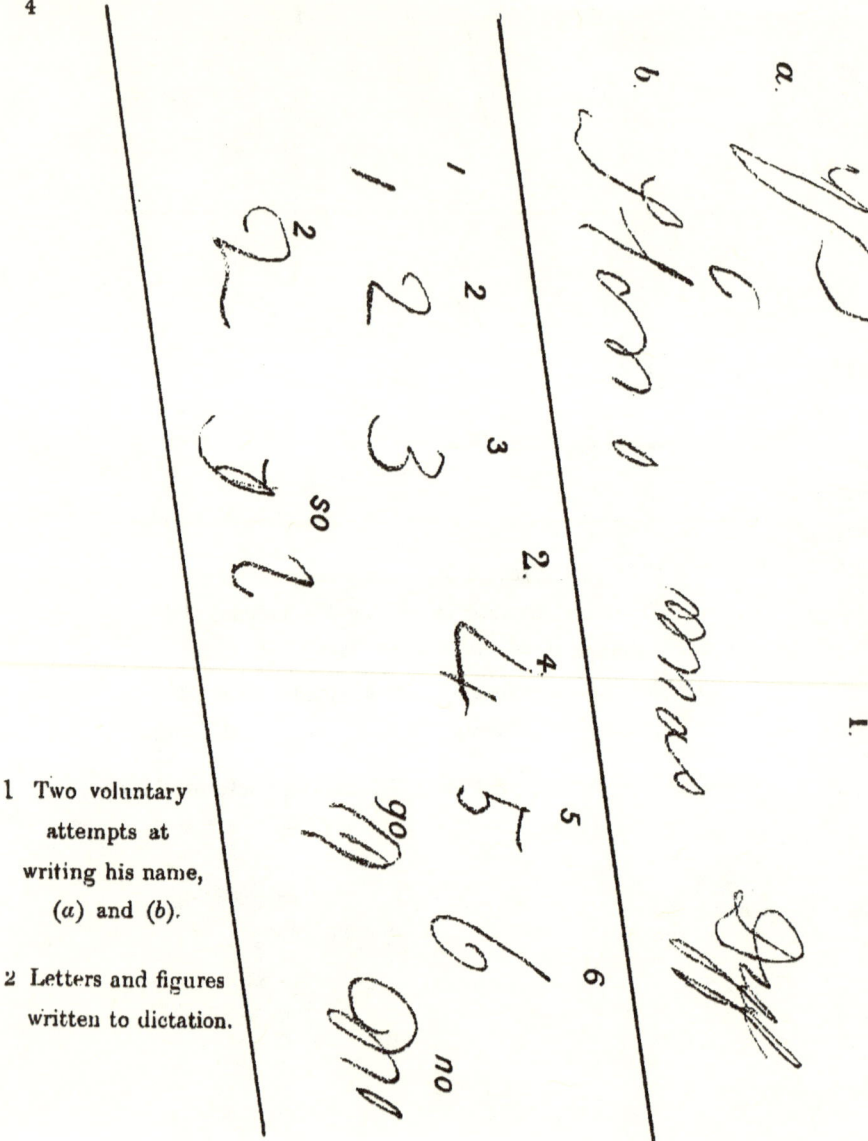

1 Two voluntary attempts at writing his name, (*a*) and (*b*).

2 Letters and figures written to dictation.

Fig. XXVII. Writing of Case XVI. on 17th Oct., 1896.

3.

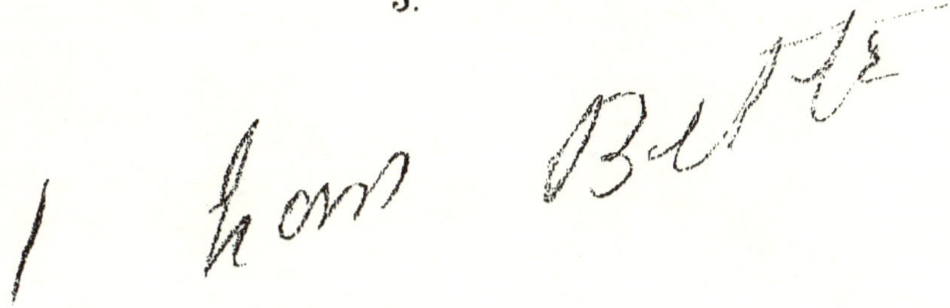

3. Attempts to write "I am better" to dictation, October 17th, 1896.

1. Voluntary writing of name.
2. Writing to dictation "I am better."

Fig. XXVIII. Writing of Case XVI. on 20th October, 1896.

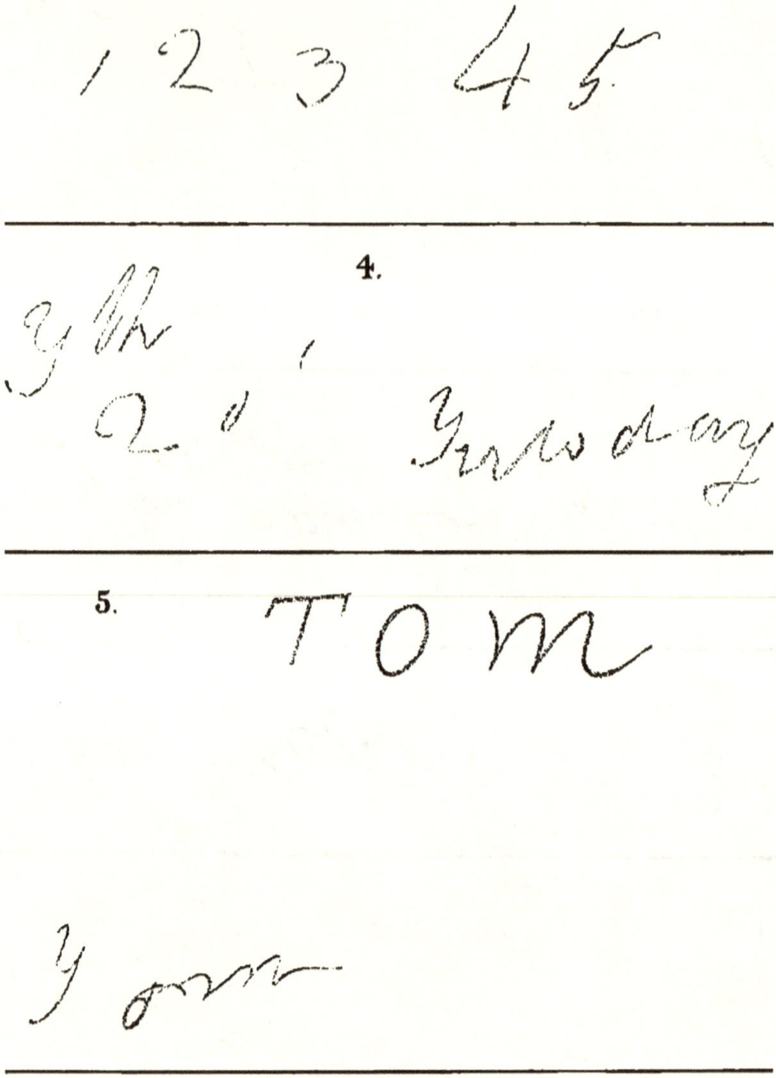

3. Writing to dictation figures "1 2 3 4 5."
4. Writing to dictation, "20th Tuesday."
5. Copy of printed word, "TOM," into written word, "Tom."

Fig. XXVIII. Writing of Case XVI. on 20th October, 1896.

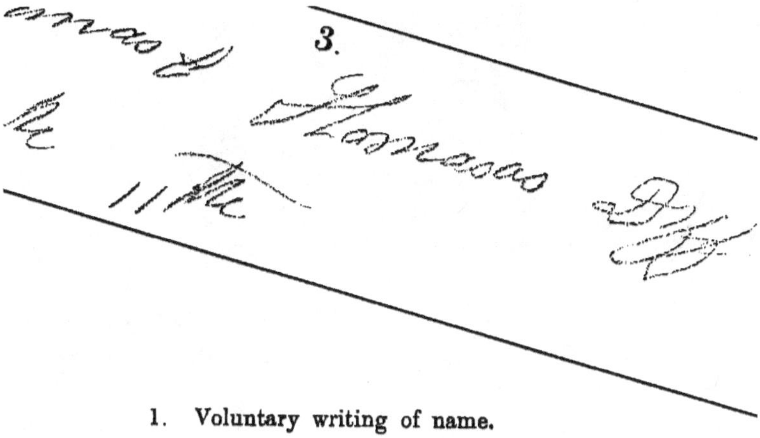

1. Voluntary writing of name.
2. Voluntary writing of date, "9th Nov."
3. Voluntary writing of name and date.

Fig. XXIX. Writing of Case XVI. on Nov. 9th, 1896.

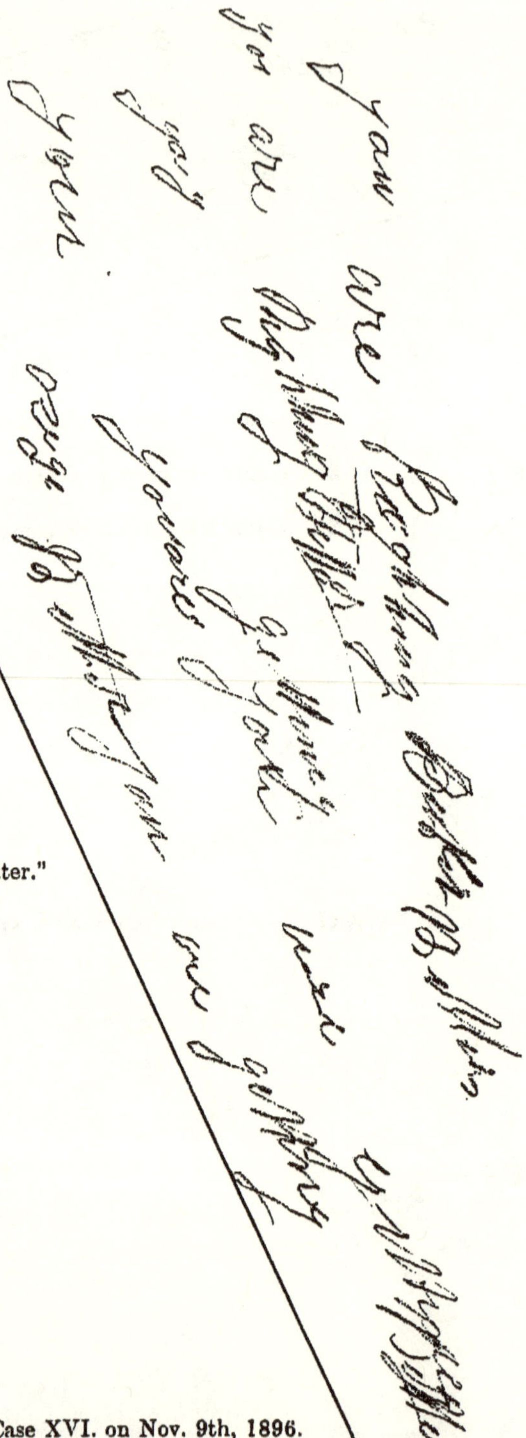

4. Several attempts at writing to dictation, "You are getting better."

Fig. XXIX. Writing of Case XVI. on Nov. 9th, 1896.

name or address. He understood what was said to him, as, for instance, when asked to put out his hand and grasp the doctor's hand, he did it slowly and deliberately. He could not read when the words "Put out your tongue" were written; he apparently did not understand them. When 1, 2, 3, were written, he could not say "one," but said "two" and "three" with difficulty. On A, B, C, being shown to him, he called B "three," but gave no answer to A and C. This was an example of what he frequently did in subsequent examinations: after he pronounced one word, the same word was given in answer to subsequent questions (word-intoxication). He was tested as to his writing, and specimens of it are shown in Fig. 25. When asked to write his name, it was seen that he began the T all right, but he often produced several T's in succession; on several occasions four to six successive T's were written. The same thing was shown on writing to dictation and to copy. This is a form of paragraphia and "letter-intoxication" in writing. After he had got the first letter, D, of his surname, he usually wrote the rest of the name rapidly, and as it were automatically. This is seen in Fig. 25 (1), where he was asked to write his name. In (2) he was asked to write 1, 2, 3, 4, 5, 6, to dictation, and the result was that he wrote T for 1, an attempt at T for 2 and an attempt at T for 3, D for 4, T for 5, and wrote Du for 6. When asked to copy PUT he wrote six T's in succession.

On the 16th it was noted that improvement in his speech began on the night before, and that it was still better in the morning. He could now tell his name and address correctly. Said he felt better, put out his tongue and shook hands more promptly when asked. Spoke still with evident effort, but more distinctly. Complained of a pain in his back. Asked how he was, said, "Mending a bit." Could tell the day of the week, named all the days of the week in order, and the numbers up to ten. No difficulty shown in the mere pronunciation of these, but hesitancy in recalling how they should be pronounced. His reading was tested, and it was found that he could read aloud some words, as, for instance, " Lord " and " Thy," from a book. The words " Give me your hand " were then written down, and he said they were " Lord," " Thy," " Lord." The figures 1, 2, 3, were then written down, and he was asked what each was separately. He said 1 was " Lo," 2 was " Lo," 3 was " three," 4 was " four." He was now asked what 1 was, and he said " one," and 2 he called " two." On being asked again what 1 was, he said " two"; 2 he said " three, isn't it?" 3 he called " three," 4 he called " three," 1 he called " three." In a final attempt he named them " one, two, three, four." The following letters were then written down, and he was asked to name them in succession. The answer he gave is put under each letter :—

T.	H.	O.	M.	A.	S.
"Three."	"H."	"Nothing."	"M."	"Four."	"N."

On the S being pointed to and the question put if it was N, he said, " No." " Is it P ?" He said, " No." " Is it S ?" He said, " That's S." The voluntary writing of his name and address are shown in Fig. 26 (1) and (2). He repeated the T. and wrote Duff fairly well. His address was a repetition of many of the letters in his name. The words " I am better " were then dictated to him, and what he wrote is seen in (3). The figures 1, 2, 3, were then dictated, and the result is seen in (4). He was then asked to copy 1, 2, 3, and he wrote "T. Duff," as in (5).

October 17th.—Speech slightly better. Said himself that he felt much better. When asked what difficulty he formerly had with speech, he explained that he felt no difficulty with his mouth and lips, but that he knew what he wanted to say and couldn't do it. Patellar reflexes found both exaggerated. His attempts at writing voluntarily and to dictation are seen in Fig. 27. They show slight improvement on previous efforts.

October 18th.—Did not feel so well to-day. Complained of numbness, coldness, and prickling sensations in his legs and feet. These went off after he was given a hot water bottle.

October 19th.—He felt better. Could speak fairly well, but had slight hesitancy between the words. On spelling over words to him he could tell what they were. He also could spell words pronounced to him, and said he could read now well, although he could not do so a few days ago. From the day of his admission he never used signs to indicate what he meant, but he now used his muscles of expression and his hands to indicate his meaning. When asked about this he said that he never thought about using signs, and thought he must not have been able to use them, or he would certainly have done so.

October 20th.—His writing is seen in Fig. 28.
The voluntary attempt at his name is seen in (1).
Writing to dictation "I am better" is seen in (2).
Writing to dictation 1, 2, 3, 4, 5, is seen in (3).
Writing to dictation "20th, Tuesday" is seen in (4).
Copy of the printed word TOM is seen in (5).

It will be seen that there is considerable improvement in his writing, and it will also be noted that in copying he was able to convert printed letters into manuscript letters, showing that it was not merely done as a tracing, but the letters reached his intelligence.

October 28th.—His eyes were examined ophthalmoscopically and no change detected.

November 3rd.—He left the hospital speaking as he usually did, but in much the same condition as regards his writing. He was asked to come back on November 9th, when his speech was found to be normal and he could read slowly. His writing is seen in Fig. 29. Voluntary writing of his name and date is seen in (1) and (2) and (3). Dictation of "You are getting better" is seen in (4). He was asked to repeat it over and over again. It will be seen that his writing had improved somewhat since he went out of the hospital.

This, as will be seen, is one of those cases of motor aphasia with agraphia in which the motor aphasia rapidly disappeared and the agraphia remained. I believe that those cases are due to Broca's convolution recovering, whilst the fibres from Broca's convolution to the graphic centre or centres for the hand remain involved, so that these cases I hold, are cases of supra-pictorial graphic aphasia. This case at first had certainly impairment of his ability to read, but whether this was entirely due to his motor aphasia, or whether there was not also some cortical word-blindness, one could not definitely say. I believe that he could not read because he could not recall the articulatory images of the words, as they are very necessary, as I have previously pointed out, for reading. The fact that he could read when he recovered his speech rather tends to show that the difficulty in reading was all due to the motor aphasia. In that case the visual word centre had nothing to do with his agraphia, and the fact that in copying when recovering he was able to convert printed letters into manuscript letters also favours this view, although at the very beginning of his illness his agraphia was so complete that he could only write part of his signature, and he showed paragraphia and letter and word intoxication so much that his graphic centre for the first few days could do nothing more than write his signature and often repeated the letter T over and over again in the same monotonous shape. The case is also of very great interest from being such a complete motor aphasia of the pictorial variety, but one which was very temporary in duration. His case suggested at first toxæmia as a cause, but there was no albuminuria, and the further progress of the case showed that it was more probably organic in origin. Hysterical mutism was also suggested, but, as I have previously pointed out, hysterical mute cases are infra-pictorial in type and there is no agraphia. The case was therefore in all probability organic in origin, but whether due to thrombosis, embolus, or hæmorrhage it is impossible to say.

A case which has a very direct bearing on cases such as these has recently been reported by Professor Grasset of Montpellier [1] under the title of aphasia of the right hand in a deaf mute. The patient was a deaf mute who was able to converse well with his hands before his illness, using his right hand for forming the letters. He had never learned to speak with his mouth, but could read and write well. For two years he had showed symptoms

[1] Grasset, *Le Progrès Médical*, October 31, 1896.

of cerebral softening without initial apoplexy, due probably to thrombosis of the Sylvian artery. He could use his right arm sufficiently well to do such acts as to raise his hand to his mouth, etc., but there was total loss of the power of right manual speech, either speech as used by the deaf and dumb or writing. He could, however, form the deaf and dumb letters with his left hand. Professor Grasset comes to the conclusion that in deaf mutes a centre becomes developed in the cerebral cortex which presides over manual speech, but this centre is quite distinct from the centres for the ordinary movements of the arm and hand. The two centres must be separable from each other, as in this case they were capable of being pathologically disassociated. The manual language centre is allied physiologically to that for writing. Are they allied anatomically, and ought they to be located in the second instead of the third left frontal? Grasset finally concludes that his case supports these hypotheses, but does not prove them. The case also supports the views which I have endeavoured to bring forward in the previous pages; but I would only say this, that in the case of Grasset, although the manual speech centre (the psycho-motor manual speech centre) may have been destroyed, the true graphic centre may not necessarily have also been destroyed, as the case is exactly analogous to a suprapictorial graphic aphasia, or even a motor aphasia, as it will be remembered that agraphia results, either from destruction of the psycho-motor articulatory centre, or from a lesion in the fibres connecting that centre to the true graphic centre. In deaf mutes, therefore, one would expect agraphia to result from either a destruction of the psycho-motor manual speech centre, or from a lesion of the fibres connecting that centre to the true graphic centre.

The case, therefore, does not necessarily show that the true graphic centre can be anatomically separable from the centres for the hand, although it strongly tends to show that the manual speech centre in deaf mutes can be. In all probability such psycho-motor manual speech centre is not in the third frontal convolution, but higher up in the near neighbourhood of the centres for the hand, and probably therefore in the second left frontal, as supposed by Grasset.

Is it possible from a study of derangements of writing in aphasic cases to localise the position of the lesion, and to say what form of aphasia the patient suffers from? I believe that in most cases it is.

1. If the patient is paralysed on the right side, he is, from the aphasic point of view, absolutely agraphic as regards his right hand, but is able to trace or write slowly with his left hand. If the paralysis is due to lesions subcortically or in the internal capsule, he may show mirror writing with the left hand.

2. If the lesion is supra-pictorial, that is, between the centre of Broca and the writing centre or the centres for the hand, or if the lesion is in Broca's convolution alone, then the patient is not able to write words as a whole, except probably the most familiar ones, such as his signature. It is possible, however, that a very expert writer, or a writer who is distinctly *auditive*, may be able to write words, but as a rule he will only be able to write letters or very short and familiar words such as his signature, and in addition to this paragraphia he

will show probably marked letter-intoxication, the most familiar letters such as his initials appearing again and again. The letters, however, are fairly well formed, provided the visual word centre be intact. He writes, however, not necessarily the same letters as he may speak if Broca's convolution is intact.

3. If the lesion is between Broca's centre and the auditory centre, then the patient will have paragraphia of words and word-intoxication. As Broca's convolution remains connected with the graphic centre, he is able to form words by speaking and also by writing, but as these centres are cut off from the auditory centre, he is not able to speak and to write the proper word, and so the most marked symptoms are paraphasia and paragraphia. He writes, however, the same words as he speaks.

These are the symptoms in conduction aphasias.

4. If the lesion is in the auditory word centre, he shows much the same symptoms as the last, but he has more difficulty in recalling words (amnesia verbalis), and in addition he cannot hear words, and therefore cannot write to dictation.

5. If the lesion is in the visual word centre, he shows most marked agraphic symptoms. He is not able to recall the shapes of letters, and therefore if he is able to attempt to write at all the letters are very imperfectly formed, or they may be formed automatically by the graphic centre. He can trace lines from copy probably, although perhaps imperfectly, but is not able to copy print into written characters.

6. If the lesion is infra-pictorial visual (word-blindness), he is able to write voluntarily and write to dictation, but not able to copy perfectly.

The conclusions we are now able to draw from a study of the whole subject of agraphia are these :—

1. That agraphia and disorders of writing may be symptoms of any of the types of aphasia.

2. That there have been no true agraphias alone proved by a post-mortem examination to be due to a destruction of a special graphic centre.

3. That if cases of paralysis of the right hand be considered as agraphias, then many post-mortems have shown that the centres for the hand are in the middle of the ascending frontal and ascending parietal convolutions.

4. That the fact that no authenticated case of agraphia pure and simple, verified by post-mortem examination, has been recorded, tends to show that if there is a graphic centre it is not pathologically separable from the centres for the hand.

5. That the cases on record where agraphia remains after return of speech in motor aphasia are probably due to lesion in the fibres joining the psycho-motor articulatory centre to the graphic centre or centres for the hand.

6. That a theoretical study of writing, as well as a study of mirror writing, tends strongly to the conclusion that there is a special graphic centre in the left cerebral cortex.

CHAPTER X.

DISTURBANCES OF THE MUSIC FACULTY, AMUSIA, ETC.

WE have now considered all the different varieties of aphasia, and have been able to localise more or less the different varieties to particular parts of the cerebral hemispheres. I wish now to consider shortly another faculty very closely allied both theoretically and clinically to the speech faculty, viz. the faculty of music.

Music can be received, retained or stored up, and produced by the cerebral hemispheres just as speech is. It is received by the auditory and the visual route, and is produced by the vocal and oral articulative mechanism and the hand just as speech is. But there is one great difference between speech and music, viz. that whilst in written speech the hand is used for writing, in music the hand is used for writing notes, but to a much greater extent for the production of music by playing instruments which have been devised for producing music. And it is not only one hand that is used for this production of music, but sometimes two, sometimes the mouth in addition, and sometimes the feet, according to the particular instrument that is played.

From what I have previously said, then, it will be seen that it is necessary to suppose the existence of specialised centres in the neighbourhood of the ordinary centres for the movements of the particular part of the body used in playing. The music faculty must be therefore quite as complicated a mechanism as, if not more so than, the speech faculty.

But it is only a few who have educated their cerebral hemispheres to produce music in various ways. All have not trained voices, although all can produce a musical voice of some kind. All have not learned to write musical notation, any more than all have taught themselves to read it, and many have never learned to play a musical instrument. The part of the musical mechanism which is probably most universal is the faculty of hearing it. Probably almost every one hears music as music, but there are enormous differences in the powers which people possess, not only in appreciating it, in the sense of its giving pleasure, but in the powers they possess of recognising its pitch and other qualities. In other words, people differ in "having an ear" or not "having an ear" for music.

The music faculty is very closely associated with the speech faculty, and disturbances of the one are very apt to be accompanied by disturbances of the other. Although closely associated, they appear, however, to be quite distinct, and the centres appear to have quite a distinct localisation in the hemispheres, because we find some cases of aphasia without amusia, and some amusias without aphasia.

In Case VII., the case I have described of conduction aphasia, although the patient had a considerable amount of word-deafness, his hearing for music was quite unaffected. He sat for hours listening to a piano, and the slightest mistake in a note was at once detected.

In Case IV., a case of word-deafness, there was a peculiar derangement of the music faculty, viz. what I have called "a hallucination of melody," where the patient heard distinctly a popular song ringing in her head, and was able to reproduce it by whistling. The fact that the sound was so complex a sound as a melody showed that it was cerebral in origin and not due to derangement of the labyrinth. As Gowers[1] pointed out recently, subjective auditory sensations of labyrinthine or peripheral origin are not so complicated as those of central origin may be.

The whole question of amusia in its relation to aphasia has recently been very carefully investigated by Professor J. G. Edgren[2] of Stockholm, who has from medical literature on aphasia collected fifty-two cases, and shown the state of the musical faculty in each case. Many of these cases are most interesting ones, and taken altogether they show the most wonderful varieties of symptoms, but Edgren is able to classify them into three groups :—

I. Comprising cases 1 to 24, where there was aphasia in some form present, but no amusia.

II. Comprising cases 25 to 46, where there were present one or more forms of amusia and one or more forms of aphasia.

III. Comprising cases 47 to 52, where there was present some form of amusia, but no aphasia.

From these it will be seen that whilst in a large number of cases (little less than the half) both amusia and aphasia were present in the same case, and in a large number (nearly a half) some form of aphasia was present without any amusia, there were very few cases indeed (six out

---

[1] *Lancet*, November 14, 1896.
[2] *Amusie. Deutsche Zeitschrift für Nervenheilkunde*, VI. 1895.

of fifty-two) where there was amusia without any form of aphasia.

These results and a careful study of each individual case show that, although the centres for music are near the speech centres, they are not exactly in the same position. Case 52 was one of Edgren's own observation, and was a case of tone-deafness which had word-deafness also at first, but the word-deafness disappeared, leaving only the tone-deafness.

At the post-mortem a lesion was found in the anterior two-thirds of the first and anterior half of the second temporo-sphenoidal convolutions, parts that were also included in the lesion in Bernard's case of tone-deafness, which Edgren also quotes.

He therefore concludes that that is the position of the music-hearing centre, viz. immediately in front of the word-hearing centre.

The following is a summary of the conclusions which he draws from a consideration of the whole question of amusia :—

1. The musical faculty, just as the speech faculty, can be entirely or partially destroyed by pathological processes of one kind or another, and when partially destroyed the faculty can be resolved into its different components, whereby special forms of amusia arise.

2. The different forms of amusia possess a certain degree of clinical independence both in their relationship to one another and in their relationship to aphasia.

3. The clinical forms of amusia appear to be analogous to the clinical forms of aphasia, and are frequently but not necessarily accompanied by the analogous forms of aphasia.

4. Amusia can be present without aphasia, and aphasia without amusia.

5. It is probable that special clinical forms of amusia (at least certain of them) possess a certain anatomical independence, and that the lesions producing them can be localised in the neighbourhood of the places where the lesions producing the corresponding forms of aphasia are considered to be localised, but nevertheless not in the identical locality.

6. For a special form of amusia, viz. tone-deafness, it is highly probable that the lesion which produces it is in the first or in the first and second temporal convolutions on the left side in front of the area injury to which produces word-deafness.

These are the conclusions of Edgren from a study of a large number of the cases in medical literature, from which it will be seen that in all probability the musical faculty as well as the speech faculty is situated in the left cerebral hemisphere only, and although the auditory centres for ordinary sounds are in both hemispheres, that the specialised centre for the recognition of musical tones, etc., as well as that for words, is in the left hemisphere only.

Disturbances of the Faculty for Interpretation and Production of Signs (Pantomime Language), Amimia, Paramimia, etc.

It has been found that some patients, although aphasic, understand and produce pantomime or gesture language quite well, and, on the other hand, some have lost all knowledge of gesture language (*amimia*).

Some, again, put a wrong interpretation on gestures or

may not produce the correct gesture, as, for instance, they may nod their head instead of shake it when they wish to say "no," and *vice versa*. This is called *paramimia*.

Some of the cases I have recorded possessed gesture language perfectly, although very markedly aphasic, as Cases IV. and V., the latter of which cases conversed for seventeen years almost entirely by signs. Case XVI., on the other hand, for several days at the beginning of his illness had lost all power of producing language by signs; even his power of using the muscles of his face in order to produce what is called expression seemed to be lost. Probably the centres for interpretation of gesture language are in the occipital lobes in both hemispheres, and not only in the left, as the written word centre is, and therefore are not so often entirely destroyed.

CHAPTER XI.

APHASIA FROM A SURGICAL POINT OF VIEW.

I HAVE in several parts of this work pointed out how important it is for the surgeon to possess a very exact knowledge of aphasia. The subject has not occupied so important a place in our text-books of surgery as it ought to. In recent years cerebral surgery has made great advances, owing to the most encouraging results got by some of our brilliant operative surgeons. Now the first essential for a surgeon who has to do with cerebral disease, in whatever form, is to locate exactly the lesion that is causing the symptoms which he wishes to relieve.

Of all the symptoms which cerebral lesions produce there are none more important, and few are so important, as those which produce disturbances of the speech faculty.

If we look, for instance, at the superficial area alone of the left hemisphere, it will be seen that if we draw a boundary line which would include all the speech centres within it, the area so included would occupy more than a third, and very nearly a half, of the whole superficial area of the outer surface of the left hemisphere (see Fig. 30).

A lesion of any size within that area would be very apt to produce some disturbance of speech, the disturbance

APHASIA AND THE CEREBRAL SPEECH MECHANISM. 245

varying, as we have seen, according to the precise position of the lesion. And not only do cortical lesions produce speech disturbances, but, as we have seen, subcortical lesions and lesions in the white matter of the cerebrum also produce speech disturbances, and these disturbances vary according to the precise position of the subcortical lesion. I have not drawn that boundary line so as to include the whole of the occipital lobe, which might fairly

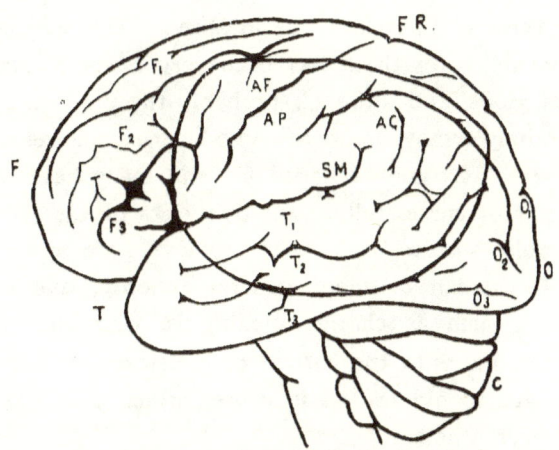

FIG. 30.—LATERAL SURFACE LEFT HEMISPHERE.

The dark line encloses an area in which a lesion of any size is very apt to produce some form of speech disturbance.

be included as within the speech area, because, as we have seen, lesions in the occipital lobe almost always produce some form of word-blindness, or symptoms associated with word-blindness and the subject of aphasia. The importance of the consideration of aphasia, therefore, to the surgeon cannot be over-estimated.

Many affections which truly belong to surgery, and not to medicine, are apt to occur in the cerebral hemispheres.

I have no intention of entering into a description of surgical cerebral affections, but I shall only mention briefly a few of the surgical affections which may produce aphasic symptoms. Perhaps the most important of these are those due to traumatic causes: accidents of various kinds to the head, producing concussion, fractures, hæmorrhages, inflammation, and abscesses. It is very essential that these be accurately localised.

And it need hardly be also emphasised how important it is for cerebral tumours to be localised. The subject of the removability of these has been very much discussed in recent years, and although probably the proportion of those entirely removable with a good permanent result is not so great as could be hoped for, still many have been removed most successfully. Another class of case where considerable success has been obtained are cases of either Jacksonian or more general epilepsy, due to a local cause, such as chronic meningitis, with adherence of the membranes to the cortex, or exostoses, or spicules of bone due to old traumatic causes which give rise to irritative symptoms.

The importance of the subject being recognised, can any method be laid down for the surgeon for the investigation of a case producing aphasic symptoms?

I take it that the three most important questions that a surgeon has to answer when he investigates a cerebral case are these:—

1. What is the nature of the lesion?
2. Where is it located?
3. Is it cortical or subcortical?

Having answered these questions he is in a position to decide as to how the case is to be treated, whether by operation or otherwise. Now although a study of aphasia may not give him very much help to decide as to the first question, an accurate knowledge of the symptoms produced by each variety of aphasia is most essential in order that the second and third questions may be accurately answered. I do not for a moment wish to state that a study of aphasia would give no help to decide the first question, viz. the nature of the lesion. Indeed in one of my cases (Case IX.), when the diagnosis lay between multiple cerebro-spinal sclerosis, general paralysis, and pachymeningitis, the fact that the patient had certainly a cortical word-blindness went a very long way to show that the cause was a pachymeningitis. This of course was not a surgical case, but the same argument applies to surgical cases, as it might have been surgical.

But whilst a knowledge of aphasia may not give much help in deciding as to the first question in cases of left cortical affections it is very important in order to answer the second and third.

2. In affections of the right hemisphere a lesion might possibly be so situated that the absence of certain aphasia symptoms might give the indication as to which hemisphere the lesion was situated in. These cases, however, cannot nearly be so numerous as the cases where the positive evidence of aphasia necessarily locates the lesion on the left side, except of course in left-handed persons.

Having therefore ascertained that there is present some speech affection, the next thing that has to be ascertained is as to which of the five great groups of aphasia cases it belongs to, whether auditory, visual, motor, graphic, or conduction.

Now that can easily be ascertained by getting an answer

to each of the twelve questions I have previously drawn out.

These questions, however, include almost the complete investigation of each case, and it is sometimes not very easy in surgical cases getting an answer to all of them.

By studying the "Table of Summary of Results" which I have previously drawn up (page 92) it will be seen that there is a certain symptom common to all auditory cases, viz. (question 3) he cannot understand words spoken; a symptom common to all visual cases, (question 6) he cannot understand words written; a symptom common to all motor cases, (question 7) he cannot speak voluntarily; and a symptom common to all graphic cases, (question 10) he cannot write voluntarily.

If therefore it be ascertained that a patient cannot understand what is spoken to him, he suffers from some form of auditory aphasia, or word-deafness.

If he cannot understand written or printed words, but can understand spoken words, he suffers from some form of visual aphasia, word-blindness.

If he cannot speak voluntarily, he suffers from some form of motor aphasia; and if he cannot write voluntarily, he suffers from some form of graphic aphasia.

If he can understand spoken words and written words, and can speak voluntarily and write voluntarily, but shows imperfections in these, and especially if he shows paraphasia and paragraphia, he suffers from conduction aphasia.

It is very essential that the questions should be answered in the order given above, because he may, for instance, not be able to understand written words because he cannot recall the auditory images of the words, owing to his having auditory aphasia, and he may not be able to write because he has visual aphasia or motor aphasia. It is therefore taken for granted that the types which precede have been ascertained to be excluded before a diagnosis is made of any particular type.

If he has some form of auditory aphasia, the lesion must involve the posterior half of the first left temporo-sphenoidal convolution; and if he suffers from visual aphasia, the lesion must involve the posterior part of the left supra-marginal convolution, the angular gyrus, or occipital lobe. If motor aphasia, the lesion must be in the region of the posterior part of the third left frontal convolution; and if graphic aphasia alone, without any other form of aphasia, the lesion may be between the third left frontal and the second left frontal, in the second left frontal, or in the motor centres for the hand across the middle of the ascending frontal and ascending parietal convolutions. If he suffers from conduction aphasia, the lesion is probably in the neighbourhood of the island of Reil and the Sylvian fissure.

3. Having therefore ascertained the locality of the lesion, the next point, and a very important one it is for the surgeon, is to ascertain whether the lesion causing the aphasia symptoms is in the cortex or is in the fibres under the cortex.

The answer to this question must very frequently decide the further question, viz. Can the cause of the symptoms be removed by surgical interference?

Whether the lesion is cortical or subcortical ought therefore to be ascertained, and I believe that it is quite possible in many uncomplicated cases to ascertain this. Limited lesions producing symptoms are easiest located, but although in many cases one would not be able to say exactly how much of the cortex or of the fibres leading to the cortex or away from the cortex was involved, still one can say with a considerable degree of certainty that the cortical region of a particular area is involved, or is not involved, in the lesion.

Case IX. is a case in point, where there can be little doubt that the angular gyrus was involved in the lesion, however much more of the cerebral cortex may have been also affected. Also in Case V., where the diagnosis was verified by the post-mortem, one could say with certainty that the cortex of the first temporo-sphenoidal convolution and of the angular gyrus was affected, however much more. The post-mortem revealed that not only these regions but nearly the whole of the temporo-sphenoidal lobe was also destroyed. How therefore are we to ascertain a cortical from a subcortical lesion in each of the four varieties?

In Auditory Aphasias, if the lesion is subcortical, the auditory word centre not being destroyed, the patient cannot hear words nor understand words spoken, but he can understand written words and can read aloud; whereas in cortical auditory aphasias, with the word-hearing centre destroyed, the patient cannot hear words nor understand words spoken, but in addition he cannot understand written words nor read aloud.

This is because, as I have previously pointed out, it is necessary to revive the auditory images of the words in order to understand written words (that is, read intelligently) and to read aloud.

The lesion producing a subcortical auditory aphasia must be a very limited one, as the course of the fibres from the ordinary auditory centre on the left side to the special auditory centre (the word-hearing centre) must be a very short one, and it is necessary to interrupt these fibres as well as the fibres from the opposite side in order to produce a subcortical auditory aphasia.

The cases producing subcortical auditory symptoms alone are therefore very few; and most auditory aphasia cases are also cortical, and are therefore situated in the posterior half of the first temporo-sphenoidal convolution. In connection with auditory aphasia it is necessary to remember also that amnesia of nouns may be a marked symptom, and in that case the naming mechanism is involved, an important part of which, as I have shown, is in all probability a little lower down than the auditory word centre, viz. in the second and third temporo-sphenoidal convolution. If the patient showed difficulty in recalling names or in naming objects at sight without having word-deafness, the lesion would probably be found to be at a lower level in the temporal lobe than the first temporal; and if the patient showed a marked difficulty in naming objects at sight, probably the lesion would be subcortical or deep in the substance of the posterior part of the temporal lobe.

If the patient showed tone-deafness, the lesion probably would also involve the anterior two-thirds of the first and anterior half of the second temporo-sphenoidal convolutions.

In Visual Aphasias, if the lesion is cortical, the patient, in addition to being word-blind, is not able to write voluntarily nor to dictation. The part involved by such a lesion is the angular gyrus and posterior part of the supra-marginal convolution.

If the lesion is subcortical, the patient is word-blind, but can write voluntarily and to dictation. He copies, if at all, simply by tracing; he has usually also hemianopsia and hemiachromatopsia. The lesion producing this may be subcortically to the angular gyrus; but a lesion in the substance of the occipital lobe or in the cortex of the occipital lobe, and passing in sufficiently far to interrupt the fibres from the visual centres both of the same and the opposite side, might produce it, so that one could not be certain of the extent of a lesion producing an infra-pictorial visual aphasia. All that can be said is that it is situated in the occipital lobe, or immediately anterior to it.

In Motor Aphasia, if *cortical* the patient would not be able to speak at all, except a very few familiar words, such as "yes" or "no." Such a lesion would be in the posterior part of the third left frontal convolution, and if it extended farther back, viz. into the lower parts of the ascending frontal and ascending parietal convolutions, he would show the symptoms of dysarthria, or paresis of the muscles of oral articulation of one side.

If Subcortical Motor Aphasia, the patient would not be able to speak, but he would be able to indicate how a word should be articulated, that is, the number of syllables it contained, by pressing the hand once for each syllable (*L'expérience Proust—Lichtheim*). Such a lesion is very limited in area if the only symptom, because if it extended farther back to the region subcortical to the lower parts of the ascending frontal and ascending parietal convolutions, dysarthria would result, just as in a cortical lesion of these same areas.

A cortical cannot be distinguished from a subcortical lesion of the lower part of the ascending frontal and ascending parietal convolutions, a point which Case I. and Mills' case distinctly proved. These cases show that lesions on the left side, producing dysarthria without aphasia, can be sometimes cortical, a point of very great importance to the surgeon and one which has not previously to the description of these two cases been clearly pointed out.

In Agraphia Cases pure we have not sufficient clinical evidence to show the difference between cortical and subcortical cases, but theoretically a cortical case would not know how to write in his usual handwriting; whereas a subcortical case would know how it should be written, but would not be able to do it. It is also to be noted that both visual and motor cortical cases are agraphic, and that auditory cases are agraphic to dictation. If the patient's right hand is paralysed from a cortical cause, or if he has agraphia pure, the lesion is in the posterior part of the second frontal or across the middle of the ascending frontal and ascending parietal convolutions. If the patient is agraphic with the right hand, but shows mirror writing with the left, I believe one may conclude that the cortical centres for the right hand are intact.

I think I have said enough to show how the different lesions causing aphasia can be located in the hemispheres, and if the causes of these lesions are removable, it is now, since so many different methods of cranial topography have been devised, a very easy matter to locate exactly on the outside of the cranium the position of the lesion, so that operative procedure may be undertaken for the relief of the symptoms.

BIBLIOGRAPHY.

Papers, treatises, etc., to which reference is made in this work.

Allan, Brain, Parts lxxiv. and lxxv.
Guido Banti, Afasia e sue forme.   Lo Sperimentale, 1886, t. lvii.
Bar, Aphasie et Hémiplégie Faciale Passagère.   France Médicale, 1876, p. 609.
Barlow, Brit. Med. Journ., vol. i., 1877.
Bastian, Brit. Med. Journ., vol. i., 1869, p. 394.
—— Hysterical and Functional Paralysis.
—— Med. Chir. Rev., vol. xliii., p. 299.
Bateman, Aphasia and the Localisation of the Faculty of Language.
Bouillaud, Traité Clinique et Physiologique de l'Encéphalite, 1823.
Broadbent, Brit. and For. Med. Chir. Rev., April 1866.
—— Cerebral Mechanism of Speech and Thought.   Med. Chir. Trans., 1872.
—— Med. Chir. Trans., 1878 ; vol. lxvii., 1884.
Broca, Bulletins de la Société Anatomique, August and November 1861.
Charcot, Lect. on Diseases of the Nervous System, vol. iii. (New Syd. Soc.).
J. B. Charcot et Dutil, Société de Biologie, Juillet 1893.
Chouppe, Comptes Rendus de la Soc. de Biolog., 1892, p. 642.
Dax, Gazette Hebdomadaire.   Paris, April 1865.   No. 17 (republished).
Déjerine, Comptes Rendus de la Soc. de Biolog., 1891-92.
Edgren, Amusie.   Deutsche Zeitschrift für Nervenheilkunde, vi., 1895.

Elder, Edinburgh Hospital Reports, vol. iii., 1895.
Exner, Untersuchungen über die Localisation der Functionen in der Grosshirnrinde des Menschen, 1881.
Ferrier, Functions of the Brain.
—— Med. Chir. Trans., vol. lxvii., 1884, p. 35.
—— Brain, April 1888 ; and Croonian Lectures, p. 80.
—— Philos. Trans., Part ii., 1884, and Part ii., 1885.
François Franck, Leçons sur les Fonctions Motrices du Cerveau. Paris, 1887.
Gairdner, Proceedings of the Glasgow Philosoph. Soc., 1865-68, p. 87.
Garel, Ann. d. Mal de l'Oreille du Larynx, etc., May 1886.
Garel and Dor, Ann. d. Mal de l'Oreille du Larynx, etc., April 1890.
Gogal, Ein Beitrug zur Lehre von der Aphasie. Breslau, 1873.
Goltz, Trans. Internat. Medic. Congress, 1881, vol. i.
Gombault and Philippe, Archives de Médecine Expérimentale et d'Anatomie Pathologique, May and September 1896.
Gowers, Lancet, November 14, 1896.
Hammond, Diseases of the Nervous System, 7th edit., chap. vii.
Henschen, Pathologie des Gehirns. Upsala, 1890.
—— Brain, lxi. and lxii., 1893, vol. xvi., p. 170.
Hinshelwood, Lancet, December 21, 1895.
Horsley and Beevor, Philosophical Trans. of Royal Society. London, 1890.
Horsley and Semon, Phil. Trans. of Royal Society. London, 1890.
Hughlings Jackson, Lond. Hosp. Clin. Lectures and Reports, 1864.
Kostenitsch, Deutsche Zeitschrift für Nervenheilkunde, 1893, Heft 5, 6.
Krausse, Arch. f. Anat. u. Physiol., 1884.
Kussmaul, Ziemssen, Cycl. of Pract. Med., Amer. Edition, vol. xiv.
Lichtheim, Brain, January 1885.
Lordat, Rev. pér. de la Société de Paris, December 1820, p. 317.
Mills, Univ. Med. Mag., November 1889, vol. ii., p. 69 ; 1891, vol. iv., p. 105.
—— Nervous Diseases, by American Authors. Edited by Dercum, 1895.
Monakow, Opticus u. Sehcentren. Arch. f. Psych., xvi.
Moxon, Brit. and Foreign Med. Chir. Rev., 1866.

Munk, Verhandlungen der Berliner physiol. Gesellschaft, 1878; and Ueber die Functionen des Grosshirns, Gesammelte Mittheilungen, Berlin, 1881.
Ogle, Aphasia and Agraphia. St. George's Hosp. Reports, vol. ii., pp. 83-121.
—— Med. Chir. Trans., liv., 1871.
Pick, Archiv f. Psych., Bd. xxiii., 1892.
Pitres, Revue de Médecine, 1884, p. 864.
—— Comptes Rendus du Congrès de Médecine, 1894.
James Russell, Brit. Med. Journ., 1864.
Risien Russell, Brit. Med. Journ., August 1895.
Sanders, Edin. Med. Journal, 1866.
Schäfer and Sanger Brown, Brain, January and April 1888; Proceed of Phys. Society, No. 2, 1887.
Semon, Virchow's Festschrift, Bd. iii., s. 432.
Sérieux, Comptes Rendus de la Soc. de Biolog., 1891-92.
Skwortzoff, De la Cécité et de la Surdité des Mots dans l'Aphasie.
Grainger Stewart, An Introduction to a Study of Diseases of the Nervous System.
Trousseau, Clinical Med., vol. i. (New Sydenham Soc., 1867), p. 252.
Vialet, Les Centres Cérébraux de la Vision, et l'Appareil, p. 355.
Wernicke, Der Aphasische Symptomen Complex, 1874.
—— Fortsch. der Med., ii., 1886, p. 463 (quoted by Wyllie).
Wernicke and Friedlander, Fortschritte der Medicin, Bd. i., No. 6, March 15, 1883. Quoted in Brain, April 1888, p. 19.
Wyllie, Disorders of Speech. Edinburgh, 1894.

INDEX.

AGRAPHIA, *see* Graphic Aphasia.
Alexia, *see* Visual Aphasia.
Allan, J. J., 223.
Amimia, 242.
Amnesia, Articulative, 204.
—— Verbalis, illustrative cases, 120, 128, 131, 132.
—— —— in Functional Aphasia, 115.
—— —— in Motor Aphasia, 136, 139.
—— —— in Sensory Aphasia, 120, 139.
—— —— situation of lesion in, 128, 130, 136, 139, 251.
—— —— varieties of, 138.
Amusia, 238.
Anarthria, 41, 42.
Aphasia, Auditory, illustrative cases, 97, 104.
—— —— situation of lesion in, 60, 70, 249.
—— —— symptoms, 70, 79, 80, 96, 139, 200, 248, 250.
—— Broca's, 179.
—— Conduction, illustrative case, 141.
—— —— situation of lesion in, 60, 75, 76, 150.
—— —— symptoms, 81, 88, 92, 203, 248.
—— Functional, Motor, 186, 187.
—— —— Sensory, 115.

Aphasia, Graphic, illustrative cases, 220, 228.
—— —— situation of lesion in, 60, 75, 235, 249.
—— —— symptoms, 75, 89-91, 200, 227, 235, 253.
—— Motor, illustrative cases, 180, 182, 186, 190, 197.
—— —— situation of lesion in, 40, 51, 60, 74, 189, 196, 249.
—— —— symptoms, 73, 82-85, 178, 179, 187, 203, 248, 252.
—— rapid recovery from, 96, 114, 117.
—— surgically considered, 244.
—— temporary, 184, 186, 233.
—— uræmic, 185.
—— varieties, differential diagnosis of, 77.
—— —— clinical, 59, 94.
—— —— theoretical, 66.
—— Visual, illustrative cases, 158, 161, 165, 173.
—— —— situation of lesion in, 60, 71, 152, 164, 249.
—— —— symptoms, 71-3, 85-8, 152, 157, 201, 248, 251.
Aphemia, *see* Motor Aphasia.
Aphonia, hysterical, 198.
Auditory Aphasia, *see* Aphasia.
—— centre, 20.
—— nerve, 16.
—— word centre, 54.

BARLOW, 6, 118.
Bastian, 10, 14, 121, 187.
Beevor, 29, 41.
Blind, the, mechanism of reading in, 13.
Blind-mutism, 12.
Bouillaud, 2.
Broadbent, 19, 121, 123.
Broca, 2, 58, 179.
Brown, Sanger, 17, 24.

CÉCITÉ Psychique, 176.
—— Verbale, *see* Visual Aphasia.
Charcot, 3, 122.
Child, the, development of language in, 8, 62.
Chouppe, 114.
Conduction Aphasia, *see* Aphasia.

DAX, 2.
Deaf Mutes, 11, 13, 69, 234.
Déjerine, 7, 59, 67, 152, 161, 205, 228.
Diabetes Insipidus, Aphasia in, 114.
Dysarthria, 38, 40, 42, 51.

EDGREN, 240.
Executory-motor centres, 36.
Exner, 205.
Expérience Proust—Lichtheim, 74.

FERRIER, 5, 16, 18, 24, 29.
Figures, memory for, 103, 119, 155.
Flourens, 1.
Friedlander, 17.

GESTURE language, 102, 120, 242.
Goltz, 5.
Gombault and Philippe, 207.
Gowers, 240.
Graphic Aphasia, *see* Aphasia.
—— centre, 7, 53, 205, 224, 237.
—— fibres, 53.
—— symptoms, 200, 235.

Grasset, 233.

HALLUCINATIONS of melody, 102, 240.
Hemianopsia, 23, 71, 85, 157.
Henschen, 25.
Hinshelwood, 157.
Horsley, 24, 29, 41, 42.
Hysterical Aphonia, 198.
—— Mutism, 117, 187-197, 203.

IDEATIONAL Mechanism, 60, 122.

KUSSMAUL, 6, 59, 122.

LEITUNGSAPHASIE, *see* Conduction Aphasia.
Letter-intoxication, 229.
Lichtheim, 6, 39, 63, 65.
Logamnesia, *see* Amnesia Verbalis.
Lordat, 2.

MEMORY, 9.
Mills, 17, 34, 65, 122, 128.
Mind-blindness, 176.
Mirror writing, 43, 214.
Motor Aphasia, *see* Aphasia.
Moxon, 56.
Munk, 17, 24.
Music faculty, 71, 102, 149, 162, 238.
—— hearing centre, 241.

NAMING Mechanism, 120, 140.

OBJECT-BLINDNESS, 176.
Ogle, 57, 58.
Optic fibres, 21, 153, 156.
—— nerve, 20.
Oral articulative centre, 29, 31, 36, 51.
—— —— fibres, 41, 42.

PARAGRAPHIA, 75, 76, 80, 81, 82, 91, 103, 200.

INDEX.

Paramimia, 243.
Paraphasia, 75, 80, 81, 82, 103, 119, 200.
Pitres, 7, 187, 226.
Propositionising centre, 36.
Pseudo-bulbar paralysis, 41, 42, 189.
Psycho-motor speech centre, 31, 36, 51, 54.
—— graphic centre, *see* Graphic centre.

RENDU, 185.
Respiratory speech centre, 28.
Right hemisphere, education of, 6, 113, 117, 181.
Russell, James, 58.
—— Risien, 30.

SCHÄFER, 17, 24.
Semon, 29, 42.
Sérieux, 7, 151.
Sighing as a symptom in cerebral cases, 28, 50.
Speech Mechanism, auditory route, 15.
—— —— centres concerned, 54.
—— —— graphic production route, 52.

Speech Mechanism, motor speech route, 27.
—— —— schema of, 61.
—— —— visual route, 20.
Spelling, 211.
Surdité Verbale, *see* Auditory Aphasia.
Surgical aspect of Aphasia, 244.

TROUSSEAU, 3.

UTTERANCE centre, 36.

VISUAL Aphasia, *see* Aphasia.
—— perceptive centre, 24, 26, 54, 153.
—— word centre, 24, 54, 154.
Vocal articulative centres, 30, 36, 51.
—— —— fibres, 41, 42.

WERNICKE, 5, 17, 58, 66, 113, 116, 214.
Word-blindness, *see* Visual Aphasia.
Word-deafness, *see* Auditory Aphasia.
Word-intoxication, 103.
Wyllie, 31, 36, 56, 66, 93, 98, 115, 121, 128.

London: H. K. Lewis, 136, Gower Street, W.C.